ISBN 978-1-397-32710-9
PIBN 11374408

ANNOUNCEMENT

OF THE

COLLEGE OF

Physicians  Surgeons

OF ONTARIO,

FOR THE ACADEMIC YEAR 1893-94.

BY AUTHORITY.

REGISTRY OFFICE:

COLLEGE OF PHYSICIANS AND SURGEONS OF ONTARIO,

SOUTH-EAST CORNER BAY AND RICHMOND STREETS,

TORONTO.

ANNOUNCEMENT

OF THE

COLLEGE OF

PHYSICIANS AND SURGEONS

OF ONTARIO,

FOR THE ACADEMIC YEAR

1893-94.

BY AUTHORITY.

REGISTRY OFFICE:

COLLEGE OF PHYSICIANS AND SURGEONS OF ONTARIO,

SOUTH-EAST CORNER BAY AND RICHMOND STREETS,

TORONTO.

June, 1893.

CONTENTS.

THE COUNCIL

OF THE

College of Physicians & Surgeons of Ontario.

TERRITORIAL REPRESENTATIVES.

J. L. BRAY, M.D., Chatham, Ont............. Western and St. Clair.
J. FULTON, M.D., St. Thomas, Ont............ Malahide and Tecumseth.
J. HENRY, M.D., Orangeville, Ont............. Saugeen and Brock.
J. A. WILLIAMS, M.D., Ingersoll, Ont.......... Gore and Thames.
D. L. PHILIP, M.D., Brantford, Ont........... Erie and Niagara.
T. MILLER, M.D., Hamilton, Ont............. Burlington and Home.
A. J. JOHNSON, M.D., Toronto, Ont............ Midland and York.
R. B. ORR, M.B., Toronto, Ont............... King's and Queen's.
A. RUTTAN, M.D., Napanee, Ont............. Newcastle and Trent.
H. W. DAY, M.D., Belleville, Ont............ Quinte and Cataraqui.
A. F. ROGERS, M.D., Ottawa, Ont............ Bathurst and Rideau.
D. BERGIN, M.D., Cornwall, Ont.............. St. Lawrence and Eastern.

COLLEGIATE REPRESENTATIVES.

W. BRITTON, M.D., Toronto, Ont............. Univ. of Toronto.
J. W. ROSEBRUGH, Hamilton, Ont............ " Victoria College.
V. H. MOORE, M.D., Brockville, Ont.......... " Queen's College.
W. T. HARRIS, M.D., Brantford, Ont......... " Trinity College.
SIR JAMES GRANT, Ottawa, Ont. .... " Ottawa.
J. THORBURN, M.D., Toronto, Ont............ Toronto School of Medicine.
F. FOWLER, M.D., Kingston, Ont.............. { Royal College of Physicians and Surgeons, Kingston.
W. B. GEIKIE, M.D., Toronto, Ont............ Trinity Medical College.
A. G. FENWICK, M.D., London, Ont .... Western Univ., London.

HOMŒOPATHIC REPRESENTATIVES.

GEORGE LOGAN, M.D., Ottawa, Ont.
G. HENDERSON, M.D., Strathroy, Ont.
C. T. CAMPBELL, M.D., London, Ont.
L. LUTON, M.D., St. Thomas, Ont.
E. VERNON, M.D., Hamilton, Ont.

Medical Registration Office of the College of Physicians and Surgeons of Ontario,
South-East corner Bay and Richmond Streets, Toronto.

OFFICE HOURS : 2 to 4 p.m.

ROBERT A. PYNE, M.D., M.C.P.S.O., Toronto, Ont.,

Registrar.

OFFICERS

OF THE

College of Physicians & Surgeons of Ontario

FOR 1893-94.

President ...... C. T. CAMPBELL, M.D., London, Ont.
Vice-President .. D. L. PHILIP, M.D., Brantford, Ont.
Treasurer ...... W. T. AIKINS, M.D., Toronto, Ont.
Registrar ...... R. A. PYNE, M.D., Toronto, Ont.

BOARD OF EXAMINERS FOR 1893-94.

DR. F. LeM. GRASETT, Toronto, Ont.... *Anatomy, Descriptive.*

DR. R. W. GARRETT, Kingston, Ont.... *Theory and Practice of Medicine.*

DR. A. A. MACDONALD, Toronto, Ont.. { *Midwifery, Operative, and other than Operative, and Puerperal and Infantile Diseases.*

DR. A. S. FRASER, Sarnia, Ont......... *Physiology and Histology.*

DR. W. BURT, Paris, Ont.............. { *Surgery, Operative, and other than Operative.*

DR. W. J. MITCHELL, London, Ont..... *Medical and Surgical Anatomy.*

DR. G. ACHESON, Trenton, Ont......... { *Chemistry, Theoretical, Practical, and Toxicology.*

DR. H. B. SMALL, Ottawa, Ont......... *Materia Medica and Pharmacy.*

DR. D. O. R. JONES, Toronto, Ont....... { *Medical Jurisprudence and Sanitary Science.*

DR. C. O'REILLY, Toronto, Ont......... { *Assistant Examiner to the Examiner on Surgery.*

DR. R. K. KILBORN, Kingston, Ont..... { *1st Assistant Examiner to the Examiner on Medicine.*

DR. GEO. PETERS, Toronto, Ont... .... { *2nd Assistant to the Examiner on Medicine, Pathology and Therapeutics.*

DR. C. |E. JARVIS, London, Ont........ *Homœopathic Examiner.*

STANDING COMMITTEES OF COUNCIL

OF

College of Physicians & Surgeons of Ontario

1893-94.

REGISTRATION COMMITTEE.

DR. ROSEBRUGH (*Chairman*), DR. MOORE,   DR. VERNON.
" JOHNSON,   " ORR,

RULES AND REGULATIONS.

DR. DAY (*Chairman*),   DR. LUTON,   DR. MILLER.
" FOWLER,   " THORBURN,

FINANCE.

DR. THORBURN (*Chairman*),   DR. HENDERSON, DR. WILLIAMS.
" FULTON,   " RUTTAN,

PRINTING.

DR. JOHNSON (*Chairman*),   DR. HENRY,   DR. BRITTON.
" FENWICK,   " LUTON,

EDUCATION.

DR. HARRIS (*Chairman*),   DR. GEIKIE,   DR. ROGERS,
" BERGIN,   " LOGAN,   " THORBURN,
" BRAY,   " MOORE,   " WILLIAMS.

PROPERTY.

DR. BRITTON (*Chairman*),   DR. HENRY,   DR. THORBURN.

COMMITTEE ON COMPLAINTS.

DR. FOWLER (*Chairman*),   DR. HENDERSON, DR. MILLER.
" HENRY,   " JOHNSON,

EXECUTIVE.

DR. CAMPBELL (*Chairman*),   DR. PHILIP,   DR. JOHNSON.

The PRESIDENT and VICE-PRESIDENT are *ex officio* Members of all Committees, and the Chairman of any Committee is *ex officio* a Member of any Sub-Committee thereof.

COMMITTEE ON DISCIPLINE.

DR. DAY (*Chairman*),   DR. BRAY,   DR. LOGAN,
Belleville, Ont.   Chatham, Ont.   Ottawa, Ont.

OFFICERS

OF THE

College of Physicians & Surgeons of Ontario

FROM 1866 TO 1893-94.

PRESIDENTS.*

1st.	John R. Dickson	from	1866 to 1867
2nd.	John Turquand	"	1867 — 1868
3rd.	James A. Grant	"	1868 — 1869
4th.	William Clark	"	1869 — 1870
5th.	William H. Brouse	"	1870 — 1871
6th.	Chas. W. Covernton	June,	1871—Dec. 1871
7th.	William Clark	Dec.†	1871 — 1872
8th.	J. F. Dewar	from	1872 — 1873
9th.	William Clark	"	1873 — 1874
10th.	M. Lavell	"	1874 — 1875
11th.	E. G. Edwards	"	1875 — 1876
12th.	Daniel Clark	"	1876 — 1877
13th.	Daniel Clark	"	1877 — 1878
14th.	D. Campbell	"	1878 — 1879
15th.	J. D. Macdonald	"	1879 — 1880
16th.	W. Allison	"	1880 — 1881
17th.	D. Bergin	"	1881 — 1882
18th.	J. L. Bray	"	1882 — 1883
19th.	G. Logan	"	1883 — 1884
20th.	H. W. Day	"	1884 — 1885
21st.	D. Bergin	"	1885 — 1886
22nd.	H. H. Wright	"	1886 — 1887
23rd.	G. Henderson	"	1887 — 1888
24th.	J. H. Burns	"	1888 — 1889
25th.	J. G. Cranston	"	1889 — 1890
26th.	V. H. Moore	"	1890 — 1891
27th.	J. A. Williams	"	1891 — 1892
28th.	F. Fowler	"	1892 — 1893
29th.	C. T. Campbell	"	1893 — 1894

VICE-PRESIDENTS.

1st.	Wm. H. Brouse	from	1866 to 1870
2nd.	Chas. W. Covernton	"	1870 — 1871
3rd.	James Hamilton	"	1871 — 1872

* The President and Vice-President, Treasurer, and Registrar of the College are elected at the Annual Meeting of the Council, and hold office until their successors are elected.

† Dr. Wm. Clark was elected December 12th, 1871, at a special meeting of the Council in consequence of the resignation of Dr. C. W. Covernton.

4th. D. CAMPBELL	....	"	1872 — 1873
5th. JOHN MUIR	....	"	1873 — 1874
6th. E. G. EDWARDS	....	"	1874 — 1875
7th. E. M. HODDER	....	"	1875 — 1876
8th. D. CAMPBELL	....	"	1876 — 1877
9th. D. CAMPBELL	....	"	1877 — 1878
10th. W. ALLISON	....	"	1878 — 1879
11th. G. LOGAN	....	"	1879 — 1880
12th. D. BERGIN	....	"	1880 — 1881
13th. J. L. BRAY	....	"	1881 — 1882
14th. W. B. GEIKIE	....	"	1882 — 1883
15th. H. W. DAY	....	"	1883 — 1884
16th. E. W. SPRAGGE	....	"	1884 — 1885
17th. R. DOUGLAS	....	"	1885 — 1886
18th. G. HENDERSON	....	"	1886 — 1887
19th. J. H. BURNS	....	"	1887 — 1888
20th. J. G. CRANSTON	....	"	1888 — 1889
21st. V. H. MOORE	....	"	1889 — 1890
22nd. J. A. WILLIAMS	....	"	1890 — 1891
23rd. F. FOWLER	....	"	1891 — 1892
24th. C. T. CAMPBELL	....	"	1892 — 1893
25th. D. L. PHILIP	....	"	1893 — 1894

TREASURER.

W. T. AIKINS .... from 1866

REGISTRARS AND SECRETARIES.

HENRY STRANGE.....................from May 3rd, 1866, to Sept. 2nd, 1872
THOS. PYNE .... " Sept. 2nd, 1872 — July 15th, 1880
ROBERT A. PYNE.. .... " July 15th, 1880 —

College of Physicians & Surgeons of Ontario.

Announcement for the Academic Year 1893-94.

"THE COLLEGE OF PHYSICIANS AND SURGEONS OF ONTARIO" is the name adopted by the Medical Profession of the Province of Ontario in its corporate capacity. As every legally qualified medical practitioner in the Province is a member of this College, it is not an institution for the teaching of medicine.

The Medical Profession of Ontario was first incorporated under this name by an Act of the Parliament of Canada, passed in 1866. This Act was subsequently repealed by the Legislature of Ontario in 1869, and now the affairs of the Profession in this Province are regulated by an Act passed in 1874 (37 Vic., cap. 30), commonly known as the "Ontario Medical Act," and further amended in 1887, 1891 and 1893.

By this Act, the "COUNCIL OF THE COLLEGE OF PHYSICIANS AND SURGEONS OF ONTARIO" is empowered and directed to enact by-laws for the regulation of all matters connected with medical education; for the admission and enrolment of students of medicine; for determining from time to time the curriculum of the studies to be pursued by them, and to appoint a Board of Examiners before whom all must pass a satisfactory examination before they can be enrolled as members of the College, and thus be legally qualified to practise their profession in the Province of Ontario.

The Council, moreover, has power and authority conferred upon it by this Act to fix the terms upon which practitioners of medicine, duly qualified in other countries, may be admitted as members of the College of Physicians and Surgeons of Ontario, this being the only mode in which they can become legally entitled to practise their profession in this Province.

For the information and guidance of students of medicine, the Profession and the public generally, the Council, in conformity with the Ontario Medical Act, hereby promulgates for the year 1893-94 the REGULATIONS which herein follow, repealing all others heretofore in force.

Regulations for 1893=94.

Section I.

MATRICULATION.

1. Everyone desirous of being registered as a Matriculated Medical Student in the Register of this College, except as hereinafter provided, must on and after the 1st day of November, 1892, present to the Registrar of the College the Official Certificate of having passed the Departmental Pass Art Matriculation Examination, and in addition Physics and Chemistry, whereupon he or she shall be entitled to be so registered upon the payment of twenty dollars, and giving proof of identity.

2. Graduates in Arts, in any University in Her Majesty's Dominions, are not required to pass this examination, but may register their names with the Registrar of the College upon giving satisfactory evidence of their identity and certificate of qualifications, and upon paying the fee of twenty dollars.

3. Every Medical Student after matriculating shall be registered in the manner prescribed by the Council, and this will be held to be the preliminary to his Medical studies, which will not be considered to begin until after the date of such registration.

Section II.

MEDICAL CURRICULUM.

1. On and after the first day of July, 1892, every student must spend a period of five years in actual Professional studies, except as hereinafter provided : and the prescribed period of studies shall include four Winter Sessions of six months each and one Summer Session of ten weeks. The fifth year shall be devoted to Clinical work, six months of which may be spent with a Registered Practi-

tioner in Ontario, and six months at one or more Public Hospitals, Dispensaries, or Laboratories devoted to Physiological or Pathological research, Canadian, British, or Foreign, attended AFTER being registered as a Medical Student in the Register of the College of Physicians and Surgeons of Ontario,—" But any change in the curriculum of studies fixed by the Council shall not come into effect until one year after such change is made."

Homœopathic Students who attend four sessions at any Medical College where nine-month sessions are taught, to be held equal to four Winter Sessions and one Summer Session of this college. This shall not in any way interfere with the Practical and Clinical work as prescribed by the Medical Council of Ontario for the fifth year.

2. Graduates in Arts or Science of any College or University recognized by the Council, who shall have spent a year in the study of Physics, Chemistry and Biology, and have passed an Examination in these subjects for degrees in Arts or Science, shall be held to have completed the first year of the five years of Medical Study, and will only be required to pass three years after graduating in attendance upon Medical studies, and having spent one year thereafter in practical Clinical work before being admitted to their FINAL Examination.

No tickets for Lectures will henceforward be accepted by the Council unless it is endorsed thereon that the pupil has attended at least 75 per cent. of each course of said Lectures, as shown by the teacher's own Roll.

3. Application for every Professional Examination must be made to the Registrar of the College of Physicians and Surgeons of Ontario two weeks prior to Examinations. No application will be received unless accompanied by the necessary tickets and certificates, and by the Treasurer's receipt showing the fees have been paid.

4. Each "Six Months' Course" shall consist of not less than Fifty Lectures, and each "Three Months' Course" of not less than Twenty-five Lectures.

5. Every Student must attend the undermentioned courses of

Lectures in a University, College, or School of Medicine approved of by the Council, viz.:

Two courses of not less than six months each (in the different years) upon

ANATOMY.
PRACTICAL ANATOMY.
PHYSIOLOGY (including Histology).
THEORETICAL CHEMISTRY.
MATERIA MEDICA AND THERAPEUTICS.
PRINCIPLES AND PRACTICE OF MEDICINE.
    "   "   "   " SURGERY.
MIDWIFERY AND DISEASES OF WOMEN.
CLINICAL MEDICINE.
    " SURGERY.

One course of not less than six months each, upon

MEDICAL JURISPRUDENCE.
MEDICAL, SURGICAL AND TOPOGRAPHICAL ANATOMY.

Two courses of not less than three months each (in different years) upon

DISEASES OF CHILDREN.
PRACTICAL CHEMISTRY (including Toxicology).

One course of not less than three months each, upon

SANITARY SCIENCE.
PRACTICAL PHARMACY.

One course of ten Lectures upon

MENTAL DISEASES.

One course of fifty Demonstrations upon

PHYSIOLOGICAL HISTOLOGY.

6. Every candidate will be required to prove that he has carefully dissected the adult human body.

7. The following are the Text-books recommended by the Council in the various branches:

GENERAL TEXT-BOOKS.

ANATOMY—Gray, Quain.
PHYSIOLOGY—Kirke, Foster, Yeo.
CHEMISTRY—Roscoe, Attfield, Remsen and Jones.

MATERIA MEDICA—Ringer, Mitchell Bruce, Hare's Therapeutics, British Pharmacopœia.

SURGERY—Bryant, Treeves, Mansell Moulin, Walsham—4th edition, Erichsen.

MEDICINE—Roberts, Hilton Fagge, Osler.

MIDWIFERY AND DISEASES OF WOMEN—Skene, Mundé, Playfair, Galabin.

MEDICAL JURISPRUDENCE AND TOXICOLOGY—Taylor, Guy and Ferrier.

PATHOLOGY—Green, Woodhead, Coats.

SANITARY SCIENCE—Wilson, Louis C. Parke.

DISEASES OF CHILDREN—Eustace Smith, Ashby and Wright.

HOMŒOPATHIC TEXT-BOOKS.

MATERIA MEDICA—Hahnemann, Hering.

MEDICINE AND THERAPEUTICS—Baehr's, Arndt, Raue's Pathology and Diagnostics, Lilienthal.

SURGERY—Franklin, Helmuth.

MIDWIFERY—Guernsey, Ludlam.

8. Also must have attended the practice of a General Hospital for twenty-four months during the first four years of study.

9. Also must have attended six cases of Midwifery.

10. Also must, before being registered as a member of the College of Physicians and Surgeons of Ontario, have passed all the Examinations herein prescribed; and attained the full age of twenty-one years.

11. Graduates in Medicine from recognized Colleges outside the Dominion of Canada, who desire to qualify themselves for registration, must pass the Matriculation required by the Council; and must attend one or more full Winter Courses of Lectures in one of the Ontario Medical Schools, and must complete fully the Practical and Clinical Curriculum required by the Council after the fourth year, and shall pass before the Examiners appointed by the Council all the Examinations hereinafter prescribed, so as to complete fully the Curriculum.

12. That British Registered Medical Practitioners on paying all

fees and passing the Intermediate and Final Examinations be registered, provided they have been domiciled in Britain for five years after becoming so registered.

Section III.

EXAMINATIONS.

1. The Professional Examinations are divided into three parts : a " Primary," " Intermediate," and "Final."

2. The Primary Examination shall be undergone after the second Winter Session, and the Intermediate after the third or fourth Winter Session, the Final after the fifth year.

3. The following branches shall be embraced in the Primary Examination :

    a. ANATOMY.

    b. PHYSIOLOGY AND HISTOLOGY.

    c. CHEMISTRY (Theoretical and Practical).

    d. MATERIA MEDICA AND PHARMACY.

4. Every Candidate for the Primary Examination will be required to present, with his Lecture Tickets, a certificate of having undergone and passed an Examination at the School he has attended at the close of his first Winter Session on Primary Branches. Also a Certificate of ability to make and mount Microscopic Specimens.

5. Each Candidate for Final Examination must present a Certificate of attendance at six Post-Mortem Examinations, and a Certificate of ability to draw up a Report of a Post-Mortem Examination ; and a Certificate of having reported satisfactorily Six Cases of Clinical Medicine, and Six Cases of Clinical Surgery, and of having attended twenty-five Pathological Demonstrations, and of having passed his Intermediate Examination. The certificates to be signed by the Teachers referred to upon these subjects, or the Practitioner holding Post-Mortem. Also, all Candidates shall (except Arts Graduates) present a Certificate of having passed at the close of their third Session in the College or School they may have attended, an Examination in such parts of Medicine, Surgery, and Midwifery as may be thought

advisable by the Faculties of the respective Colleges or Schools. This Examination is not in any way to interfere with any of the Examinations of the Council.

6. The following branches shall be embraced in the Intermediate Examination :

  a. MEDICAL, SURGICAL AND TOPOGRAPHICAL ANATOMY.
  b. PRINCIPLES AND PRACTICE OF MEDICINE.
  c. GENERAL PATHOLOGY AND BACTERIOLOGY.
  d. SURGERY, other than Operative.
  e. SURGERY, Operative.
  f. MIDWIFERY, other than Operative.
  g. MIDWIFERY, Operative.
  h. MEDICAL JURISPRUDENCE, INCLUDING TOXICOLOGY AND MENTAL. DISEASES.
  i. SANITARY SCIENCE.
  j. DISEASES OF CHILDREN.
  k. DISEASES OF WOMEN.
  l. THERAPEUTICS.

7. The Primary and Intermediate Examinations shall be "Written" and "Oral." The Final, "Oral" and "Clinical."

8. The following branches will be embraced in the Final Examination :

  a. CLINICAL MEDICINE.
  b. CLINICAL SURGERY (including Vaccination).
  c. DISEASES OF WOMEN.
  d. DISEASES OF CHILDREN, MEDICAL AND SURGICAL.

9. Any Candidate who makes 60 per cent. in three or more branches, but fails in the others, shall receive credit for the subjects so passed, and be compelled to pass in the other branches only at a subsequent Examination.

10. Candidates who intend to be examined by the Homœopathic Examiner in special subjects, shall signify their intention to the Registrar at least two weeks previous to the commencement of the Examination, in order that he may provide means of preventing their identification by the other Students, or by the Examiners.

11. In the event of any Candidate signifying his intention to the Registrar to be examined and registered as a Homœopathic Practitioner, due notice of such must be submitted to the Registrar, so that the Examinations may be conducted by the parties appointed for that purpose ; prior to the acceptance of such notice from the Candidate, the usual fees must be paid. In the event of any Candidate present-ing himself for such Examination, due notice must be given by the Registrar to the special Examiner.

12. A Professional Examination will be held in Toronto on the second Tuesday in September, 1893. Candidates who have failed in a former Examination to pay a fee of twenty dollars for this Exam-ination. The next Professional Examinations will be held in Toronto and Kingston on the second Tuesday in April, 1894.

Section IV.

FEES.

1. The following scale of fees has been established by the Council of the College of Physicians and Surgeons of Ontario :

a. Registration of Matriculation $20 00

b. Primary Examination 20 00

c. Final Examination, including Registration 30 00
> These fees are to be paid to the Treasurer of the College before each Examination.

d. Registration of Persons duly qualified before 23rd day of July, 1870 . . . . 10 00

e. Registration of Persons duly qualified after 23rd day of July, 1870 . . . . 25 00

f. Registration of Additional Degrees or Titles 2 00
> This fee is only payable when the additional titles are registered at different times, but any number of such titles as are allowed to be regis-tered, may be put on record at the first regis-tration, for the registration fee.

g. Diploma of Membership of the College $5 00

> This Diploma is granted free of charge to all those members of the College who attain their membership by passing the Examinations of the College. All other members may obtain it on application to the Registrar, and paying the above-named fee.

h. Annual Assessment due by Members of the College for the year 1892, payable to the Registrar.. 2 00

> This fee is payable by every member of the College on or before the last day of December, in each year, to December, 1892.

Fees after 1st of July, 1889 :

a. Registration of Matriculation.................... 20 00
b. Primary Examination......................... 30 00
c. Intermediate and Final Examination, including registration.................................... 50 00

> This is not to affect any Student who is registered as a Matriculate prior to 1st July, 1889.

2. All fees must be paid in lawful money of Canada to the Treasurer of the College.

3. No Candidate will be admitted to any Examination until the fee for such Examination is paid in full.

4. Candidates who have failed in any Professional Examination shall pay a fee of Twenty Dollars for each subsequent Examination.

Section V.

EXAMINATIONS.

Rules for the Guidance of the Board of Examiners.

1. The Registrar or Deputy Registrar must be present at every Examination.

2. At the end of each Written Examination upon any Subject, the answers to the Questions are to be handed to the Registrar, who will open the envelopes, in which they are hereinafter directed to be

enclosed, and to each set of papers affix a number by which the author will be known to the Examiners during the Examination. The Registrar will then deliver the papers to the Member of the Board of Examiners appointed by the Council to examine upon the Subject.

3. The papers, when delivered to the Member of the Board of Examiners appointed by the Council to examine upon the Subject, are to be by him examined, and the relative value of answers marked by means of numbers in a Schedule which will be furnished to him by the Registrar, ranging for the Primary Subjects as follows :

4. That the percentage in the Primary branches be as follows, ranging from 0 to 100 on all subjects :

	Honors.	Pass.
Anatomy	75	50
Physiology and Histology	75	50
Chemistry—Theoretical and Practical	75	50
Materia Medica and Pharmacy	75	50

INTERMEDIATE.

Medical, Surgical and Topographical Anatomy	0 to 100
Principles and Practice of Medicine	0 to 100
General Pathology and Therapeutics	0 to 100
Surgery, other than Operative	0 to 100
Surgery, Operative	0 to 100
Midwifery, other than Operative	0 to 100
Midwifery, Operative	0 to 100
Medical Jurisprudence, Toxicology and Mental Diseases	0 to 100
Sanitary Science	0 to 100
Diseases of Children, Medical and Surgical	0 to 100
Diseases of Women	0 to 100
Therapeutics	0 to 100

Marks required for Honors and Pass :

	Honors.	Pass.
Medical, Surgical and Topographical Anatomy	75	50
Principles and Practice of Medicine	75	50
General Pathology and Therapeutics	75	50
Surgery, other than Operative	75	50
Surgery, Operative	75	50
Midwifery, other than Operative	75	50
Midwifery, Operative	75	50

Medical Jurisprudence, Toxicology and Mental

    Diseases 75 50

Sanitary Science 75 50

Diseases of Children, Medical and Surgical ... 75 50

Diseases of Women....................... 75 50

That the percentage in the Final branches be as follows : o to 100 on all subjects. Honors 75, Pass 50.

5. The value awarded by the individual Examiners to the answers of Candidates are not to be subject to revision, except by an appeal by the Candidate to the Council, when special cases of hardship may seem to have occurred.

6. The Examiners shall return the Schedules to the Registrar, with values inserted, within seven days of notice to be sent by the Registrar. From these values a general Schedule is to be prepared by the Registrar, and no change of value can be made after such Schedules have been returned by the Examiners to the Registrar. The General Schedule so prepared is to be examined as to its correctness by the President, and the results announced by the President.

7. Papers on the Homœopathic subjects are to be finally submitted to the Examiner approved of for that purpose by the representatives of that system in the Council.

8. All Oral Examinations are henceforth to be as Clinical, Demonstrative and Practical as possible, and the Candidate shall be known to the Examiners by number only.

9. That it be an instruction to the Examiners, in the questions in their respective subjects, to confine themselves to the text-books in ordinary use (see page 15 of this Announcement), also that in referring to diseases or operations of any kind, the names of such diseases or operations most commonly in use should be employed.

10. That it be an instruction to the President that he shall in no case report a Candidate as having passed an examination when on any subject he makes less than the minimum of marks set by the Council for a pass on that subject. But in any case where he thinks there are special reasons for granting a license to such candidate, he shall report the same to the Council for its action.

Rules for Candidates when in the Examination Hall.

11. Each Candidate shall receive from the Registrar a Programme containing a list of subjects upon which the Candidate is to be examined, and it will admit him to the Examination Hall during the progress of the Examinations upon such subject, but at no other time.

12. Candidates must write the answers to the questions given by the Examiners, legibly and neatly upon one side only of each page of a book, which will be furnished to each candidate, and the number given with each question is to be put at the head of the answer to it, in such a manner as to have the first page facing outward to the view; they are then to be folded once, and enclosed in an envelope, on the outside of which each candidate is to write his name. The packet is then to be handed to the Registrar, or some one deputed by him. Neither signature, number or sign, by which the writer could be recognized by the Examiner, is to be written or marked upon any portion of the book to be enclosed in the envelope.

13. The questions of the Examiners in the Homœopathic subjects will be handed in writing, at the beginning of the General Examination on the same subject, by the Registrar, to such candidates as have given him notice in accordance with Section III., sub-secs. 8, 9. They shall write the answers to these questions in the same hall with the other candidates, and hand their papers, when finished, to the Registrar in the same manner as provided for the other candidates, to be by him given for examination to the Homœopathic member of the Board of Examiners appointed to examine on that subject.

14. If any abbreviations are used in answering the questions, candidates must be careful that they are such as are generally understood, or which cannot be mistaken.

15. No candidate will be allowed to leave the hall after the questions are given out, until his answers have been handed in.

16. No candidate will be allowed in the hall during the hours of examination, except those who are actually undergoing examination.

17. Any candidate who may have brought any book or reference paper to the hall, must deposit it with the Registrar before the examination begins.

18. Candidates must not communicate with each other while examinations are going on, either by writing, signs, words, or in any manner whatever.

19. Candidates must at all times bear themselves towards the Registrar and Examiners with the utmost deference and respect; and they will not be permitted in any manner to manifest approbation or disapprobation of any member of the Board of Examiners during the progress of the examination.

20. Candidates must not only conduct themselves with decorum while any examination is going on, but they will be held strictly responsible for any impropriety of conduct during the whole progress, both of the Written and of the Oral Examinations.

21. Any infraction of the above rules will lead to the exclusion of the Candidate who is guilty of it from the remainder of the examination ; and he will not receive credit for any examination papers which he may have handed to the Registrar previous to his being detected in such misconduct.

22. And be debarred from further privileges at the discretion of the Council.

LIST OF STUDENTS OF MEDICINE

WHO HAVE PASSED

The Matriculation Examination

BEFORE THE EXAMINERS APPOINTED BY THE COUNCIL, AND REGISTERED
AS MATRICULATES WITH THE

College of Physicians and Surgeons of Ontario.

Abbott, Clarence.........Toronto 1883
Adamson, H. A............Ottawa 1889
Addison, W. L. T........Armory 1892
Aiken, A. W.........Orangeville 1890
Airth, H. W............Renfrew 1886
Aitchison, William ....St. George 1870
Alexander, D. B........Huntley 1882
Alexander, G......... ..Huntley 1884
Alexander, L. H.....Owen Sound 1892
Alexander, W. E., Hemmingford, Q 1892
Alexander, W. H.. ....Toronto 1889
Alexander, W. J.....Thornbury 1887
Alexander, W. W., Hemmingford, Q 1892
Allen, William G......... Perth 1875
Allen, Thomas...........Toronto 1888
Allin, J. H..... ....Collingwood 1892
Allingham, A. W.....Warkworth 1884
Alway, F. J............Vittoria 1891
Alway, J. H...........Grimsby 1890
Alway, R. D............Grimsby 1889
Alway, William R........Simcoe 1891
Anderson, J. J..........Kingston 1883
Anderson, N............Toronto 1890
Anderson. R. ....Hornby 1886
Ardiel, L. M..........Thorndale 1887
Argue, John F..........Leitrim 1891
Arkell, E. H .... St. Thomas 1892
Armstrong, Moore .....Kingston 1873
Arnold, H. T..........'..Watford 1885
Arnold, John R. ......Harriston 1880
Atkinson, V. T.......... Nelson 1875
Austin, G. H........Lansdowne 1891
Aylen, Walter W.........Quebec 1885
Aylsworth, A. C....Mount Forest 1884

Babbitt, W......Parrsboro', N.S. 1888
Badgerow, G. W........Eglinton 1890
Baily, Eli H........Mount Forest 1881
Baker, E.............Springfield 1892
Bain, W. L.............Parkdale 1884
Baldwin, H. F..........Toronto 1877
Banting, W. T..........London 1888
Barber, Robert A..........Berlin 1880
Barclay, Thomas........Hamilton 1871
Barker, A. N...........Kingston 1890
Barlee, H. J. W........Montreal 1888
Baston, John ....Kingston 1870
Basken, J. T..........Stittsville 1890
Bayne, C. W............Ottawa 1887
Bayne, John G.........Newbury 1891
Beamish, George.......Port Hope 1876
Beasley, W. J...........Weston 1892
Beattie, D. A.............Galt 1888
Beatty, A. A..........Toronto 1892
Beatty, E. D.......South March 1891
Beaudry, J. S..........Montreal 1883
Bedell, T. C. .....Hillier 1892
Beemer, W. C..........Simcoe 1888
Belanger, R. U..........Ottawa 1892
Belch, J. A ....Kingston 1887
Beckett, James.......Thamesville 1890
Bellamy, A. W....North Augusta 1888
Bell, A. W.............Toronto 1857
Bell, Basil H.....New Edinburgh 1886
Bell, B. C............St. George 1891
Bell, J. C.. ....Strathroy 1877
Bell, John C..............Nairn 1881
Bell, J. H............Camlachie 1891
Bell, T. H............Peterboro' 1892

3

Bell, A................Agincourt 1892
Belton, W. J..........Kingston 1885
Bennett, Henry .... Picton 1875
Bennie, Robert.........Sudbury 1892
Bentley, F. M........Newmarket 1887
Berry, George H.........Oakleaf 1892
Berry, R. P..............Lindsay 1883
Berwick, G. A.........Farnham 1888
Berwick, R. H......Cowansville 1887
Bethune, F. H..........Seaforth 1892
Bickstead, Morris.....Morrisburg 1874
Bier, Thomas H........Brantford 1891
Birge, A. H ....Toronto 1891
Birks, William R........Prescott 1891
Birmingham, F. H......Kingston 1888
Blewett, W. J......Little Britain 1886
Blewett, W. G.........Lindsay 1892
Block, B. F ....Kingston 1891
Blow, T. J.......South Mountain 1892
Blunt, H. W.....Knowlton, Que. 1888
Boddy, James ....Toronto 1889
Bollen, P... .... .Chicago 1885
Bollen, C..............Chicago 1885
Boileau, F. X......Sturgeon Falls 1890
Bolton, T. B.............Toronto 1881
Booth, John A........ Brantford 1890
Boucher, R. P........Peterboro' 1892
Bouck, C. A............Inkerman 1891
Bonter, G. S..............Trenton 1869
Bosanko, Arthur.....Gravenhurst 1875
Bowan, Hector A.........Albion 1873
Bouillon, A........... Montreal 1890
Bowles, G. H.......... Sandhill 1888
Bourns, W. H.........Kingston 1888
Boyce, B. F.........Warkworth 1888
Bowbeer, W. C..........Simcoe 1889
Bowie, Innes..............Embro 1890
Boyd, W. B...........Uxbridge 1890
Boyle, J. F.............Toronto 1892
Bradley, J. L..............Airlie 1892
Bradshaw, Kate ....Toronto 1892
Brereton, C. H........Schomberg 1892
Brennan, William H.......Toronto 1875
Brewster, William ......Toronto 1873
Bridgman, O. M.........London 1882
Brien, J. W.............Toronto 1888
Britton, Fred ....Brantford 1892
Broad, R..............Coboconk 1892
Brown, Campbell .....Acton Vale 1870
Brown, Harry...........London 1870
Brown, Charles ....Carleton Place 1892
Brown, J. A..... ......Kingston 1882
Brown, C. O..Lauranceville, Que. 1878
Brown, Kent A....St. Catharines 1881
Brown, E...............Cobourg 1886
Brown, James E.........Tyrone 1881

Brown, F. W.........Brockville 1888
Brown, G. W.............Lyons 1892
Brown, W. F............Medina 1892
Brown, J. N............Medina 1889
Bruce, F.,New Lathrop, Mich.,U.S. 1889
Bryce, W. ....Keene 1892
Buchan, D ....Galt 1892
Buchanan, H. M.......Kingston 1885
Buck, Katie L ....Peterboro' 1892
Buck, R. A ....Avonbank 1888
Burden, F. L...........Newbury 1885
Burnham, J. H.......Peterboro' 1887
Burns, T. B.............Toronto 1875
Butler, Charlton ......Strathroy 1876
Butler, John A ....Lindsay 1892
Bull, John H.....Weston 1890
Burd, W. S.........Parry Sound 1892
Burrows. Frederick N......Bath 1880
Burk, John A.......Amherstburg 1892
Burt, George S...........Toronto 1892
Byers, W. G. M.......Gananoque 1890

Caldwell, H. J...........Toronto 1881
Callander, C. N.........Kirkton 1888
Cameron, Alex. D....River Raisin 1878
Cameron, D. A......Wallacetown 1892
Cameron, Duncan ....Perth 1873
Cameron, Duncan,
    85 Hayter St., Toronto 1870
Cameron, John D ......L'Orignal 1892
Cameron, Duncan ......Strathroy 1880
Cameron, J. B. Montague,
    Prince Edward Island 1872
Campbell, A. W...Montreal, Que. 1831
Campbell, A. L........Kingston 1883
Campbell, Bryon ....Parkhill 1890
Campbell, David 1879
Campbell, G. G......Truro, N.S. 1888
Campbell, James .....:...London 1873
Campbell, George J ....Blyth 1893
Campbell, P. M........Kingston 1892
Carbert, Joseph A....Orangeville 1870
Calton, William H......Toronto 1875
Carry, Chester ....Florence 1870
Case, J. H..............Colborne 1872
Cassidy, William ,......Toronto 1884
Carter, L. H..............Picton 1884
Carroll, R. W.........Stratford 1889
Carlaw, T. W.........Warkworth 1889
Carron, F. B.........Brockville 1892
Caven, James...........Toronto 1892
Chabot, J. L...........Ottawa 1885
Chambers, W. J.........Paisley 1881
Christie, Andrew........Bradford 1880
Christin, J. A ....Montreal 1892
Chance, J. Broomley....Brantford 1876

Chestnut, George................ 1866
Chevrier, G. R............Ottawa 1891
Church, F. W. H......Hull, Que. 1888
Church, A. H ....Montreal 1892
Churchill, B. P ....Toronto 1892
Clare, H...............Chapman 1892
Clark, D. A............Agincourt 1890
Clarke, E. A.............Aylmer 1887
Clark, F. G. R ......Collingwood 1871
Clark, J. A. M........Ridgetown 1891
Clarkson, Frederick A...Seaforth 1891
Clark, W. H...........Meaford 1883
Clark, J. L.............Waterloo 1883
Clark, William J........Toronto 1891
Clayes, George ....Brockville 1892
Clemes, S. R........Collingwood 1892
Cleaver, John C........Kingston 1875
Cleaver, William F.... Kingston 1875
Clinton, George ......Wellington 1875
Close, James A............ 1869
Clindinin, S. L..........Brighton 1892
Cloutier, F..............Kingston 1884
Coffee, R. H.................... 1883
Cole, J. A.............Freelton 1880
Coleman, F ....Toronto 1890
Coleman, H. Kay..... Gananoque 1876
Coleman, Mary E......West Hill 1880
Coleman, T..............Seaforth 1886
Collfas, W. F.........Morriston 1892
Collins, E. P...........Princeton 1892
Collison, G. W....Dixon's Corners 1892
Conerby, M..............Trenton 1886
Connell, W. T..........Kingston 1890
Connolly, B. G ....Trenton 1890
Cooke, C. F ....Gesto 1886
Cook, E. L. B............Toronto 1876
Cook, J. D ....Paris 1875
Cook, George E......Morrisburg 1892
Cooke, Sheldon R......Aultsville 1878
Cooper, J. J...........Chatham 1887
Coote, Frank ....Montreal 1885
Corbett, R T......... Port Hope 1890
Corson, Douglas ......Woodstock 1881
Cosford, John B.........Toronto 1876
Coulthard, W. L.........Picton 1890
Cowan, J. J ....Goderich 1880
Cowley, Daniel K.......Ottawa 1876
Cowper, J. A ....Welland 1890
Craft, R. A...........Fish Lake 1890
Cranston, J. G.........Arnprior 1891
Crawford, D. T ....Thedford 1892
Crawford, John..........Toronto 1890
Crosby, Arthur ....Uxbridge 1880
Crosby, F. H ....Uxbridge 1884
Cron, William ....Batteau 1890
Cumberland, Thos. ..Mono Centre 1880

Curzon, Edith M ....Toronto 1890
Cuzner, Mark R....Aylmer, Que. 1878
Cunningham, J. A. ..Parry Sound 1892
Cunningham, J. D. ......Osborne 1892
Currie, M ....Picton 1893
Curtis, James .....Middlemarch 1892

Dady, Ralph ....Toronto 1877
Dales, F. A.............Sanford 1888
Darling, Elsie L ....Rosedale 1892
Dargavel, J.............Durham 1887
Darling, R. E ....Warkworth 1889
Dancey, J. H .... .Aylmer 1892
Davis, H. C............Dundas 1892
Davis, Murdock L........Norham 1872
Davis, R. J ....Smith's Falls 1871
Davis, T. B......Wakefield, Que. 1880
Davis, W. 1872
Davis, J. J ....London 1893
David, W. C...........Kingston 1885
Davidson, Allan...........Burns 1890
Davies, P. H...........Rosedale 1888
Day, A. R..............Guelph 1888
Deacon, G. R ....Stratford 1892
Deacon, J. D ....Pembroke 1885
Dean, W. E. ....Toronto 1892
DeCow, D. M............Dresden 1881
Deeks, W. E.....Montreal, Que. 1889
Delaney, W. F......\..Peterboro' 1885
Denis, A. ....Vaudreuil, Que. 1889
Devitt, T. G ....Bobcaygeon 1890
Dewar, Alexander ......Montreal 1887
Dillabough, H. W.....Hamilton 1891
Dickson, G. J ....Paisley 1892
Dingham, H ....Picton 1871
Disney, H. C...........London 1880
Doan, W ....New Sorum 1888
Doherty, Charles E......Eglinton 1891
Doherty, George........Markham 1875
Donovan, Patrick. ..Campbellford 1876
Donovan, E. J.........Kingston 1881
Donald, William........Goderich 1881
Doogherty, J. W. ....Eden 1881
Dorais, U. A...........Montreal 1884
Dougan, R. P...........Thorold 1886
Douglas, Alexander ....Avon 1872
Douglas, A. E.........Warwick 1889
Douglas, James H.......Norham 1876
Dow, J. D ....Pembroke 1881
Downes, C. H...........Toronto 1885
Downing, Jos. J ....Kingston 1891
Doyle, C. S............. Toronto 1885
Doyle, J. M.........Caledonia 1892
Drain, J. F ....Campbellford 1891
Drennan, Jennie G......Kingston 1890
Drummond, P .. .. .. .Almonte 1884

King, John E	Elder's Mills	1889
Keith, W. D	Toronto	1892
Kyle, R. J. L	Winchester	1892
Kerr, J. J	Cobourg	1892
Kemp, H. G	Brighton	1891
Kelly, J. K.	Almonte	1892
Kirby, T. W	Toronto	1892
Knight, C. E	Napanee	1892
Lang, Abner J	King	1876
Livingstone, Joseph	Carlisle	1871
Lusk, C. W.	Gorrie	1877
Luton, Albert	Mapleton	1871
Luton, Robert	Mapleton	1870
Lewis, Thomas W	Iroquois	1877
Loring, Jonathan B	Sherbrooke	1877
Loughead, ——	Belleville	1878
Loucy, George A		1879
Lander, T. H	London	1880
Lundy, Frederick G	Newmarket	1880
Leitch, A. L.	Bowood	1880
Lawton, Thomas M	Warwick	1880
Lannin, John N	Toronto	1881
Latimer, W.	Marshville	1882
Law, D	Palmerston	1885
Leary, E.	Britannia	1882
Lindsay, James	Limehouse	1881
Livingston, Mary	Kingston	1882
Longeway, A. F	Montreal	1882
Luke, E.	Manilla	1883
Lesperance, J.	Montreal	1883
Livingston, J. S	Belleville	1886
Lucas, M. F	Grimsby	1886
Laurie, C. N	Toronto	1885
Lawson, Alice	Toronto	1887
Laird, C. J	Guelph	1888
Lapp, T. B	Baltimore	1888
Lockhart, A	Kingston	1888
Ludwig, A	Heidleberg	1889
Lennox, Eleanor G.	Toronto	1889
Leitch, A. E.	Dutton	1889
Locke, John A	Kingston	1889
Laycock, R. G	Embro	1889
Lane, M. S	Toronto	1889
Lochead, J.	Montreal	1890
Langford, W	Brampton	1890
Lawson, J. A	Brampton	1890
Lineham, D. M.	Newry	1890
Large, S. H	Queensville	1890
Lawrason, L.	Dundas	1890
Livingstone, H	Alliston	1880
LeRosignol, W. J	Toronto	1891
Lee, F. J	Bethany	1891
Lyle, W. D	Morrisburg	1892
Laidlaw, W. C	Toronto	1892
Lane, G. A	Toronto	1892

Leith, J. D.	Dromore	1892
Louergan, W. J	Rutherford	1892
Large, R. W	Queensville	1892
Lander, S. E	Durham	1892
Lynch, D. P.	Montreal	1892
Lee, J. P	Toronto	1892
Macdonald, Hugh	Guelph	1871
Markle, V. Alfred	Millgrove	1874
Martin, M	Toronto	1876
Masson, J	Cobourg	1871
May, William B	Toronto	1877
Meldrum, P. Gordon	Ashburn	1872
Murray, S. S.	Nelson, Co. Halton	1873
Miller, Alexander	Goderich	1877
Miller, ——	Toronto	1874
Mills, R. G	Newbury	1874
Mitchell, John C.	Newtonville	1872
Morden, James G	Carlisle	1874
Moore, John T	Yorkville	1876
Moore, William	Owen Sound	1877
Morrison, James J	Sarnia	1875
Morrow, Charles		1869
Morton, John A. McD.	Kingston	1873
Morton, W. C	Waterdown	1871
Munn, William Albert	Lynn	1873
Munro, Duncan E.	Wardsville	1877
Munro, L. S	Fergus	1875
Murphy, E N	Penetanguishene	1871
Musgrove, W. J	St. Catharines	1877
Murgatroyd, R. G	Smithville	1877
Mather, Charles L	Warkworth	1878
Metherell, S. L.	Little Britain	1879
Martin, J. Francis, Charlottetown, P.E.I.		1880
Moore, Thomas A.	Kingston	1880
Midgley, James E	St. Thomas	1881
Macdonald, John	Guelph	1881
Morris, Samuel	Strathburn	1881
Murray, W. H	Galt	1881
MacLean, D. W	Kingston	1885
Macpherson, W. A	Fingal	1883
Malcolm, H	Harrisburg	1883
Marshall, Alice A	Brockville	1885
Metcalf, W. F.	Bayside	1884
Morgan, V. H	Aultsville	1882
Morrow, C. N	Russell	1884
Mustard, J. W.	Uxbridge	1883
Morgan, E. M.	Renfrew	1886
Morgan, L. E	Kerrwood	1886
Marr, A. W	Westmeath	1886
Mabee, C. O	Odessa	1883
Mundie, J.	Toronto	1885
Masales, M. L	Erin	1884
Morphy, A. G	London	1886
MacKechnie, W. G	Brighton	1886

Montgomery, W	Perrytown	1887
Mullock, L. J	Waterdown	1887
Moore, J. M	Belleville	1887
Mackenzie, A. J. L.	London	1887
Martin, S. H.	Waterloo	1887
Murphy, R	London	1887
McLennan, D. N	Kingston	1888
Munro, L. W	Caledonia	1888
Macdonald, M. S	Montreal	1886
MacKay, Thomas E.	Kingston	1887
Murray, W. O. S.	London	1887
Meikle, W. F.	Morrisburg	1888
MacNee, E	Perth	1888
MacLean, J. D	Meaford	1889
MacKendrick, H. F	Toronto	1889
Marr, Dell	Ridgetown	1889
MacKay, R. B	Montreal	1889
Maloney, P. J.	Ennismore	1889
Moss, F. H	Toronto	1889
Murray, Allie G	Strathroy	1889
Morden, F. W	Picton	1890
MacCarthy, George S.	Ottawa	1890
Moore, John	Kingston	1890
Mahan, John W	Brampton	1890
Myers, Ambrose R	Kingston	1890
Massey, Hamish	Toronto	1890
Morrison, L. T	Windsor	1891
Martin, C. E	Toronto	1891
Millichamp, G. E	Toronto	1891
Musson, George	Toronto	1891
Macklin, A. H	Stratford	1891
Mallock, N	Marvelville	1891
Marselis, E. H	Morrisburg	1891
Miller, H. W	Orillia	1891
Mackay, A.	Creemore	1892
Marquis, S. A	Brantford	1892
Martin, J. E..East Saginaw, Mich.		1892
Moles, E. B	Arnprior	1892
Moffatt, William..Carleton Place		1892
Murray, H. G	Owen Sound	1892
Mills, George B.	Fergus	1892
Morris, James S	Oshawa	1892
MacCallum, W. G	Dunnville	1892
MacMillan, Margaret L.	Toronto	1892
Matheson, John	Martintown	1892
Menzies, R. D	Kingston	1892
Macallum, Margaret	Toronto	1892
More, George	Kirkton	1892
Malloch, W. J. O	Meaford	1892
Mullin, J. H.	Hamilton	1892
Mooney, T..	Kingston	1892
Milburn, J. A	Peterboro'	1892
Membery, G. G	Toronto	1892
Moore, R	Laskay	1892
Monteith, J. D	Stratford	1892
Moxwell, G. B	St. Thomas	1892

Milligan, A	Toronto	1891
Metcalf, A. A.	Almonte	1892
McAlpine, D	Kilmartin	1874
McCollum, A	Toronto	1875
McCrae, Henry	Portsmouth	1872
McDiarmid, Andrew	York P.O.	1873
McDiarmid, John	Toronto	1872
McDonald, Alexander	Paisley	1877
McIlvaine, Samuel	Orillia	1875
McKibbon, Arch	Rollin's Mills	1876
McKinnon, John A.	Toronto	1876
McLean, Arch. M	Portsmouth	1872
McLeod, Duncan	Keepen	1871
McRae, John C	Port Colborne.	1875
McTavish, P. F	Toronto	1873
McBride, John	Toronto	1877
McNulty, M	Dixon's Corners	1877
McDuffy, John W	Stanstead	1887
McPherson, Graham A	Toronto	1878
McLean, John Douglas	Ottawa	1887
McVicar, John	Brantford	1873
McCammon, C. Gordon		1876
McMichael, James.	Gorrie	1880
McCulloch, James	Norval	1880
McPhail, Duncan P..Iona Station		1880
McGhie, George S.,		
Elgin P.O., Co. Leeds		1880
McCullough, George	Georgetown	1880
McKerroll, John	Harriston	1880
McKillop, Alexander	Crosley	1881
McKay, Kenneth W..St. Thomas		1881
McIntyre, C. J	Port Hope	1881
McDonald, George	Ingersoll	1881
McAndrew, G. C	Renfrew	1885
McCollum, E. P	Duart	1883
McDonald, G	Tilsonburg	1883
McFarlane, M	Ottawa	1883
McKay, W	Collingwood	1883
McKinnon, N. C.	Sonya	1882
McLean, John	Florence	1882
McLeary, J. A	Watford	1882
McLennan, D	Dunvegan	1883
McLurg, J. A.	Falkirk	1883
McNeece, J	Brampton	1884
McEwan, F	St. Thomas	1885
McGregor, J	Longwoods	1884
McColl, D	Merritton	1885
McArthur, F. T	London	1886
McDonald, J. N	Moosejaw	1884
McDonald, P. A	Alexandria	1885
McFarlane, M. J	Ridgetown	1886
McKechnie, J	Claude	1886
McGuire, J. C.	Trenton	1887
McCrimmon, A. A	St. Thomas	1887
McCullough, F. F	Port Severn	1886
McArthur, E. L	Thorold	1887

McFarlane, W. ....Dunnville 1888
McGinnis, J..............London 1887
McCrimmon, F..........London 1887
McCuen, J. A .. ..Guelph 1887
McLaren, A. P.........Port Elgin 1887
McPherson, W. A......Esquesing 1887
McEwen, W. H..........London 1887
McIntyre, H..........St Thomas 1887
McCuaig, J. A..........Kingston 1887
McCollum, Annie......Gananoque 1888
McGrath, G. .... Frankford 1888
McIntosh, J. F..North
    Grosvenordale, Conn., U.S. 1889
McLennan, K............Kenzon 1889
McCarthy, D. S .... Orangeville 1889
McIlwraith, K..........Hamilton 1889
McKenzie, R. T ....Montreal 1889
McCrae, T ....Guelph 1889
McIntosh, L. Y. ......Strathmore 1889
McNaughton, J. A......Cornwall 1889
McClenahan, D. A.......Tansley 1890
McMillan, J. A ....Strathroy 1890
McKee, J. F.............Aurora 1890
McKechnie, R. E. ......Montreal 1890
McColgan, R . ... .Elora 1890
McCollum, W. J. ....Toronto 1890
McEvay, Thomas ......Montreal 1891
McDonnell, J ....Belleville 1891
McDonald, William..........Galt 1891
McPherson, D. W........Toronto 1891
McEwen, A ....Kingston 1891
McCormack, F. ....Toronto 1891
McEachern, J. S........Cashtown 1891
McDonald, H. G.......Kingston 1891
McDermid, A......... Coldwater 1891
McKechnie, W. B......Aberdour 1891
McGannon, A. V .....Brockville 1891
McKeown, H. A........Kingston 1892
McPherson, C. F. S.....Prescott 1892
McMurrich, J. B. ....Toronto 1892
McDougall, T. A......Ailsa Craig 1892
McKenty, J. E..........Montreal 1892
McKee, T. H. ....North Glanford 1892
McCash, E. A. .... Lucan 1892
McEwen, D ....St. Elmo 1892
McCraig, A. S . .....Collingwood 1892
McDermott, J. W .....Eganville 1892
McLaren, P. S ......Owen Sound 1892
McKee, C. S ....Peterboro' 1892
McRossie, T. D..........Napanee 1892
McCormick, A. H......Brantford 1892
McKenzie, D. C. .... Durham 1892
McLennan, John ......Port Hope 1892
McLean, A. M..........Bradford 1892
McCallum, E. D ......Gravel Hill 1892
McLennan, R ....Kingston 1892

McLaren, A ....Kingston 1892
McLaren, R. W ...... .Kingston 1892
McQuarrie, J. K.....Orangeville 1892
McRobbie, D. G........Shelburne 1892
McInnes, N. W..........Vittoria 1892
McConnell, J. H..........Toronto 1892
McCarter, J. M.........Almonte 1892
McNamara, A. T ....Toronto 1892

Nellis, J. Meloux .....Brantford 1871
Nealon, Edward A 1879
Ney, George S 1879
Nelles, C ....Brantford 1883
Normon, J. O............Toronto 1884
Nichol, T. S............Montreal 1884
Nelles, A. B............Ingersoll 1887
Nelles, W. J. ....Caledonia 1888
North, E ....Pringer 1885
Newberry, W. F. H., London, Eng. 1889
Nichol, A. H............Listowel 1891
New, C. F. ....London 1891
Noble, R. T ....Norval 1891
Northcott, W. S.......Belleville 1891
Nicholl, R ....Listowel 1891
Nichol, W. H..........Brantford 1892

O'Connor, George........Cobourg 1875
Oliver, Albert ....Mitchell 1878
O'Brien, Tim ....Brudenell 1880
Oliver, A. J..........Cowansville 1886
O'Rielly, J. J. ....Vestor 1883
Orr, J. E .. ..Mount Elgin 1883
Ogden, W. E. ......Niagara Falls 1888
Outwater, S. W ....Montreal 1888
O'Connor, W ....Toronto 1886
Oliver, J. H.........Sunderland 1891
Oronhyatekha, W. A ...Deseronto 1888

Page, William ....Napanee 1872
Parnell, J. H. ....Kingston 1871
Perks, William.. .....Port Hope 1876
Perkins, O. S.,
    Metamora, Mich., U.S.A. 1873
Perry, P ....Port Hope 1872
Phillips, C....Scotland, Co. Brant 1873
Philip, William........Frankford 1869
Porter, John G............Guelph 1870
Preston, Richard F....New Boyne 1871
Purcell, Alexander ....Wardsville 1877
Purdy, A. M...........Kingston 1869
Patterson, Richard L ....Morpeth 1887
Phippen, S. S. C. ....Parkhill 1878
Petit, Emerson B.......Windham 1879
Porter, Thomas..........Jarvis 1880
Powell, Frederick H ......Ottawa 1881
Parent, C. E...........Montreal 1882

Rounie, J. A ....Toronto 1892
Rogers, F. E............Brighton 1892
Robertson, D. M ... Hawkesbury 1892
Reid, J. B............St. George 1892
Ritchie, W. J............Whitby 1892

Sanders, Ernest C ......Kingston 1871
Scott, Walter ....Dundas 1871
Scot., W .:...... .Auburn, Huron 1872
Sharpe, John William .....Simcoe 1875
Shave, John R.......... London 1877
Sibbett, Adam.........Kingston 1874
Smith, Albert S.........Sterling 1873
Smith, George.............Berlin 1870
Smith, John ....Chaudiere 1873
Stark, John H. .. ..Toronto 1877
Stone, George W............. ... 1873
Stowe, Emily H.. ....Toronto 1871
Stumph, D. B. J.....λ..Stratford 1873
Sutherland, D. E. ......Bradford 1876
Strange, John Henry...Kingston 1877
Shannon, Lewis W.....Kingston 1877
Smellie, Kinian C. ......Montreal 1887
Stark, John ....Bolten 1878
Scott, George Hope.......Ottawa 1878
Stewart, Peter...........Milton 1878
Sheridan, Samuel .....Columbus 1878
Scott, John Milan..Carleton Place 1878
Shaver, William Henry ....Wales 1878
Stuart, Andrew E ......Sandwich 1881
Shepherd, Byron E. ......London 1881
Sands, E. ....Kingston 1885
Saunders, J. B.........Montreal 1881
Schoff, F ....McGillivray 1882
Sinclair, C. M........West Lorne 1883
Spencer, E. M....Tavistock, Eng. 1882
Staples. L. E............Kingston 1883
Stevens, F. M ....Montreal 1883
Sullivan, A. J. F ....Toronto 1885
Sutherland, A. R......Woodstock 1882
Sandison, F............Toronto 1885
Sinclair, L. G.........Tilsonburg 1886
Snider, E. T......... ..Kingston 1885
Stevenson, E. V.........London 1885
Smith, J. G ....Belleville 1886
Speers, A. A ....Toronto 1886
Strathy, H. E...........Toronto 1886
Scott, A. P. ....Montreal 1886
Smiley, W. N..St. Lambert, Que. 1886
Sangster, J. A ....Port Perry 1887
Smith, J. L ....Arthur 1886
Smith, W. D ....Plantagenet 1886
Smith, C........West Winchester 1887
Spencer, A. M..........Harriston 1886
Shaw, J. W. ....Brussels 1887
Sparling, A. J ....Montreal 1887

Sanson, R. D. B.........Toronto 1885
Smith, H. S.............Toronto 1885
Springle, J. A ....Montreal 1884
Skimin, Nellie.........Kingston 1887
Sandison, E ....Cannington 1887
Smale, W. M. B........Wroxeter 1888
Skey, W. R.............Alymer 1888
Sicard, J. D .. ..Angers, Que. 1884
Sinclair, Jennie ....Madoc 1886
Stockhouse, A ....Kingston 1887
Seager, James. ....Rochesterville 1887
Stevenson, W. E....Mount Forest 1888
Sullivan, D. V.........Kingston 1888
Senkler, W. J......St. Catharines 1888
Seymour, W. H.........Toronto 1889
Spankie, J. C. ....Kingston 1889
Smith, R. J.............Toronto 1889
Scane, J. W .... Chatham 1889
Stinson, J. C.,
        Franklin, Penn., U.S. 1889
Shaw, G. F. ....Montreal 1889
Spotswood, W. A. J..Plantagenet 1889
Sproatt, Alan..........Toronto 1889
Singleton, A. B ...... Newboro' 1889
Smyth, Charles E ..St. Catharines 1890
Scott, Walter H........Caledonia 1890
Storey, F G...........Norwood 1890
Shurie, J. S.............Trenton 1890
Sinclair, H. H. ....Walkerton 1890
Shirra, Jennie S........Caledonia 1890
Symington, Maggie P....Brighton 1890
Sutherland, G. A.......Lakeside 1890
Smith, S. R. B.........Brighton 1890
Sneath, T. S.......... .Midhurst 1890
Shier, D. W..........Cannington 1890
Stevenson, H. A.........London 1890
Smuck, W. J...........Renforth 1890
Smith, R. H. .....St. Catharines 1890
Shaver, H. E. ....Stratford 1891
Small, A. A.............Toronto 1891
Shaw, R. W. .... .Lotus 1891
Sills, C. H..............Picton 1891
Shepard, C. A. ....Toronto 1891
Slack, T. J ....Quebec 1891
Stevens, O. H.,
        St. Felix de Valois, Que. 1891
Sutherland, J. A........Hamilton 1891
Stanbury, R. B. J ....Bayfield 1891
Sharpe, W. D ....London 1891
Shaw, M. A ....Overton 1891
Smith, F. W ....St. George 1892
St. Pierre, A. D ....Montreal 1892
Sneath, C. R ....Toronto 1892
Scott, W. A............Ottawa 1892
St. Charles, W. P ......Belleville 1892
Schmidt, G. A. ....Tavistock 1892

Shouldice, J. H ....Hamilton 1892
Stewart, George ....Springfield 1892
Stands, W. W ....Sunbury 1892
Smith, C. H ....Bradford 1892
Snider, R. O.............Toronto 1891
Smith, D. K. ....Toronto 1892
Segsworth, John.....Streetsville 1892
Smith, R. A ....Durham 1892
Skinner, Emma L ......Davisville 1892
Scott, Frank N .... Toronto 1892
Silcox, W. L ....Toronto 1892
Scott, F. A. ....Hastings 1892
Steele, W. H............Arnprior 1892
Steele, F. C ....Orillia 1892
Somers, R. H............Toronto 1892
Snyder, T........ ..... .Preston 1892
Shillington, A. T......Kemptville 1892
Stevenson, W. J.........London 1892
Sinclair, Christina .... Ottawa 1892
Stuart, W. A..Clarenceville, Que. 1892

Taber, R. W. H ....London 1874
Teller, R. F ....Montreal 1876
Thompson, G. W. ......Hamilton 1877
Thompson, S. F..........Toronto 1875
Thompson, J. M ....Clarke 1871
Titchworth, Ira. ....Hartford 1874
Teows, Peter ....Toronto 1875
Travers, William R............. 1865
Trumpour, John R ....Peterboro' 1875
Tudhope, James .. ..Orillia 1875
Taylor, Walter Mume ..Chatham 1879
Taylor, William..Box 795, Toronto 1879
Thompson, J. A..........Manilla 1880
Thompson, J. F.......Binbrook 1881
Thompson, C. E ......St. Thomas 1882
Thompson, D.... ....Deans 1883
Thompson, J. M.......Strathroy 1883
Toole, C. A ....Elder's Mills 1883
Trigge, A..............Hamilton 1883
Tyndall, Mary E........Montreal 1885
Taylor, Frederick ......Kingston 1884
Thomas, H. B............Barrie 1884
Telfer, W. J. .... .Burgoyne 1886
Thompson, P. W........Rosedale 1885
Tegart, A ....Tottenham 1887
Taylor, T. H. ......Grand Valley 1887
Taylor, T. T............ Chatham 1887
Tye, W. H. ... .Chatham 1888
Teeter, R. G ....Teeterville 1888
Taplin, M. M..........:...Addison 1888
Tuffard, W. H. P.,
          Northfield, Centre 1888
Thomson, W. A ....Caintown 1889
Temple, H. P. R........Toronto 1889
Tremblay, E. C........Wauregan 1889

Towner, George H........Toronto 1890
Thomson, W. P..........Toronto 1890
Thomas, C. H...........Toronto 1890
Tait, N. J.. ....St. Thomas 1890
Tremayne, F. G......Sutton West 1890
Tonkin, E. W ....Oshawa 1892
Tremayne, H. E..........Mimico 1891
Thomson, F. L.........Mitchell 1891
Teetzel, William M....St. Thomas 1891
Turner, Adelaide........Kingston 1892
Thorne, J. S............Belleville 1892
Tetreau, T. ....Ottawa 1892
Thomson, C. G ....Hyawatha 1892
Taylor, W. H...........Toronto 1892
Thomson, J. W ....Toronto 1892
Tyndall, J. E.....Richmond Hill 1892
Thompson, J. A....Kinnear's Mills 1892

Vanstone, William T..Dorchester 1877
Vale, Frank,
     9 Pembroke Street, Toronto 1878
Van Velsor, Wallace...,Rondeau 1880
Vidal, E. C..... St. John's, Que. 1885
Vail, Hattie B ....Sarnia 1889
Vaux, Leonard .... Brockville 1891
Verth, Annie .... Toronto 1892

Walker, Peter B. ....Perth 1875
Walsh, G.,Mayville,Tuscola,Mich. 1875
Weir, Charles...........Thorold 1874
Whitehead, Alexander....Toronto 1870
Willoughby, George. ....Colborne 1879
Wilson, Henry H. ......Kingston 1872
Wyatt, W. C....Custom's Corners 1874
Wood, James S. ....Kingston 1878
Whiting, John. ....Brantford 1878
Williams, Joseph ....London 1878
Wilson, Charles James 1879
Warren, Edward................ 1879
Whetham, James .. ..Toronto 1880
Wright, Henry ....Toronto 1883
Wait, G. N ....Harriston 1881
Walker, N ....Toronto 1884
Watson, John C ....Belleville 1885
Watson, W. R........Waterdown 1883
Weld, O. ....London 1882
Williams, E. P. ....Ottawa 1883
Williamson, W. P......Buckhorn 1884
Willmott, W. E..........Toronto 1885
Wilson, C. W........Cumberland 1881
Wonder, W. M ....St. Catharines 1883
Woodruff, T. A ....St. Catharines 1883
Woolway, E. W.......St. Mary's 1884
Wright, H. A ....Guelph 1882
Wright, W. ....Kingston 1882
Welsh, H. A. ....Quebec 1886

Williamson, H. M ....Guelph	1886	Williams, J. A....Carleton Place 1891
Watson, G.C.......Hawkesbury	1885	White, E. B............Chatham 1891
Whyte, J. J............Lancaster	1885	Wood, D. M...........Kenmore 1892
Ward, W. L...............Acton	1884	Weisbrod, S. L ....Aylmer 1892
Wideman, H. B.......Ringwood	1887	Weeks, E. C. ....Mosa 1892
Whitely, R .:..........Goderich	1887	Webster, B. E.........Kingston 1892
Wilson, A.. ....Kingston	1887	Westman, S. H ....Toronto 1892
Woods, C. R ....Brockville	1887	Webb, Alfred...........Toronto 1892
White, J. W..........St. Mary's	1887	Weir, W. H... .....Brantford 1892
Willoughby, G. A. F.,		Wasley, W. J.......Newmarket 1892
Saskatoon, N.W.T.	1886	White, W. C ......Woodstock 1892
Wickman, L. G ....Toronto	1885	Wallbridge, F. G. ......Belleville 1892
White, James G...... Thessalon	1884	Whiteley, A. G. ....Goderich 1892
Watson, N. M.....Williamstown	1887	White, R. W. K.......Hamilton 1892
Windell, J. D.............Lotus	1888	Walker, H. ....Belleville 1892
Walker, W G.........Stratford	1888	Wade, George H........Brighton 1892
Wardell, H. A. ....Dundas	1888	Weaver, W. J............Toronto 1892
Wheeler, J. W.........Kingston	1888	Willson, Jennie M. ......Toronto 1892
Watson, R. ....Newmarket	1888	White, R. B.........Pembroke 1892
Williamson, T ... .Picton	1888	Walker, R. J ....Strathroy 1892
Watson, N. M.....Williamstown	1888	
Wickson, D. D ....Toronto	1889	York, F. E ....Aurora 1883
Wilson, J. T. ....London	1889	Yeomans, P. H ....Mount Forest 1888
Webb, C. W ....Melbourne	1889	Yates, H. B...........Brantford 1888
Wood, P. B.............London	1890	Yourex, Ed. L.........Belleville 1886
Wilson, Thomas.........Toronto	1890	Young, William Howie 1869
White, P. D ....Glencoe	1890	Young, G. S. ....Markham 1881
Wells, R. B............Toronto	1890	Young, T. A ....Brougham 1891
Ward, Marjory ....Kingston	1890	York, H. E ....Montreal 1892
White, F. A.............Orwell	1890	Yeo, W. T. ....Little Britain 1892
Wilson, George B ....Toronto	1890	Young, W. Y...........Toronto 1892
Wilson, W T...........Dundas	1890	
Wiley, Walter. ....Wisbeach	1890	Zimmerman, Solomon ....Toronto 1876
Weir, Janet M.........Kingston	1888	Zangg, A. A. C. ....Montreal 1883
Wallace, H. E ....Port Elgin	1891	

LIST OF STUDENTS OF MEDICINE

WHO HAVE PASSED

The First Year's Examination

OF THE

College of Physicians and Surgeons of Ontario.

Bosanko, S. A.................................1877
Neilson, A 1877
Shaw, Frank 1877
Shepherd, O. B 1877
Steffins, John.................................1877
Atkinson, H. H...............................1878
Baker, George W 1878
Campbell, James 1878
Cotton, Robert 1878
Cooper, R. E 1878
Dupuis, James.................................1877
Haken, George W............................1878
Holcomb, S. D...............................1878
Houston, D. W 1878
Island, Robert 1878
Keam, A. P...................................1878
Koyle, F......................................1878
Lang, W. A...................................1878
Mewburn, F. H..............................1878

Milne, G. L...1878
Munro, Lawrence 1878
Mickle, Herbert..................................1878
McConnell, B. J...................................1878
McCauley, John....................................1878
McDonald, Walter................................1878
Poole, ˙W. H 1878
Reid, W. D 1878
Serviss, T. W......................................1878
Sullivan, Thomas.................................1878
Watson, M. J 1879
Burton, R. J. F....................................1879
Carson, S. H 1879
Fairbairn, F. W....................................1879
Harvie, John C 1879
Higginson, Henry................................1879
Kerr, Henry..1879
Mordy, A. A 1879
McLachlan, D. A 1879
O'Keefe, Henry 1879
Shaw, Alexander...... 1879
Smith, Edwin A...................................1879
Wilson, Herbert C...............................1879

LIST OF STUDENTS OF MEDICINE

WHO HAVE PASSED

The Second Year's Examination

OF THE

College of Physicians and Surgeons of Ontario.

Aikins, William Heber..........................1878
Black, James 1878
Christie, J 1878
Donovan, J. C 1878
Eccles, R. M 1878
Hunter, J. B 1878
Lindsay, Ninian...........................1878
Marsh, Edward 1878
Montgomery, W. A. D......................1878
Sutherland, W. R.........................1878
Van Norman, H. C........................1878
Beatty, Wm...............................1879
Empey, C. T.............................1879
Ferguson, J 1879
Hatton, E. T 1879
Meikle, Hamilton 1879
McCracken, C. L.........................1879
Ross, J. W..............................1879
Smith, H. W 1879
Thompson, G. B.........................1879
Wilson, Robert 1879
Witherspoon, W 1879
Harris, A. B 1881

LIST OF STUDENTS OF MEDICINE

WHO HAVE PASSED

The Third Year's Examination

OF THE

College of Physicians and Surgeons of Ontario.

Cross, W. J 1879

Howitt, F. W................................1880

Montgomery, D. W...........................1881

Nicholson, M.A..............................1879

LIST OF STUDENTS OF MEDICINE

WHO HAVE PASSED

The Primary Examination

OF THE

College of Physicians and Surgeons of Ontario.

Bell, James	1876	Brown, W. M	1883
Betts, Alfred H	1876	Logan, J. R	1883
Burton, W. H	1874	Murray, T. W	1883
Cameron, D. H	1876	Phillips, J. R.	1883
Cameron, L. D.	1877	Wattam, G. S	1883
Cannon, Gilbert	1876	Wilson, A. B.	1883
Cluxton, Frederick C.	1870	Charlesworth, W. H.	1884
Cormon, John W	1874	Simenton, G	1884
Dunsmore, John	1876	Smith, C. J	1884
Glasgow, James H	1876	Wilson, W. A	1884
Gray, J. W	1872	Green, W. D.	1885
Greer, Thomas E	1875	Gardiner, A. W.	1885
Henderson, Kenneth	1876	Hotson, A	1885
Howey, William	1877	Thompson, A. B	1885
Lewis, Ford	1877	Woodhull, F.	1885
McArthur, J	1877	Dowson, W. H.	1886
McCrimmon, John	1877	James, Charles	1886
McIlmoyl, Henry Allen	1875	Stockton, G. S	1886
McKinley, J. H.	1877	Berry, R. P	1887
Rae, George W.	1874	Brown, J. F	1887
Stevenson, Charles S	1875	Cross, J. A	1887
Stevenson, Sabin	1875	Campbell, J. F	1887
Ferguson, A. H.	1880	Cooke, W. H.	1887
Ferrier, James	1880	Edgar, A. E	1887
Herrington, A. W	1880	Ferguson, F. F	1887
McCarthy, W. T	1880	Hotson, J. M	1887
Ogden, H. V	1880	Johnston, T. H	1887
Panton, A. C.	1880	Kennedy, J. D.	1887
Denike, G. H	1881	Mason, H	1887
Johnston, Joseph	1881	Mitchell, D.	1887
Snider, S. H	1881	Millman, M. G	1887
Graham, George	1882	McKellar, A.	1887
Menzies, John	1882	McBride, J	1887
Thompson, A. S	1882	McCammon, S. H.	1887
Walmsley, P. C.	1882	Ogden, J. P	1887

Johnston, H. A	1892	Downing, A.	1893
Kingston, C. M	1892	Drummond, C. A	1893
Livingstone, H	1892	Douglas, W.	1893
Lawson, J. A	1892	Delahey, F. C.	1893
Lapp, L	1892	Downey, R. A.	1893
Morden, F. W	1892	Dow, Jennie I	1893
Mencke, J. R	1892		
Mulligan, F. W.	1892	Elliott, Geo.	1893
McIlwaith, K. C	1892	Elliott, Geo. A	1893
McClenahan, D. A	1892		
McCallum, Annie	1892	Ford, J. N	1893
McNaughton, J. A	1892	Fleming, S. E.	1893
McCrae, T	1892	Fleming, Maggie A	1893
McKee, J. F	1892	Featherstone, H. M	1893
McCollum, W. J	1892	Farley, F. J.	1893
McKendrick, H. F	1892	Flaherty, T.	1893
McIntosh, L. Y	1892		
New, C. F	1892	Graham, E. D	1893
Parfitt, C. D	1892	Gray, G. B	1893
Procter, E. L	1892	Gibson, A.	1893
		Grant, F. E	1893
Ryan, Eva	1892	Greenwood, A. B	1892
Richardson, A	1892		
		Hunter, A. J	1893
Shirra, Jennie S	1892	Hastings, R. J	1893
Seager, J	1892	Hutchison, J. C	1893
Smyth, C. E	1892	Hodgson, T. C	1893
Sinclair, J. P	1892	Hewson, T. B	1893
Scott, W. H	1892	Hill, Jennie	1893
Sparling, A. J	1892	Hurdon, Elizabeth	1893
		Hulet, Gertrude	1893
Thomas, C. H	1892	Hacket, W. A	1893
Thomson, W. P	1892	Hall, G. W	1893
		Hagar, F. C	1893
Wells, R. B	1892	Hogg, D. H	1893
Windell, J. D	1892		
White, P. D	1892	James, J. F	1893
Amyott, N. J	1893	King, James	1893
Arrell, W	1893	King, R	1892
Agnew, T	1893	Kellam, E. T.	1893
Armstrong, H. E	1893	Klotz, M. O.	1893
Allen, Mary E	1893	Kerr, T	1893
Allen, J. R	1893		
Alger, H. H	1892	Lambert, A. C	1893
		Lancaster, J. R.	1893
Baker, M.	1893	Lamont, J. G	1893
Bean, S. B	1893	Lipsey, R. M	1893
Ball, W. A.	1893	Langrill, A. S	1893
Burt, Ellen A. A	1893		
		Merritt, A. K	1893
Chapin, C. D	1893	Monteith, J. D	1893
Cuthbertson, H. A	1893	Macklin, Daisy	1893
Chapman, W. J	1893	Murphy, S. H.	1893
Carter, Chas	1892	McIntosh, J. W.	1893

MEMBERS

OF THE

College of Physicians and Surgeons of Ontario

WHO HAVE ATTAINED THEIR MEMBERSHIP

BY PASSING THE

FINAL EXAMINATION

BEFORE THE

Board of Examiners

Appointed by the Council of the College.

Adams, S. A. J	Kinmount	1887
Adams, W. A	Lakefield	1876
Alexander, R. A	Stoney Creek	1871
Alguire, D. O.	Lunenburg	1873
Alt, A	Toronto	1877
Anderson, J. B.	Watford	1875
Armstrong, F. R.	Stouffville	1874
Arnott, H.	Brampton	1870
Armour, J	Hastings	1877
Atkinson, J. S	Hamilton	1875
Adair, J	Oshawa	1878
Algie, J	Ayr	1879
Ashby, T. H.	Woodbridge	1878
Abbott, R. H.	Stoney Point	1879
Anderson, J. D.	Port Perry	1879
Armstrong, G. S	McKellar	1879
Ames, F. H. S.	Martin's Town	1880
Anderson, J	Hamilton	1880
Allen, W. L.	Ridgeway	1880
Aikens, H. W.	Toronto	1881
Alexander, F. R	Ottawa	1881
Anglin, W. G.	Kingston	1883
Addison, J. L.	St. George	1884
Anderson, J. E. W.	Boston	1884
Acheson, G	Toronto	1887
Aikins, N.	Caistorville	1887
Applebe, J.	Belle Ewart	1887
Armstrong, W	Zephyr	1887
Avison, O. R.	Toronto	1887
Allen, A. G.	Desoronto	1887
Anglin, J. V.	Kingston	1887
Amos, T. A.	West McGillivray	1887
Arthur, E. C.	Brighton	1888
Ardagh, A. E.	Barrie	1888
Anderson, C. N.	Comber	1888
Auld, L.	Toronto	1888
Almas, W. E.	Hagersville	1889
Anderson, R. K.	Hornby	1889
Armstrong, W. J.	Bayfield	1889
Armstrong, H. W	Ballieboro'	1889
Adams, E. H.	Toronto	1890
Agar, J. S.	Chatham	1890
Agar, Mary L.	Chatham	1890
Aldrich, A. G.	Port Hope	1890
Archer, D.	Burketon	1890
Ardagh, A. P.	Barrie	1890
Arnall, H. T.	Barrie	1890
Auld, J. C.	Forest	1890
Abraham, C. F. P.	Hamilton	1891
Almas, J. S.	Hagersville	1891

Amyot, J. A.	St. Thomas	1891
Arthur, J. L.	Shanty Bay	1891
Ashbaugh, J. A.	Aylmer	1891
Anderson, H. B.	Apsley	1892
Awde, A. E.	Toronto	1892
Armstrong, M. A. V.	Bayfield	1892
Archer, Robt	Milton, Dakota	1892
Austin, J. H.	Brampton	1893
Alway, R. D.	Grimsby	1893
Backhouse, John B.	Simcoe	1870
Bain, Hugh Urquhart	Angus	1875
Baird, J. G.	Montreal	1872
Ball, Jerrold	Meaford	1874
Balmer, J. S.	Oakville	1874
Barkwell, R. H.	Port Hope	1874
Bates, S. L.	Bowmanville	1871
Beeman, Milton J	Selby	1873
Beemer, N. H.	Brantford	1874
Bell, Forest F.	Amherstburg	1870
Bell, Robert	Carleton Place	1870
Bell, Samuel	Alliston	1874
Bennett, J. H.	Toronto	1875
Bentley, R. J.	Kettleby	1877
Birdsall, S. E.	Canboro'	1876
Bonner, H. A.	Albion	1877
Black, Wm. S.	Barrie	1871
Bowen, G. H.	Kingston	1877
Bowerman, A. C.	Toronto	1876
Boyle, W. S.	Bowmanville	1872
Brattan, J. R.	London	1875
Bray, Alfred	Angus	1874
Brent, H.	Port Hope	1874
Brereton, W. J.	Bradford	1871
Brett, R. G.	Arkona	1874
Brewster, N.	Ridgeway	1873
Bridgland, S.	Bracebridge	1870
Brien, Jas.	Essex Centre	1870
Britton, Wm.	Brantford	1875
Brock, Wm.	Jarvis	1875
Brown, Miles	Winchester	1871
Buchanan, Geo.	Rodgerville	1871
Burgess, T. J.	Toronto	1870
Burnham, G. H.	Peterboro'	1875
Burns, W. J.	Streetsville	1876
Buchart, J. L.	Ingersoll	1877
Burt, W.	St. George	1870
Byam, J. W.	Campbellford	1875
Baines, A. M.	Toronto	1878
Bennett, Henry	Peterboro'	1878
Bentley, W. H	Newmarket	1878
Bonnar, J. D.	Kingston	1878
Burt, Franklin	Paris	1878
Black, Fergus	Uxbridge	1879
Beeman, Thos	Centreville	1879
Bremner, W. W.	Minesing	1879

Baldwin, J. B.	Toronto	1879
Butler, Billa F.	Stirling	1879
Brown, J. L.	Chesterville	1879
Bowlby, D. A.	Simcoe	1879
Brooke, D. E.	Chatham	1879
Boileau, Jules M.	Crysler	1880
Bowman, Geo.	Penetanguishene	1880
Boyce, W. W.	Warkworth	1880
Brownlee, Milne	Millbrook	1880
Buchner, D. C.	Delhi	1880
Berry, F. R. R.	Simcoe	1881
Bingham, Geo. S.	Waterloo	1881
Baugh, Jas	Hamilton	1881
Beck, G. S.	Orillia	1882
Bedard, E.	Pembroke	1882
Bell, J. F.	Toronto	1882
Bentley, F.	Toronto	1882
Bentley, L	Toronto	1882
Book, E. H.	Drummondville	1882
Bonnar, Wm	Albion	1882
Brereton, T. G.	Bethany	1882
Brett, W. M.	Arkona	1882
Burt, J. C.	Bolton	1882
Bray, J	Enfield	1883
Bates, F. D.	Hamilton	1883
Belt, R. W.	Brussells	1883
Bell, W. D. M.	Bear Brook	1883
Bingham, G. A	Manilla	1884
Beatty, Elizabeth R.	Lansdowne	1884
Burgess, J. A.	Toronto	1885
Baumann, A. F.	Waterloo	1885
Britton, C. H	Brantford	1885
Barber, J.	Nassagaweya	1885
Beemer, F.	New Durham	1886
Brock, L.	Guelph	1886
Brodie, G. M.	Markdale	1886
Bateman, R. M.	Port Perry	1886
Brennan, F. H	Peterboro'	1886
Bromley, E.	Pembroke	1886
Birkitt, H. S.	Hamilton	1886
Beaman, W. C	Ventnor	1886
Burdett, H. E.	St. Paul's, Minn.	1887
Brown, J. J.	Owen Sound	1887
Barnett, A. D.	Fergus	1887
Barton, S. G. T.	Toronto	1887
Bradford, A.	Vachell	1887
Begg, J. W.	Kingston	1887
Bell, J.	Caledon	1887
Balfour, J. D.	Russelldale	1887
Bolby, G. H	Berlin	1888
Bell, G.	Owen Sound	1888
Bishop, E. R.	Brantford	1888
Bechard, D	Stoney Point	1888
Bradley, W. J.	Ottawa	1888
Bibby, F. T.	Brighton	1888
Barber, W. C	Toronto	1888

Bell, S. T.	Alliston 1888	Barber, H. D.	Cobourg 1892
Baptie, G	Ottawa 1888	Brown, J. N. E	Medina 1892
Burns, R. A. E.	Toronto 1888	Bownes, T. C	Addison 1892
Bradd, F. J	Campbellford 1889	Balfe, T. H	Smith's Falls 1892
Brown, J.	Campbellford 1889	Burkholder, J. F	London 1892
Bateman, W. E.	Cresswell 1889	Bourns, W. H	Frankville 1892
Birdsall, W. W.	Delhi 1889	Burrows, J. G	Napanee 1892
Bolton, A. E	Portland 1889	Brown, P. M	Camlachie 1892
Broad, J. J	Coboconk 1889	Bentley, D. B	Forest 1892
Bowman, J. E.	Dundas 1889	Ball, F. J	Rugby 1893
Becker, H.	Crieff 1889	Brown, W. F	Medina 1893
Beeman, T. A.	Bancroft 1889	Burrows, F. J	Lambeth 1893
Bull, E.	Weston 1889	Bowie, I	Embro 1893
Bowman, G. M.	Hamilton 1889	Brodie, R.	Claremont 1893
Brown, P.	Oshawa 1889	Bird, C. H	Barrie 1893
Berdan, O. L.	Strathroy 1889	Brander, Minnie M	Priceville 1893
Bateman, F. J	Christina 1889	Blanchard, F.	Sutton 1893
Baldwin, W. W.	Toronto 1890	Bruce, R. F.	New Lathrop, Mich. 1893
Bayly, B	London 1890		
Bowes, E. J	Ottawa 1890	Caldwell, William	Brantford 1875
Brown, Minnie.	Strathroy 1890	Callaghan, R. A	Toronto 1872
Berry, J. D	Warkworth 1890	Cameron, I. H.	Toronto 1874
Bigelow, G. T.	Port Perry 1890	Cameron, K. H. L.	Cayuga 1875
Bray, R. V.	Chatham 1890	Campbell, A. L.	Brooklyn 1874
Boyes, E. T	Benbrook 1890	Carmichael, Duncan	Ottawa 1877
Bryans, W. F.	Toronto 1890	Carscallen, A. B.	Petworth 1875
Boyle, Susanna P.	Toronto 1890	Carthew, C. E	Guelph 1877
Bond, W. L	Newmarket 1890	Case, G. H	London 1875
Baker, W. A.	Stouffville 1890	Case, W. H	Hamilton 1870
Black, M. C.	Glammis 1890	Cash, Edward	Markham 1871
Burger, J. H.	Toronto 1890	Cassells, J. McN	Quebec 1875
Barker, L. F.	Ingersoll 1890	Clarke, R. A	Oakville 1872
Boyes, E. J	Toronto 1890	Clarke, John	Peterboro' 1872
Bell, J. H.	Colborne 1890	Claxton, William	Verona 1876
Baker, T. C.	Chatham 1890	Clement, John	Streetsville 1871
Beatty, A. C.	Elizabethville 1890	Cole, H. J.	Brantford 1871
Bedard, J. A.	St. Eugene 1890	Cook, A. B.	Welland 1875
Bell, J. C	Strathroy 1890	Copeland, W. L.	St. Catharines 1872
Bowie, E. F	Toronto 1890	Cornell, C. M. B	Toledo 1872
Bueglass, A. S.	Bright 1890	Cotton, J. H	Garafraxa 1875
Barnhart, W. N.	Mitchell Square 1891	Coverton, T. S.	Toronto 1875
Beath, T	Columbus 1891	Cowan, G. H.	Princetown 1871
Bennett, T. E.	Toronto 1891	Crawford, Allen	Yorkville 1870
Bolster, L. E.	Orillia 1891	Crozier, J. B	London, Eng. 1872
Bowie, R. A.	Brockville 1891	Cameron, J. D.	Glengarry 1878
Boyd, G.	Toronto, 1891	Campbell, A. D.	Toronto 1878
Brown, W. A.	Chesterville 1891	Clarke, C. K	Toronto 1878
Burritt, C. H.	Lyndhurst 1891	Clinton, George.	Prince Edward 1878
Boultbee, A.	Toronto 1892	Cornell, S. A	London 1878
Bowles, G. H.	Sandhill 1892	Cornell, Warner.	Arkona 1878
Bissonette, J. D.	Napanee 1892	Craig, H. A	North Gower 1878
Boyce, B. F.	Norham 1892	Comfort, William	Ridgeville 1878
Bruce, H. A.	Port Perry 1892	Chisholm, Thomas	Fergus 1879
Beattie, D. A.	Galt 1892	Clapp, R. E	Lochiel 1879
Blain, E. B.	Hamilton 1892	Caughlin, J. W	St. Thomas 1879
Bensley, R. R.	Hamilton 1892	Chappell, W. F.	Thorold 1879

Cattanach, A. J. . . . . .Fergus 1879
Chisholm. Alexander. . . . . . .Lochiel 1879
Campbell, A. W. . . . . .Toronto 1880
Chown, H. H. . Emerson, Manitoba 1880
Clark, W. S. . . . . .Toronto 1880
Clemens, G. H. . . . . .Blair 1880
Clements, L. B. . . . . .Breslau 1880
Colquhoun, George . . . . . .Iroquois 1880
Cotton, James M. .Burnhamthorpe 1880
Cameron, Paul . . . . .Lancaster 1881
Clarke, J. G . . . . .Meaford 1881
Cameron, Alexander . . . . . .Vachel 1882
Charlton, W. J . . . . .Weston 1882
Cleland, G. S. . . . . .Niagara 1882
Clendenan, G. W. . . . . .Jordan 1882
Cornell, A. P . . . . .Kingston 1882
Coulter, R. M . . . .Richmond Hill 1882
Clarke, H. S . . . . .Toronto 1883
Cuthbertson, William . . . .Toronto 1883
Collver, M. K . . . . . . .Wellandport 1883
Casgrain, H. R. . . . . .Windsor 1883
Chafee, C. W. .·. . . . . .Toronto 1883
Carleton, W. H . . . . .Hamilton 1883
Case, T. E. . . . . .Exeter 1883
Cryan, John. .North Williamsburg 1883
Canfield, F. D . . . . .Ingersoll 1884
Carveth, G. H. . . . . .Orono 1884
Clerk, J. W. . . . . .Kinsale 1884
Campbell, D. . . . . . .Ontario, N.Y. 1884
Cochrane, J. M . . . . .Toronto 1884
Cook, E. M . . . . .Belleville 1884
Coughlan, Richard . . . . . .Hastings 1884
Courtney, J. D. . . . . . . .Hamilton 1885
Cowan, T. C. . . . . .Iona 1884
Corlis, M. A. . . . . .St. Thomas 1885
Cane, F. W . . . . .Newmarket 1885
Cunningham, H. C. . . . . .Kingston 1885
Couch, J. A. . . . . .Queensboro' 1885
Campbell, Frank . . . . .Wiarton 1885
Conerty, J. M . . . .North Augusta 1886
Caven, W. P . . . . .Toronto 1886
Cruickshank, G. R . . . . . . .Weston 1886
Clemison, J. McD. . . . .Wellington 1886
Casselman, J. P. .N. Williamsburg 1886
Collins, Cornelius. . . . . .Peterboro' 1886
Carruthers, J. B. . . . . .Barrie 1886
Cullen, L. F. . . . . .Woodstock 1886
Cassidy, J. I. . . . . Goldstone 1886
Cassidy, G. A . . . . .Moorefield 1886
Campbell, T. F . . . . .Newbury 1886
Cale, W. F. . . . . .Mitchell 1886
Cuthbertson, C. R. . . . . . . .Toronto 1886
Campbell, J. F. . . . . .Toronto 1886
Creggan, J. G. . . . . .Kingston 1886
Cornell, S. S . . . . . . .Farmersville 1886
Charteris, C. R. . . . . .Chatham 1887

Collins, A. E . . . . . .St. Catharines 1887
Cameron, Daniel . . . . .Perth 1887
Cameron, J. M. . . . . .Galt 1887
Campbell, Edwin. . . . . .Port Perry 1887
Caron, G. G. . . . . .Aylmer 1887
Clouse, Elias. . . . . Simcoe 1887
Clarke, W. H. . . . . .Meaford 1887
Campbell, A. W . . . . . . .Montreal 1887
Cline, L. F. . . . . .Springfield 1888
Campbell, D. M . . . . . .St. Thomas 1888
Carson, Miss Susie. . . . . .Strathroy 1888
Chamberlain, W. P. . . .Morrisburg 1888
Cummings, S. . . . . .Hamilton 1888
Connell, J. C. . . . . .Kingston 1888
Cowan, F. P. . . . . .Toronto 1888
Craine, Miss Agnes . .Smith's Falls 1888
Conroy, C. P . . . . .Martintown 1888
Campeau, W. J. . . . .Amherstburg 1888
Campbell, D. W. . . . . .Petrolia 1888
Clutton, W. H. . . . . .Dunlop 1888
Castleman, A. L. . . .Williamsburg 1888
Crosthwaite, G. K. . . .Bartonville 1889
Campbell, J. . . . . .Mapleton 1889
Collins, J. H. . . . . .Whitby 1889
Campbell, J. T . . . . .Whitby 1889
Carruthers, John. . . . . . . .Cayuga 1889
Chambers, G. . . . . .Woodstock 1889
Clark, C. P. . . . . .St. Mary's 1889
Chapple, H. . . . . .Newcastle 1889
Crawford, J. . . . . .Glencoe 1889
Clapp, W. H . . . . Toronto 1889
Carson, Jennie S. . . . . . . .Strathroy 1889
Creaser, J. A. . . . . . . .Owen Sound 1889
Channonhouse, R. C . . . .Eganville 1889
Cooper, R. M . . . . .London 1889
Cline, C. A. . . . . .Belmont 1889
Carbert, G. B . . . . .Orangeville 1889
Coutlee, H. N . . . . . .Sharbot Lake 1889
Cornu, F. . . . . .Montreal 1889
Clerihew, E. M. . . . . .Kingston 1889
Chisholm, W. P. . . . . . . .Hamilton 1889
Comfort, F. S. . . . . .Campden 1890
Coleman, A. H. . . . . .Belleville 1890
Cullen, T. S. . . . . .Sarnia 1890
Chrystal, R. J. . . . . .Avonton 1890
Clarke, F. R. . . . . .Colborne 1890
Coughlin, C. B. . . . . .Hastings 1890
Carveth, C. B. . . . . .Port Hope 1890
Copeland, E. M. . . . . .Ealing 1890
Cunningham, D. . . . . .Kingston 1890
Clendenan, C. W. . . . . .Toronto 1890
Coon, D. A. . . . . .Elgin 1890
Cunningham, F. W. . . . . . .Hespeler 1890
Cameron, W. A. . . . . . .Smith's Falls 1891
Campbell, J. W. . . . . .Kingston 1891
Carmichael, A. . . . . . . .Spencerville 1891

Chown, A. P. ....Kingston 1891
Clemesha, J. C. ....Port Hope 1891
Clendenan, A. E.........Cambray 1891
Clune, P. J..............Wooler 1891
Crawford, R. J. ....Owen Sound 1891
Campbell, W. A. ....Whitby 1892
Chabot, J. L. ....Ottawa 1892
Crawford, W...............Galt 1892
Clark, A. M. ......Wellandport. 1892
Chambers, Annie ......Port Elgin 1892
Chalmers, A. P.............Poole 1892
Crichton, A..............Toronto 1892
Closson, J. H.............Toronto 1892
Clark, D. A. ....Agincourt 1892
Chevrier, G. R. ....Ottawa 1892
Cooke, G. H. ....Chesley 1892
Clingan, G...............Toronto 1892
Chambers, W............Toronto 1893
Campbell, L. H. ....Bradford 1893
Campbell, N ....Cookstown 1893
Carlaw, T. W.........Warkworth 1893
Calder, R. M..........Grimsby 1893
Countryman, J. E. ....Tweed 1893
Creighton, J. K........Millstown 1893
David, A........ ...Port Lambton 1874
Davinson, Alex...........Berlin 1877
Day, Jonathan.......Port Hope 1877
Day, W. D. P. W....Harrowsmith 1874
DeCow, A...........Thamesville 1870
Dee, J. M. ....Stamford 1872
De La Mater, R. H. .....Fonthill 1871
Deynard, A. B............Picton 1875
Dingham, W. E. ... ...Milford 1875
Dingwall, A. M. ....Mount Hope 1875
Donaldson, John ....Singhampton 1872
Dorland, Jas.........Adolphuston 1872
Douglas, Alex............Avon 1876
Douglas, W. J. ....Norman 1876
Dowsley, D. H.......Owen Sound 1870
Dumble, T. H. ......Gananoque 1877
Dumble, W. C. ......Owen Sound 1870
Dunsmore, J. McA.......Mitchell 1870
Dafoe, Wm...............Toronto 1878
De Lom, H. A. ....London 1878
Duggan, F. J.........Lloydtown 1878
Dunfield, J.............Peterboro' 1878
Davies, R. A.....Easton's Corners 1879
Dryden, J. R. .. ..Eramosa 1879
Dowling, J. F.........Eganville 1879
Duck, W. B...........Morpeth 1879
Des Rosiers, *dit* Lafreniets, Alex. N.
　　　　　　　　　Clarence Creek 1880
Dickson, J. F. ....Goderich 1880
Duncan, J. H............Bayfield 1881
Davidson, J. G. ....Lynden 1882
Day, L. E.............Harwood 1882

Dickson, C. R......Wolfe Island 1882
Dowsley, G. C. ....Wingham 1882
Duncan, J. T.............Toronto 1882
Drake, F. P............Kingsmill 1883
Dickson, W. F.........Ingersoll 1883
Derby, W. J............Rockland 1883
Davis, W. N. ....Aylmer 1884
Duff, H. R. ....Kingston 1884
Doolittle, P. E ....Toronto 1885
Dales, J. R. ....Dunbarton 1885
Dewar, P. A.......Essex Centre 1885
Dwyer, A. W ....Elgin 1885
Drummond, H. E......Pontypool 1886
Dunton, Daniel ....Britannia 1886
Dickison, G. J.........Mildmay 1886
Dow, W. G. ....Fergus 1886
Dow, Wm. .. ..Barnett 1886
Dixon, M. L ....Frankville 1886
Dame, A. A........ .....Jordan 1886
Dobie, D. A.........Strathburne 1887
Dryden, G. F.........Rockwood 1887
Durand, C. F...........Toronto 1887
Dickson, Miss Annie....Brockville 1887
Downing, W. H........Kingston 1888
Dawson, F. J............Toronto 1888
Dewar, C. P...........Ottawa 1888
Dewar, M. C... .. ..Weston 1889
Daird, W. C...........Kingston 1889
Dixon, W. A............Toronto 1889
Dickinson, G. A ....Zion 1889
Duff, John.............Inverary 1889
Davis, Lelia A.............King 1889
Dela, H. J ....Moorefield 1889
Douglas, S............Marshville 1890
Drake, F. A.......South Cayuga 1890
Dinwoody, J. A .....Clover Hill 1890
Dolan, J. F............Belleville 1890
Danby, J. J............Ottawa 1890
Day, S. D...........St. Thomas 1891
Dow, J. ....Fergus 1891
Dunning, M ....Orangeville 1891
Day, A. R. A ....Guelph 1892
Davis, S. N..............York 1892
Dwyer, R. J. ....Toronto 1892
Dymond, Bertha .... Toronto 1892
Duncan, J. H............Emery 1893
Darling, R. E.........Warkworth 1893
Douglas, T.............Harrison 1893
Doan, W.............New Sarum 1893

Eakins, J. E ....Newbury 1875
East, C.................Moray 1873
Edwards, O. C.........Clarence 1883
Ellison, S. B.........St. Thomas 1873
Esmond, J. J..........Belleville 1877
Evans, H. E. ....Pembroke 1878

Emerick, F.	Simcoe	1878
Edwards, J. S.	London	1879
Ellis, Judson	St. George	1880
Emory, C. Van N.	Galt	1881
Eastwood, W. F.	Whitby	1882
Emory, W. J. H.	Burlington	1883
Elliott, J. E.	Toronto	1884
Ewing, Wm.	Hawkesbury	1885
Ellis, D. D.	Tilbury Centre	1885
Eberts, D. W.	Chatham	1885
Eadie, A. B., jun	Toronto	1886
Eadie, A. B., sen	Toronto	1886
Edmison, A. H	Roseneath	1886
English, W. M.	London	1886
Earl, E. H.	Port Hope	1886
Ego, Angus	Sutton West	1886
Eastwood, J. H	Whitby	1887
Erritt, A. I	Merrickville	1887
Easton, C. L.	Smith's Falls	1887
Evans, E...	Seaforth	1887
Eaton, J. M.	Lakeview	1888
Embury, Miss E	Napanee	1888
Earley, W. J.	Owen Sound	1889
Emery, G. F.	Gananoque	1889
Elliott, A. R.	Belleville	1889
Egbert, W	Dunnville	1889
Emmerson, A. T	Peterboro'	1889
Elliott, H. C. S	Toronto	1889
Ellis, T. H	Pembroke	1890
Ellis, A. D.	Norwich	1890
Echlin, E. B	Copetown	1891
Edgar, J. W	Hamilton	1891
Empey, W. A	Winchester	1891
Ewing, F. J	Seaforth	1891
Evans, J. A. C	Bradford	1892
Earl, W. M	Bishop's Mills	1892
Elliott, W	Mitchell	1893
Farewell, Adolphus	Oshawa	1874
Farewell, G. W	Stouffville	1874
Farley, Jno. J.	Ottawa	1877
Faulkner, George W.	Belleville	1871
Fenwick, Kenneth N	Kingston	1874
Field, Bryon	Toronto	1877
Fisher, David M	Toronto	1877
Forest, Wm	Mount Albert	1871
Francks, Wm	Port Elgin	1877
Fraser, Alex. C	Wallaceburg	1877
Fraser, Donald B.	Shakespeare	1874
Fraser, Duncan	Shakespeare	1874
Fraser, John	Strabane	1871
Freel, Eugene I	Markham	1875
Freeman, Wm. Clarkson	Scotland	1877
Fulton, Jas.	Fingal	1876
Faulkner, D. W	Holloway	1878
Forbes, John M	Caledonia	1878

Fraser, John R	Hawkesbury	1878
Fraser, Henry Donald	Pembroke	1881
Fisher, Richard M	Toronto	1882
Freel, Ira Albert.	Markham	1882
Fairchild, Rich. Melvin	Brantford	1883
Frost, Robt. Samuel.	Kinmount	1883
Freeman, Wm. Francis	Milton	1883
Fierheller, G	Parry Sound	1886
Foster, Chas. Manley	Toronto	1884
Fraser, Robt. Nelson	Westmeath	1884
Ferguson, Jas	Cumberland	1884
Feilde, Ed. Cazalet	Prescott	1884
Ferguson, John	Berlin	1885
Ford, Henry Bernice	Bouck's Hill	1885
Fox, Wm. Henry	Mono Road	1886
Fraser, John Wilson	London	1886
Foley, Declan Ed.	Westport	1886
Forster, Jas. Moffat	Oakville	1886
Forin, Alex	Belleville	1886
Freeman, Albert Ed	Invermay	1887
Free, Ed. John	Campbellford	1887
Funnell, Ada Alferetta	Trenton	1887
Fraser, Jas. Mitchell	Hawkesbury	1887
Fish, Wm. Am	Newtonbrook	1887
Foster, Alonzo Barton	Waterford	1887
Fere, G. A.	Toronto	1888
Fisher, J. H. C. F	Bailieboro'	1888
Fisher, A. J	Wiarton	1888
Francy, C. H	Gormley	1888
Ferguson, J. G.	Cookstown	1888
Ferguson, T. A	Toronto	1888
Fraser, J. B	Brockville	1889
Fitzgerald, T. A.	Millbrook	1889
Fraser, S. M.	London	1889
Ferguson, W. S	Avonbank	1890
Ferguson, R.	London	1890
Forfar, J. E.	Toronto	1890
Fletcher, W. J	Toronto	1890
Flatt, C. E	Millgrove	1890
Fairfield, C. A. D	St. Catharines	1890
Freeland, A.	Ottawa	1890
Funnell, Rozelle V	Kingston	1890
Ferguson, W. D. T	Rocklands	1890
Fairchild, C. C.	Brantford	1891
Farmer, G. D	Ancaster	1891
Field, A. B	Blackstock	1891
Fotheringham, J. T	Toronto	1891
Forrest, J	Mount Albert	1892
Forrest, R. F	Mount Albert	1892
Fowler, R. V	Colborne	1882
Fenton, F.	Toronto	1892
Ferguson, M	Harriston	1892
Foster, Mattie I	Welland	1892
Fraleigh, A. E	Arva	1882
Foley, J. G	Westport	1892
Futcher, T. B	St. Thomas	1893

Hamilton, Alexander ...Onondaga 1871
Hamilton. J. R. ....Stratford 1872
Hamilton, Robert........Athlone 1874
Hanover, William. ......Almonte 1876
Harris, W. T ....Onondaga 1874
Hart, J. M..............Wilford 1871
Harvey, W. A..... ....Harriston 1875
Heally, L. D..........Springfield 1874
Henderson, A. A. ... .Ottawa 1871
Henning, N. P ....Tyrell 1871
Hickey, S. A ....:Aultsville 1876
Higgins, E. M....... ....Ottawa 1877
Higginbotham, Wm..Bridgewater 1871
Hill, Alfred H........Woodstock 1877
Hobley, Thomas..........Toronto 1875
Hockridge, T. G.....Newmarket 1874
Hodge, George ....Orono 1870
Holmes, F. L........Farmersville 1877
Holmes, T. G ....Holmesville 1875
Honeywell, William......Toronto 1877
Hopkins, E. L .....Stoney Creek 1875
Hourigan, A. B........Peterboro' 1877
Howitt, Henry.......... Guelph 1874
Hudson, Samuel .. ..Roslin 1871
Hunter, John..........St. George 1875
Hartman, Jacob.......Hamilton 1878
Howe, F. M ....Cartwright 1878
Hutchinson, T. S......... Exeter 1878
Hamilton, C. J..........Goderich 1879
Henderson, W. H.....Kingston 1879
Horton, R..N........New Dublin 1879
Hossie, T. R... .. ...Cataraqui 1879
Hanna, Frank ......Lansdowne 1876
Hunt, Henry. ......Williamstown 1879
Hyde, J. G............Stratford 1879
Hamil, W. E. ....Aurora 1880
Hoig, D. S..............Oshawa 1880
Howie, W. H.........Courtland 1880
Hart, G. C. ....Osnabruck Centre 1880
Heyd, H. E ....Brantford 1881
Hall, J. B. ....Toronto 1881
Hanbidge, William ....Dunblane 1882
Henwood, A. J ....Brantford 1882
Hansler, J. E............Fonthill 1883
Hislop, Robert ....Detroit 1883
Hearn, Richard.........Toronto 1883
Hickey, D. C. ....Kingston 1883
Hall, W. R. ....Chatham 1884
Hixon, E. F...........Priceville 1884
Hamilton, W. H.......Stratford 1884
Hunt, C. W ....Listowel 1884
Herald, John ....Kingston 1884
Hall, E. A ....Hornby 1884
Harrison, W. S. ....Milton 1885
Hamilton, H. J ....Brampton 1885
Harvie, A. R ....Orillia 1885

Howell, J. H............Fonthill 1885
Hawley, H. H. ....Trenton 1885
Hanks, A. R............Florence 1885
Harkin, F. McD....Vankleek Hill 1885
Hunter, J. W ....Buffalo 1886
Hillier, Reil..............Cottam 1886
Heggie, W. C.........Brampton 1886
Hunt, George..........Rosemont 1886
Hart, J. W............Fleetwood 1886
Hay, W. W ....Watford 1886
Hopkins, W. B.......Marshville 1886
Hamilton, J. H ....Hillsburg 1886
Hamilton, J. A. ....Woodhill 1886
Heath, F. C............Brantford 1886
Hanna, J. E.....North Gower 1886
Hughes, P. H ....Leamington 1886
Hoover, J. H ....Aylmer 1887
Hopkins, R. R. ....Harrison 1887
Halstead, T. H......Mount Forest 1887
Hawke, Benjamin....Hawkesville 1887
Hart, M. W ....Prescott 1887
Hay, H. R ....Listowel 1887
Hall, William...........Lloydtown 1887
Hunter, A. J ...Rochester, Mich. 1888
Hotson, A. N...........Innerkip 1888
Hart, J. F ....Prescott 1888
Harris, W. H ....Canton 1888
Hæntschell, C. W......Pembroke 1888
Horsey, E. H. ....Ruthven 1888
Hanvey, C. B. H......St. Thomas 1888
Hyttenranch, L. J........London 1888
Hutton, John ....Priceville 1888
Hotson, Alex ....London 1888
Hoare, C. W ....Walkerville 1888
Howitt, J. A...........Gourock 1888
Henderson, D ....Bradford 1889
Halliday, A. H. ....Bellwood 1889
Hart, J. S. .. .. Toronto 1889
Harding, W. E ....Brockville 1889
Hickson, L. J..Lasalle, N.Y., U.S. 1889
Honner, R. H.............London 1889
Holdcroft, J ....Tweed 1889
Harkness, F. B.........Kingston 1889
Hamilton, C. H.........Oakville 1889
Henwood, J. M.........Toronto 1889
Hamilton, W..........Beaverton 1889
Herriman, W. C. ....Lindsay 1890
Hutchison, D. H ....Ingersoll 1890
Hayes, A. N ....Parkhill 1890
Hobbs, A. T ....London 1890
Hillary, R. M ....Aurora 1890
Harrison, G.............Toronto 1890
Hutton, Mary .. ..Forest 1890
Hodgetts, C. A ....Toronto 1890
Hill, R.................Aylmer 1890
Howell, R. G............Jarvis 1890

Holdcroft, W. T	Tweed	1890
Hanly, J. F	Waubashene	1890
Harrington, A. J	Toronto	1890
Harrison, E. D	Picton	1891
Hay, R. F	Watford	1891
Heaslip, A. W	Niagara Falls	1891
Henry, T. H	Orangeville	1891
Herriman, W. D. D	Lindsay	1891
Hett, J. E	Berlin	1891
Hilliard, W. L	Waterloo	1891
Hunter, A. C	Newcastle	1891
Hunter, W. R	Clarksburg	1891
Hutt, W. G	Aurora	1891
Hagerman, F. H	Parkhill	1892
Haig, A	Menie	1892
Halliday, V. S	Peterboro'	1892
Heggie, D. L	Brampton	1892
Henderson, E. M	Brockville	1892
Henderson, J	Warkworth	1892
Henry, A. E	Mono Centre	1892
Hough, A. H	St. Catharines	1892
Hughes, T. A. M	Ilderton	1892
Heming, T. H	Toronto	1892
Harper, J. J	Rosemont	1892
Holmes, W. L	Walkerton	1892
Hershey, J. A	Garrison Road	1892
Harvey, E. E	Newry	1893
Hopkins, J. R	Stoney Creek	1893
Harvie, J. N	Orillia	1893
Hyndman, H. K	Exeter	1893
Henderson, J. A	Orangeville	1893
Irving, W	Toronto	1874
Inksetter, D. G	Copetown	1880
Ivey, J. A	Jarvis	1889
Irwin, T. W	Pembroke	1889
Inksetter, W. E	Copetown	1890
Irwin, H	Pembroke	1890
Irwin, A. F	Chatham	1890
Irvine, Emily J	Brampton	1890
Irwin, E. E	Newmarket	1890
Irwin, T. C	Cloverhill	1890
Jackes, G. W	Unionville	1875
Jackson, F. W	Brockville	1873
Jackson, N. M	Port Lambton	1876
Jakeway, C. E	Holland Landing	1871
James, W	Mount Albert	1872
Jessop, E	Port Perry	1876
Johnson, A. J	Yorkville	1873
Johnson, W. H	Fergus	1875
Johnston, J. S	Mount Charles	1873
Johnston, T. G	Sarnia	1878
Jones, J. R	Toronto	1878
Jamieson, D	Mount Forest	1878
Judson, G. W	Westport	1880

Jamieson, J	Kars	1881
Jones, A. C	Cumminsville	1881
Josephs, G. E	Pembroke	1881
Jarvis, C. E	London	1882
Johnston, W. H	Toronto	1882
Johnston. D. A	Bridgewater	1882
Johnston, J. M	Kincardine	1882
Jacques, W	Jarvis	1883
Jackson, J. M	Arva	1882
Johnston, G. L	Winthrop	1883
Johnston, F. H	Brantford	1884
Jones, J. A	Kemptville	1884
Jones, D. O. R	Toronto	1885
Johnston, D. R	Ancaster	1886
Johnson, D	Buck's Hill	1887
James, M	Centreville	1887
Jones, S. J	Stoney Creek	1887
Jones, G. F	Lucan	1887
Johnson, J. W	Farmersville	1887
Jeffs, W. H	Hoards	1888
Jamieson, D	Kars	1888
Jamieson, T. J	Kars	1888
Jento, C. P	Brockville	1890
Johnson, D	Underwood	1891
Johnston, W. J	Carleton Place	1891
Jamieson, Alison	Wicklow	1892
Johnston, Albert	Ottawa	1892
Jones, W. A	Clandeboye	1892
James, H. J	Clayton	1893
Kains, Robert	St. Thomas	1871
Kennedy, Alex	Bath	1876
Kennedy, J. B	Welland	1872
Kennedy, William	Sandhill	1875
Kidd, Edward	Manotick	1872
King, J. S	Toronto	1876
Kitchen, Ed.	St. George	1877
Kittson, Ed. G.	Hamilton	1883
Kennedy, G. A	Dundas	1878
Kennedy, W. B	Pembroke	1878
Kidd, P. E	Kingston	1877
Kirk, G. W	Pembroke	1878
Kilborn, R. K	Frankville	1879
Kidd, T. A	Carp	1886
Kippax, J. R	Toronto	1880
Krauss, Frank.	Toronto	1883
Kidd, J. F	Kingston	1883
Kent, F. D	Bracebridge	1884
Knight, J. H	Wallaceburg	1885
Kinsley, A. B	Port Colborne	1885
Krick, C. A	Elcho	1885
Kyle, W. A	North Winchester	1885
Kester, D. W	Princeton	1886
Keane, M. J	Toronto	1887
Kennedy, R. A	Rockland	1887
Kelly, J. A. A	Woodbridge	1887

Karn, C. J. W	Woodstock	1888
Kidd, D. A	French River	1888
Kennedy, J. H	Lindsay	1888
Kerr, W	Toronto	1889
Kilborn, O. L	Kingston	1889
Kalbfleisch, F. H	Paisley	1890
Kaiser, T. E	Edgeley	1890
Kennedy, J. P.	London	1891
Kidd, W. E	Kingston	1891
Knechtel, R	Brussels	1891
Kilbourne, B	Parkhill	1892
Kirk, F. J	Kingston	1892
Koyle, F. H	Brockville	1893

Lafferty, James	Perth	1875
Lane, Joseph	North Williamsburg	1871
Lang, Hugh	Granton	1873
Lang, Wm	Keene	1871
Langstaff, G. A.	Thornhill	1878
Lawrence, Robert	Honeywood	1871
Lean, Thomas.	Cobourg	1872
Leitch, Arch.	St. Catharines	1875
Leitch, D.	St. Thomas	1870
Leslie, R. B	Toronto	1874
Lett, Stephen	Toronto	1870
Lindsay, N. J	Alvinston	1874
Locke, C. F. A	Barrie	1871
Lovekin, J. P	Newcastle	1871
Lovett, Wm	Ayr	1870
Lowey, W. H	Guelph	1874
Lumley, W. G	Delaware	1870
Lynd, Adam	Bond Head	1875
Lackner, H. G	Hawkesville	1876
Lowe, J. H	Haliburton	1878
Langstaff, J. E	Richmond Hill	1878
Langlois, Onesine	Windsor	1878
Lewis, F. W	Toronto	1878
Lehman, Wm	Ringwood	1878
Lynch, D. P	Kingston	1878
Lowry, David	Cavanville	1878
Lloyd, David	Strathroy	1879
Lefevre, J. M	Brockville	1879
Leonard, R. A	West Brook	1879
Lundy, F. B	Galt	1880
Lavell, W. A.	Newburg	1881
Lennox, L. J.	Thornton	1881
Lesslie, J. W	Toronto	1881
Lafferty, Jas.	Hamilton	1882
Lepper, W. J	Toronto	1883
Langstaff, L. G.	Thornhill	1884
Lake, A. D	Drumbo	1884
Lochart, R. J.	Hespeler	1886
Lynch, W. V	Lindsay	1885
Little, A. T	Allendale	1885
Lucy, Robt	Glen Allan	1885
Leitch, H. D	Flesherton	1885

Lundy, F. G	Sheffield	1885
Lapp, T. C	Grafton	1886
Logie, W. J.	London	1886
Logie, Wm	Sarnia	1886
Lawson, Alex	Greensville	1887
Lackner, A. E.	Hawkesville	1887
Loucks, W. F	Stirling	1887
Lawrence, F	St. Thomas	1887
Livingstone, Miss M	Kingston	1887
Langford, C. B	Kent Bridge	1888
Lammiman, B.	Solina	1888
Little, T. H	Owen Sound	1888
Lawyer, Miss Annie	Ottawa	1888
Lane, I. J	North Williamsburg	1888
Lang, C. M	Owen Sound	1888
Lanfear, H. O	Lakefield	1889
Little, W. C	Barrie	1889
Lynd, Ida E	Bond Head	1890
Lockhart, G. D	Mount Brydges	1890
Liddell, G. L.	Cornwall	1890
Lambert, E. M.	Ottawa	1891
Langrill, W. F	Oshweken	1891
Langstaff, R. L	Richmond Hill	1891
Lundy, P	Toronto	1891
Leininger, J.W	Gladwin, Mich.	1892
Lucas, M. F	Grimsby	1892
Lambert, W. H.	Arnprior	1893
Lehman, J. E.	Orillia	1893
Laird, C. J	Guelph	1893
Locke, J. A	Brinston's Corners	1893
Lockhart, A.	Sydenham	1893

MacColl, D. S	Eagle	1871
Macdonald, A. A.	Guelph	1872
Machell, H. T	King, Co. York	1873
Mackie, J. McD	Clifford	1876
Macklim, M	Markham	1877
Marlatt, C. W	Yarmouth Centre	1871
Marlatt, G. A	Yarmouth	1877
Mathieson, J. H	Embro	1871
Mattice, R. I	Moulinette	1875
Meldrum, N. W	Harrington	1873
Metcalf, W. G	Uxbridge	1872
Millar, A. H	St. Thomas	1877
Miller, L. F	Kingston	1877
Miller, T. M	Keene	1877
Minaker, Wm	Milford	1875
Minshall, H	Thamesville	1875
Mitchell, Fred	London	1874
Mitchell, J. C	Clarke	1878
Moore, C. S	London	1874
Moore, C. G	Brampton	1871
Moore, J. T	Woodstock	1874
Moore, V. H	Merrickville	1870
Moore, L. M.	Duntroon	1872
Moorehouse, H	Toronto	1871

McCallum, J. S	Dunnville	1872
McConkey, T. C.	Barrie	1874
McCurdy, Archibald	Otterville	1876
McDermid, Wm	Athol	1877
McDermitt, James	Bond Head	1870
McDiarmid, Duncan.	Malvern	1875
McDiarmid, J. C	Prospect	1875
McDonald, D. F.	Ardock	1877
McDonald, Peter	Brucefield	1872
McDonnell, Alex	Alexandria	1875
McEwan, Findlay	Toronto	1871
McFayden, Duncan	Nobleton	1877
McGregor, J. O.	Lowville	1875
McKay, Andrew	Woodstock	1871
McKay, Angus	Ingersoll	1871
McKeough, G. T	Chatham	1877
McKinnon, A. H	Norval	1877
McKinnon, A.	Ospringe	1871
McLaren, Alex.	Delaware	1874
McLaren, A. L	Sarnia	1874
McLarty, Colin.	St. Thomas	1875
McLay, P. W. McM	Toronto	1870
McLean, John	Barrie	1876
McLean, J. C.	Centre Augusta	1874
McLean, Peter	Morrison	1874
McLellan, Chas	Walton	1872
McClure, Wm.	Thorold	1875
McNicholl, Eugene	Norwood	1877
McPhedran, Alex	Toronto	1875
McRae, George	Toronto	1876
McWilliam, James	Galt	1876
McCort, T. J	Tormore	1878
McCrimmon, Wilton	Ancaster	1878
McDonagh, G. R	Carlow	1878
McGrath, John	Lucan	1878
McKay, Wm.	St. Thomas	1878
McKelvey, Alex.	Seaforth	1878
McLennan, J. H	Lambeth	1878
McNamara, G. W.	Gorrie	1879
McDiarmid, Andrew	Fingal	1878
McCullough, Geo	St. Mary's	1878
McArthur, J. A	North Bruce	1879
McIlhargy, J. J	Lucan	1879
McFadden, J. J	Stratford	1879
McLean, Peter	Jarratt's Corners	1879
McCammon, Jas.	North Augusta	1879
McCarroll, John	Barrie	1880
McGuigan, Wm	Point Edward	1880
McKenzie, B. E	Aurora	1880
McKinnon, R. J	York	1880
McWilliam, Robert	Hespeler	1880
McLain, George	Nanticoke	1881
McGannon, E. A	Prescott	1881
McCausland, H. P	Aylmer	1882
McGill, H. R	Janetville	1882
McMahon, T. F.	Fergus	1882
McPhaden, Murdock	Brussels	1882
McConochie, S. W	Bowmanville	1883
McMurchy, Archibald	Strange	1883
McGillivray, Mrs. Alice.	Kingston	1884
McLaren, D. C	Galt	1885
McGannon, M. C	Prescott	1885
McCormack, Norman.	Pembroke	1885
McKenzie, A. F.	Belgrave	1886
McAllister, J. C	Wendigo	1886
McEwen, Thomas	Hagersville	1886
McCallum, H. A	London	1886
McEdwards, Duncan	Thedford	1886
McLaughlin, Edward	Harrowsmith	1885
McCabe, J. C.	Phelpton	1886
McKenzie, John	Poplar Hill	1886
McKague, W. H.	Cobourg	1886
McVety, A. F	Kingston	1886
McGannon, T. G	Prescott	1886
McPhail, D. P.	Iona Station	1887
McCasey, J. H.	Wingham	1887
McKenzie, Thomas.	Toronto	1887
McDonald, C. D	Rodney	1887
McLurg, James	Woodstock	1887
McLean, C. H.	Barrie	1887
McKenzie, Dugald.	Dromore	1887
McFaul, A. McN.	Caledon	1887
McCullough, H. R	Georgetown	1887
McEwen, Ewen.	Franktown	1887
McDonald, A. L.	Glen Donald	1887
McCordick, A. W	North Gower	1888
McClinton, J. B. H	Black Bank	1888
McLaughlin, P	Dundela	1888
McKay, Miss M.B.	Stellarton, N.B.	1888
McGrath, E	Campbellford	1888
McLaughlin, Miss A	Toronto	1888
McFarlane, M. A.	Arnprior	1888
McDonald, J. A	Kintall	1888
McKibbon, L. G.	Teeswater	1888
McGillawee, J.	Shakespeare	1888
McLennan, D	Renfrew	1888
McMartin, D. R	Toronto	1888
McCarthy, J. G.	Sorel, Que.	1888
McDonald, D. D.	North Lancaster	1888
McFaul, J. J., sen	Toronto	1888
McCullough, T. P	Alliston	1888
McNally, T. J	Walkerton	1889
McKay, D.	Bradford	1889
McCabe, J. R..	Adelaide	1889
McLachlin, J. Y	London	1889
McFarlane, J. M	Toronto	1889
McLachlan, C	Toronto	1889
McIntosh, D. H	Carleton Place	1889
McEwen, Hugh	Carleton Place	1889
McDonald, George	Renfrew	1889
McRitchie, T. L.	Harwich	1889
McKeown, P. W. H	Toronto	1889

5

McKercher, H..........Camlachie	1889	Nunan, D................Guelph 1875
McKillop, J. T ....Beachburg	1889	Nevitt, R. B ....Toronto 1878
McConville, Isabel .....Kingston	1889	Neilson, W. J.............. Perth 1878
McNamara, C. J ..... Walkerton	1889	Newlands, Geo.................. 1879
McGillivray, C. J. ......Hamilton	1889	Nelles, D. A..........Waterford 1879
McEwen, J. A............London	1890	Noecker, C. F..........Waterloo 1886
McColl, H. A ....Georgetown	1890	Nicholls, W. R. .... Plattville 1886
McGillivray, W .... Whitby	1890	Newell, W ....Strathroy 1887
McNaughton, J. D. Worth Keppel	1890	Niemeier, O. G............Ayton 1887
McFaul, J. H............Seaforth	1890	Nairn, J. M ....Port Dover 1887
McCarty, O. C. ....Belleville	1890	Nimmo, J. H. ....Kingston 1887
McGillivray, C. F ....Whitby	1890	Norman, T. J. ....Schomberg 1887
McLeod, D. ....Cannington	1890	Neff, J. A.. ....Springfield 1888
McQueen, D. K.......... Ripley	1890	Nesbitt, W. B. ....Toronto 1888
McGregor, J. A........Longwood	1890	Nasmyth, W. W. ....Toronto 1889
McCullough, J. W. S....Dundalk	1890	Northmore, H. S. ......Cataraqui 1889
McPherson, W. A. A....Prescott	1890	Niddrie, R. J...........Hampton 1890
McDonald, A......Vankleek Hill	1890	Noble, John..............Arthur 1890
McKellar, Maggie ......Ingersoll	1890	Noble, C. T. .... Sutton West 1890
McKenty, Jas ....Kingston	1890	Nixon, A. W ....Esquesing 1891
McGee, Robt ....Collingwood	1890	Nichol, A. H............Listowel 1893
McClelland, M ....Bensfort	1891	
McColl, A. E........Campbellford	1891	Oakley, W. D. ....Plattsville 1887
McCrimmon, F. ....London	1891	Ogilvie, R. C.......... ..Toronto 1878
McCuen, J. A............Guelph	1891	O'Neil, E...............Belleville 1875
McCullough, J. S........Toronto	1891	Orr, R. B...............Toronto 1877
McCullough, O..........Everton	1891	Ogg, A. S ....Dundas 1878
McGorman, G.........St. Mary's	1891	O'Gorman, C...........Hastings 1879
McKensie, G...........Wingham	1891	O'Reilly, G............Hamilton 1879
McLaughlin, T. P......Fish Creek	1891	O'Brien, D.............Renfrew 1879
McLean, D ....Elmgrove	1891	Odlum, J......... .....Lucknow 1879
McNeill, D. G...... ....London	1891	O'Shea, J. F...........Norwood 1881
McQueen, J. ....Sheffield	1891	O'Keefe, J. F........Henderson 1882
McAsh, J. ....Varna	1892	O'Reilly, E. B..........Hamilton 1883
McCammon, F. J........Kingston	1892	Orr, J. O................Toronto 1884
McCormick, H........Walkerton	1892	Ovens, Thos.........Ailsa Craig 1884
McCoy, S. H. ....Brantford	1892	Olmstead, Ingersol ......Ancaster 1886
McCullough, H. A....Georgetown	1892	Osborne, A. B..........Hamilton 1886
McDonald, H. F..........Rodney	1892	Orton, T. H............Hamilton 1886
McDonald, P. A......Alexandria	1892	Ochs, A...............Hespeler 1887
McDonald, P. J......... ..Barrie	1892	O'Neil, T. ....Belleville 1888
McEachern, D..........Harriston	1892	Oliver, C. B..........Motherwell 1890
McEwen, W. H............Paris	1892	Old, F. J. T............Caledonia 1891
McCullough, E. F....Everton	1892	Oldright, H. H...........Toronto 1891
McPherson, D. A.......Toronto	1892	Orton, R. H ....Guelph 1891
McConaghy, F....Richmond Hill	1892	Oldham, J. H.........Marlbank 1892
McGinnis, John ....Arva	1892	Olmstead, W. E ....Ancaster 1893
McKenzie, W. J........Warwick	1893	
McGarry, J. H......Niagara Falls	1893	Park, Hugh ....Caistorville 1875
McGrath, G........Campbellford	1893	Parke, W. T............Seneca 1877
McLennan, K.........Dunvegan	1893	Parker, Jas...........Frankville 1871
		Parker, Wm............Ashton 1871
Newell, J. ....Springfield	1877	Parsons, J. H..........Yorkville 1871
Nichol, A ....Stratford	1873	Paterson, C. A.......Streetsville 1873
Nichol, Wm ....Brantford	1876	Paterson, H. ....Berlin 1872
Norton, T ....Horning's Mills	1875	Pettigrew, G. A ....Norwood 1876

Phelan, D................Ottawa 1877
Phelan, J. B. ....Toronto 1877
Phillip, T.W..........Port Perry 1870
Philip, Wm. ....Port Perry 1874
Pringle, A. R..........Unionville 1876
Potter, S ....Manotick 1875
Potter, T.. ....Hazledean 1875
Powell, N. A............Cobourg 1875
Powell, R. H..............Ottawa 1876
Preston, R..............Newburg 1878
Pringle, H. H. ....Port Perry 1877
Prosser, Wm. O. ......Newington 1877
Pomeroy, J. R.... .....Newburg 1878
Pyne, R. A..............Toronto 1878
Prouse, E..........Little Britain 1879
Park, T. J.. ....Amherstburg 1879
Patterson, R...............Ilderton 1880
Piper, J. M............. London 1880
Peters, W. F .Michipicoten Island 1882
Prevost, L. C.............Ottawa 1882
Park, John ....Saintfield 1883
Patterson, J.W.....Harrowsmith 1884
Pringle, A. F ......Mount Albert 1884
Peters, G. A. ....Toronto 1885
Paul, J. J...........Sebringville 1885
Parry, W. T. .... Dunnville 1885
Pickard, J. E.......Thamesville 1885
Palmer, G. F ....London 1885
Peaker, J.W......Burnhamthorpe 1886
Pattee, R. P.........Plantagenet 1886
Philp, T. S. ....Colborne 1887
Palmer, J. A......Richmond Hill 1887
Pirie, A. F ....Dundas 1887
Pyne, A. R..............Toronto 1887
Piper, D. H.............London 1887
Phillips, J. A ....Guelph 1887
Perfect, A. H .... Orangeville 1887
Pare, L. T. ....Sandwich 1887
Palling, J. F............Allandale 1888
Patton, J. C ....Toronto 1888
Pickering, Mrs. Annie L..Toronto 1888
Proudfoot, J. ....London 1888
Park, P. C.............Durham 1888
Paterson, J. A .....,,.Port Elgin 1889
Palmer, R. H ....Danforth 1889
Patterson, T. C..........Grafton 1889
Philp, W. S. ....Brampton 1889
Pomeroy, L. E. M ....Tweed 1889
Pratt, W. F.............Ottawa 1889
Phair, W. R. G ....Uxbridge 1889
Phelan, D ....North Gower 1890
Parker, S. G ....Toronto 1890
Pugh, W. M ....Milverton 1890
Philp, W. H ....Waldemar 1890
Patterson, C. J. ....Ottawa 1890
Page, T. ....Concord 1891

Penhall, F. W ....Port Perry 1891
Potts, R. B..... ....Toronto 1891
Parkyn, H. A............Toronto 1892
Parson, H. C ....Toronto 1892
Peters, J. B............Toronto 1893
Pease, H. D. ....Toronto 1893
Pirritte, F. W ....Toronto 1893

Quance, S. H.............Elfrid 1887
Quackenbush, Allen......Morpeth 1892
Quackenbush, A..Mountain View 1892

Rattray, C. J. .... .Cornwall 1871
Read, William. ....London 1874
Reeve, J. E.............Toronto 1878
Renwick, J. W.........Scotland 1871
Reynolds, T. N.........Meaford 1870
Richards, N. D....... Castleton 1877
Richardson, G. T ......Wyoming 1880
Richardson, Joseph ......Toronto 1875
Richardson, Samuel .....Toronto 1871
Robertson, Hugh..St. Catharines 1871
Robertson, J. A......Shakespeare 1871
Robinson, R. H........Toronto 1874
Robinson, Wesley .....Markham 1874
Rodgers, Amos. ....Ottawa 1876
Rolston, H. J.......... .Toronto 1874
Ross, Hugh............Brucefield 1872
Ross, W. D ....Ottawa 1875
Ross, R. A.............Barrie 1877
Routlege, G. A.........Lambeth 1877
Rowan, P. J ....Toronto 1870
Rutherford, James. ....Orono 1870
Rutherford, S. G. ....Shakespeare 1871
Ryerson, G. A. S ....Toronto 1878
Rankin, J. P ....Tavistock 1878
Riddell, George......Cold Springs 1888
Ross, J. F. W. ....Toronto 1887
Robson, W. T.. ....Toronto 1878
Robinson, Alexander....Beaverton 1878
Reddick, Robt..West Winchester 1878
Rowe, G. G ....Georgetown 1879
Radford, J. H. ....Perth 1880
Robinson, Jonathan ....Uxbridge 1881
Reynolds, T. W........Brockville 1881
Rogers, D. H ....Gananoque 1881
Reeve, H. H ....Minesing 1882
Riordan, B. L............Toronto 1882
Rose, David.............Simcoe 1882
Rutherford, D. B. ......Belleville 1882
Robinson, T. H. ....Nobleton 1883
Robinson, W. J. ....Fergus 1883
Ross, W. A. ....Barrie 1882
Rattray, J. C ....Cobden 1883
Ray, J. W.........Little Britain 1883
Routhier, L. G...........Curran 1884

Stewart, J. M ....Portsmouth 1882	Sinclair, D. J...Ann Arbor, Mich. 1888
Symington, T. J.....Camlachie 1882	Struthers, R. B. ....Montreal 1888
Sawers, F. H ....Peterboro' 1883	Scott, P. J ....Saugeen 1888
Stowe, Miss Augusta ....Toronto 1883	Smith W. A ....Welland 1888
Spilsbury, E. A..........Toronto 1883	Smellie, D. M...........Chesley 1888
Scott, W. O..........Mono Road 1884	Smith, A. A . ...Ridgetown 1889
Shoutts, G ....Park Hill 1884	Sangster, W. A. ....Stouffville 1889
Sangster, A............Stouffville 1884	Silverthorne, G ....Toronto 1889
Shaw, J. M..............Keene 1884	Scott, A. Y......... .....Toronto 1889
Smyth, R. A..North Williamsburg 1884	Snider, E. T............Toronto 1889
Sprague, W. E...... .Belleville 1884	Stewart, H. A ....Toronto 1889
Stewart, S ....Wallaceburg 1884	Stevens, R. H ....Detroit 1889
Spence, J ....Fergus 1884	Starr, F................Brooklyn 1889
Staebler, D. M ....Port Elgin 1884	Starr, F. N. G. ....Toronto 1889
Stewart, R. L., Jamestown, N.Y.,	Stone, J. R ....McKellar 1889
U.S.A.....-......... 1884	Sands, E ....Sandbury 1889
Stirling, J. E ... .Kingston 1884	Sisley, O ....Toronto 1889
Smith, Miss Elizabeth ..Hamilton 1884	Sheppard, C. ....Toronto 1890
Snelgrove, C. F........Griersville 1885	Springer, W. D...........Nelson 1890
Simmons, J. U ....Trenton 1885	Sifton, J. M..........Thamesford 1890
Shaver, A. M..........Innerkip 1885	Smith, D.............Belmont 1890
Scott, S ....Toronto 1885	Starr, C. L............Brooklyn 1890
Sutherland, J. G.....Cookstown 1885	Shiel, R ....Plattsville 1890
Stacey, C. E ....Fleetwood 1885	Stenton, D. K.....Port Lambton 1890
Stirling, J. A ....Kingston 1885	Stringer, T. L ....Chatham 1890
Smith, E. A. C ....Toronto 1885	Shannon, J. R ....Kingston 1890
Spankie, W ....Kingston 1885	Sherk, F. H...............Berlin 1890
Sanford, C. M ....Brighton 1886	Smith, J. L ....Monck 1890
Sanson, G ....Petrolia 1885	Speers, A. H..........Burlington 1890
Soden, J. J............Bailieboro' 1886	Spence, A. M ....Fordwich 1890
Shaw, J. P...............Orono 1886	Sargent, W. A....... ..Centreton 1891
Smith, L. G ....Glanford 1886	Scott, W. J............Renfrew 1891
Storms, D. G ....Hamilton 1886	Shannon, G. A........Orangeville 1891
Shaw, J. M ......Mallorytown 1886	Sharp, M ....Delaware 1891
Scadding, H. C..........Orillia 1886	Shaw, J. W...........Brussels 1891
Staples, C. R ....Princeton 1887	Smith, C. F ....Winchester 1891
Shillington, J. W .... Ottawa 1887	Smith, J. C.............Mitchell 1891
Stewart, W. O...........Guelph 1887	Spier, J. R ....Lindsay 1891
Shaw, W. R...........Brantford 1887	Sutherland, A. A ....Fingal 1891
Smith, J. C .....Dayton, Dakota 1887	Sutherland, J ....Strathroy 1891
Sinclair, Duncan, Tonawanda, U.S. 1887	Sinclair, L. C.........Tilsonburg 1892
Shannon, W. A.........Marmora 1887	Smith, J. R............Glanford 1892
Shannon, J. R .... Goderich 1887	Spankie, J. E...........Kingston 1892
Stevenson, A. J ....Brantford 1887	Sparling, A. J.........Pembroke 1892
Smith, R. S ....London 1887	Sullivan, D. V.........Kingston 1892
Scales, Thomas ....Kingston 1887	Saulter, W. W .... Toronto 1892
Stevenson. W. J ....Aurora 1887	Skippen, A .... .Hillsburg 1892
Stewart, George ......Cedar Mills 1887	Switzer, F. L.....Carleton Place 1892
Shepherd, H. E........Stouffville 1887	Shaw, R. W .....Hudson, Mich. 1892
Scott, W. D...........Peterboro' 1887	Smuck, J. W ....Renforth 1893
Smith, G. O. ....L'Orignal 1887	South, T. E............St. George 1893
Steele, M ....Avon Bank 1888	Sanderson, H. H ....Sparta 1893
Smith, W. H ....Toronto 1888	Stafford, E. H...........Chicago 1893
Sisley, E ....Toronto 1888	Stinson, J. C .... .Brantford 1893
Scott, J. A ....McIntyre 1888	Story, S. G ....Cedar Springs 1893
Stinson, A. W ....Codrington 1888	Shouldice, J. H. ....Hamilton 1893

Whitely, J. B ....Goderich 1883	Whiteman, G. A .....Shakespeare 1889
Woods, E. R. ....Galt 1883	Webster, T. E............Fergus 1889
Wilson, J. D............London 1883	Walsh, F ....Guelph 1890
Webster, H. E ... ... .Whitby 1884	Wright, G. ....Wheatley 1890
Watson, J. A............Toronto 1885	Walker, Hattie A ....Pitt's Ferry 1890
Wright, W. H ....Glen Allan 1885	Webster, E. H. ... .Preston 1890
Woodward, A. F ....Hawkesville 1885	Welch,H.W..Cook's Mills,Algoma 1890
Wishart, D. J. G..........Madoc 1885	Walker, A. E...............Arva 1891
Wood, E. G..........Londesboro' 1885	Watson, J ....Sherwood 1891
West, Stephen...............Ivy 1886	Webster, D. F ....Glencoe 1891
Wilson, R. J ....Toronto 1886	Webster, R. E....... Brockville 1891
Watts, E. J. ....Easton's Corners 1886	Wells, F. H ....Aurora 1891
West, Robert. ....Woodstock 1886	Wesley, J. H.........Newmarket 1891
Winnett, Frederick .....Toronto 1886	White, R. H ....Bailieboro' 1891
Wilson, G. H ....London 1886	Wilson, C. W..Buckingham, Que. 1891
Weeks, W. J ....Thorndale 1886	Walker, N ....Toronto 1892
Wright, E. W. ....Bath 1886	Wasson, H. J..........Peterboro' 1892
Waddell, W. H............Perth 1886	Way, H. J...............Toronto 1892
Walters, W. R. ....Coleman 1887	Wheeler, J. W......Wolfe Island 1892
Walsh, W. J............Guelph 1887	White, J. W ....Branchton 1892
Warner, A. F. ....Napanee 1887	Wigle, F. A. ....Kingsville 1892
Wardlaw, J. S ....Galt 1888	Wilson, J. A ....Lakelet 1892
Weir, T. P ....Toronto 1888	Wilson, W. T............Dundas 1892
Watson, G. R ....Wellington 1888	Wood, Isaac............Kingston 1892
Walker, R E............Orillia 1888	Walker, W. G........Stratford 1892
Whitney, A. W ......Morrisburg 1888	Wardell, H. A............Dundas 1893
Walker, A. D-......Shannonville 1888	Williams, J. J ....Tottenham 1893
Weagant, A. A.,	Wilson, J. A. G ......Warkworth 1893
Dickinson's Landing 1888	Wakefield, W. F. B.....Thorold 1893
Willmott, J. W........Unionville 1888	Wickson, D. D ....Toronto 1893
Wallwin, H............Toronto 1888	
Wilkins, H. P. ....Toronto 1889	Youker, W.............Halloway 1870
Wiley, J. I ....Wisbeach 1889	Young, R. C. ....Hamilton 1873
Willson, A. J. ....Berlin 1889	Young, O................Whitby 1877
Wade, R. J ....Brighton 1889	Yourex, J. McG........Belleville 1877
Wade, W. R.........Dunchurch 1889	Young, W. J ....Wingham 1884
Wills, A. E ....Belleville 1889	Yelland, A. E......... Peterboro' 1887
Wilson, H. W. ....Toronto 1889	Young, S. N ....Ridgetown 1889
Wright, W. M ....Flesherton 1889	Yeomans, H. A ....Belleville 1889
Webster, J.............Toronto 1889	Youell, J. H. G ....Aylmer 1892
Williams, H. T. H.......London 1889	
Westley, R. A......Williamstown 1889	Zwick, F ....Belleville 1890

Spring Examinations, 1893.

THEORY AND PRACTICE OF MEDICINE.

Time 2½ Hours.

15   1. Describe and give the causes of, and suitable treatment for, (*a*) Erythema Simplex, (*b*) Erythema Intertrigo, and Erythema Nodosum.

10   2. Diagnose Spasmodic from Inflammatory Croup, and state what treatment you would adopt for each.

10   3. What are the causes of Emphysema of the Lungs? How would you recognize and treat it?

10   4. Give the symptoms and treatment of Chorea. At what age is it most common? With what other affections is it frequently associated?

15   5. Give the causes, symptoms, and treatment of Gastric Ulcer.

20   6. Give, in tabular form, the diagnostic point of difference between (*a*) Hydatid of the Liver, (*b*) Abscess of the Liver, and Cancer of the Liver.

20   7. A patient is suffering from Hæmaturia. What parts of the urinary tract might it proceed from, and what symptoms would enable you to decide as to its source and probable cause?

H. J. SAUNDERS, M.D., M.R.C.S., ENG., *Examiner.*

PATHOLOGY AND THERAPEUTICS.

Time 2½ Hours.

1. What are the gross and microscopic distinctions between tubercular and syphilitic disease of the testicle? Trace the usual course of tubercular disease, commencing in the testicle and ending fatally.

2. What are the varieties of Epitheliomata? Describe the general and minute characters of each, and state what parts are most liable to be attacked by each variety.

3. Describe the general and minute changes which occur in the Spinal Cord in Locomotor Ataxia (Posterior Spinal Sclerosis).

4. State what you know of the germ of Cholera. What conditions are favourable to its development, (1) in a community ; (2) in an individual ?

5. Describe the process of Ulceration of the Bowel in Typhoid Fever.

THERAPEUTICS.

1. Describe the different methods of producing Diaphoresis. What remedies are in common use for this purpose? Give doses. Write a prescription for a diaphoretic mixture—the directions to be given in English.

2. Write brief notes on the therapeutic uses of Arsenic, Salol, Hydrogen Peroxide, Iron, Potass Nitrate, Ergot.

GEO. A. PETERS, M.B., F.R.C.S., ENG., *Examiner.*

MIDWIFERY, OTHER THAN OPERATIVE.

PUERPERAL AND INFANTILE DISEASE.

Time 2½ Hours.

1. What is Parasitic Stomatitis ? Give causes, prevention, and treatment.

2. What is Icterus Neonatorum ? When does it commonly occur ? Give diagnosis, causes and treatment.

3. What is Cholera Infantum ? Give anatomical lesions, etiology, symptoms, diagnosis, and treatment.

4. What is Puerperal Fever ? Give its causes, prevention and treatment.

5. What are the "Stages of Labour"? Give the method of management of an ordinary case from its commencement to the end of the puerperal period.

6. What is Abortion ? How do you treat a case where the ovum is expelled with the membranes unruptured ?

7. How would you diagnose Pregnancy at the fifth month from a case of Fibroid Tumour of the Uterus ?

A. A. MacDONALD, M.D., *Examiner.*

MIDWIFERY, OPERATIVE.

Time 2½ Hours.

1. Give diagnosis and treatment of a case of Abortion at the third month, the membranes having ruptured, the ovum being retained, and hæmorrhage taking place.

2. What is Concealed Accidental Puerperal Hæmorrhage? Give the circumstances under which it may occur towards the end of gestation ; give its treatment, and mention the distinction between accidental and unavoidable hæmorrhage.

3. What is Podalic Version ? Give indications for its use, and manner of performing it.

4. What are the indications for forceps delivery? Mention the usual precautions before applying the forceps, and the method of applying them when the head is in the pelvic cavity in the first position.

5. How would you endeavour to prevent laceration of the perinæum during delivery, and how treat a recent laceration through the perineal body ?

6. Under what circumstances is Craniotomy admissible ?

A. A. MacDonald, M.D., *Examiner.*

SURGERY, OTHER THAN OPERATIVE.

Time 2½ Hours.

1. Give the signs and diagnosis of four of the principal kinds of Tumours.

2. Treat a fracture of the Femur in the middle third in an adult, and in a child three years old.

3. Give concise accounts of Appendicitis and Psoas Abscess from their inception to their various terminations.

4. Give a short description of the manifestations of Tubercle as a surgical affection.

5. Diagnose the following : Intracapsular fracture of the neck of the Femur, dislocation of the head of the Radius forwards, Movable bodies in the Knee-joint and Glaucoma.

W. Burt, M.D., *Examiner.*

SURGERY, OPERATIVE.

Time 2½ Hours.

1. Describe the Operative treatment of ununited fractures of the long bones, and the patella.

2. In Strangulated Inguinal Hernia describe (*a*) the relief of the stricture ; (*b*) the treatment of the sac ; (*c*) the treatment of the contents of the sac.

3. Describe the removal of foreign bodies from the cornea and conjunctiva and the enucleation of the Eye.

4. Give indications for and describe the ligation of the brachial, ulnar, anterior and posterior tibial arteries in the middle of the arm, forearm, leg and calf respectively.

5. Give a general description of the preparation of patients for operations, and give the principal points to be attended to in the administration of the various anæsthetics.

W. BURT, M.D., *Examiner.*

MEDICAL AND SURGICAL ANATOMY.

Time 2½ Hours.

1. What structures form the Scalp, and what vessels and nerves supply it.

2. Give in their order the parts divided in a Syme's amputation of the foot.

3. If the Obturator nerve were injured, what muscles would be paralyzed and what movements of the limb would be impaired.

4. Give the course and relations of the descending colon and sigmoid flexure.

5. Give the formation, branches and relations of the superficial and the deep Palmar arch.

W. WAUGH, M.D., *Examiner.*

MEDICAL JURISPRUDENCE.

Time 2½ Hours.

1. Distinguish between feigned and real Mania ; feigned and real Epilepsy ; also between Idiocy and Imbecility : between Mania and Delirium Tremens ; Melancholia and Dementia ; Dementia and

Paresis; Monomania and Idiosyncrasy; Compression of the Brain and Coma from Alcoholism.

2. Describe a Fœtus of fourteen days; of six weeks; of three months; five months; and eight months.

3. Give the post-mortem appearance where death has resulted from —(*a*) Starvation, (*b*) Asphyxia, (*c*) Acute Alcoholism.

4. How could you distinguish between the condition of the muscles found in Catalepsy, and that occurring in Rigor Mortis; also between Strangulation and Hanging, Molecular and Somatic death? Asphyxia and Apnœa, Ecchymosis and Suggillation, Hypostatic Congestion and Inflammation of the Lungs, Liver Pleura and Ileum; also between the condition produced by Irritant Poisons and Decomposition in the Larynx and Stomach, and between the artificially inflated lungs of a new-born child, and one in which respiration had been maintained naturally for thirty minutes?

5. Describe the condition of the uterus in a case where death has resulted after delivery at full term :—(*a*) Immediately afterwards, (*b*) One day afterwards, (*c*) Three days, (*d*) One week, (*e*) Three weeks, (*f*) Six weeks.

6. Describe the proceedings of the Coroner's Inquest as ordinarily observed in this country.

7. What points should be specially noted in making a post-mortem upon the body of an individual who is supposed to have died from the effects of an irritant poison, such as Arsenic, but who was also well known to have been addicted to the excessive use of ardent spirits; also in a case where death is supposed to have resulted from the effects of a blow upon the head while the individual was in a state of profound intoxication.

R. HEARN, M.D., C.M., *Examiner.*

———

SANITARY SCIENCE.

Time 1½ Hours.

1. Describe fully the method of the disposal of sewage by "Irrigation."

2. Give a description of the "tubercle bacillus" and state how it may be propagated, the conditions of the system which favour its development or otherwise, the conditions and variations of climate which influence it, the different classes of food which may effect its development, the proofs that it is capable or otherwise of producing disease by

being taken into the blood or lungs of human beings or animals; also any general or special means to be employed in rendering it innocuous either external to the body or in the lungs.

3. Describe Tænia Bothriocephalus, Tænia Solium, Hydatids and Trichina, stating where they are found, how they obtain entrance into the body, how they are propagated, and what symptoms they give rise to.

4. Give a description and compare, the hopper closet, the pan closet, and the ship closet.

5. Mention some of the diseases which may arise from the use of water contaminated with stercoral matter, giving the names of some of the entozoa which may be found therein.

R. HEARN, M.D., C.M., *Examiner.*

ANATOMY.

Time 2½ Hours.

1. Describe the Clavicle.

2. Give the course, relations and branches of the Internal Mammary Artery.

3. Trace the Facial Nerve from its exit from the skull to its ultimate distribution.

4. Give the origin, insertion and nervous supply of the Tibialis Anticus and Posticus; Semi Membranosus; Extensor Ossis Metacarpi Pollicis; Transversalis; Levator Anguli Scapulæ.

F. LeM. GRASETT, F.R.C.S.E., *Examiner.*

PHYSIOLOGY AND HISTOLOGY.

Time 2½ Hours.

1. Describe the terminations of nerve fibres in plain and striated muscles and in the heart.

2. Describe the nervous and muscular mechanisms concerned in speaking, deglutition, and in the gastric and intestinal movements.

3. Explain the causes of the sounds of the heart, and the cardiac impulse. Why are the former heard best at certain points on the chest wall? Describe the means by which the character of the heart beat is brought into relation with the calibre of the minute arteries.

4. Give all the reasons for believing that Anabolism and Katabolism are controlled by the nervous system.

5. Explain the functions of the Membrana Tympani, Tensor Tympani, Eustachian Tube, and the Cochlea. Give the origin and termination of the Auditory Nerve.

A. S. Fraser, M.D., *Examiner.*

CHEMISTRY.

Time 2½ Hours.

1. (*a*) Explain the processes by which the composition of water has been ascertained, both by weight and volume, and its formula settled as H_2O.

   (*b*) What is meant by the "*hardness*" of water? How is it estimated, and how may hard waters be made soft?

2. (*a*) Describe a method of preparing Nitric Acid, giving the equation; and from it how may nitrous oxide (N_2O), nitric oxide (NO), acid nitrous anhydride (N_2O_3) be obtained?

   (*b*) What is a nitrate? Show how the presence of a nitrate in aqueous solution may be detected.

3. (*a*) Describe the method generally employed in the manufacture of potassium chlorate, giving the equations.

   (*b*) In a solution containing potassium chlorate and potassium chloride, silver nitrate produced a precipitate weighing 2.87 grammes; and after acting on the filtrate with nascent hydrogen a further precipitate of 0.359 grammes was produced by silver nitrate. Calculate the amount of chloride and chlorate present.

4. (*a*) What is meant by "*vapour density*," and how is it determined?

   (*b*) The density of a gaseous hydrocarbon is 15 times that of hydrogen; the weight of the carbon is 4 times that of hydrogen. What is the molecular formula of the gas?

5. Give the general method of preparation of the homologous series of hydrocarbons represented by the formula $C_n H_{2n+2}$. Show how from these hydrocarbons the following classes of compounds may be obtained :—halogen derivatives, alcohols, aldehydes, acids, simple ethers, etherial salts, mercaptans, thio-ethers, sulphonic acids, cyanides, amines, nitro-compounds.

What is the difference between the amido-acids and the acid amides? To which of the two classes does each of the following bodies belong :—glycin (glycocoll), urea, creatin, leucin, sarcosin, hippuric acid?

ATOMIC WEIGHTS.

H — 1	N — 14
Cl —35 5	C — 12
O —16	Ag —108
K--39	

GEO. ACHESON, M.A., M.B. (TOR.), *Examiner.*

———

TOXICOLOGY.

Time 1 Hour.

1. Give the symptoms of Chronic Arsenical Poisoning, mentioning any difficulties of diagnosis; and describe the post-mortem appearances.

2. Describe the symptoms and treatment of poisoning by Cannabis Indica.

3. What post-mortem appearances would lead you to conclude that a man had died from acute alcoholic poisoning? From what other conditions is it to be differentiated, and how?

4. Give the minimum fatal dose and antidote for each of the following :

(*a*) hydrargyri perchloridum, (*b*) Scheele's hydrocyanic acid, (*c*) strychnin, (*d*) oxalic acid, (*e*) saltpetre, (*f*) phosphorus.

GEO. ACHESON, M.A., M.B. (TOR.), *Examiner.*

———

MATERIA MEDICA AND PHARMACY.

Time 2½ Hours.

Candidates are requested to employ the Pharmacopœial titles
without abbreviations.

1. Name the suppositories that are officinal, and give the quantity of the active ingredients in each.

2. Distinguish between an alkaloid and a glucoside, and describe an example of each, giving the source, characters and dose.

3. Aconitum Napellus:
   Describe the parts of the plant employed, its physiological action, the officinal preparations, and the strength of each.

4. Iodum. Name the officinal salts and preparations, and give the strength of the latter.

5. Spiritus Ætheris Nitrosi ; Acidum Tannicum ; Hydrargyri Perchloridum. Name some substances that are incompatible with the above, and explain the changes that are produced.

H. BEAUMONT SMALL, M.D., *Examiner.*

PROCEEDINGS

AT MEETING OF

MEDICAL COUNCIL OF ONTARIO

IN JUNE, 1893.

TUESDAY, *June 13th*, 1893.

The Medical Council of the College of Physicians and Surgeons of Ontario met this day, Tuesday, the 13th June, 1893, at 2 p.m., in accordance with the by-laws of the Council.

The President, Dr. Fife Fowler, in the chair, called the Council to order. The Registrar called the roll. All present except Sir James Grant and Dr. Miller.

Dr. Fowler now addressed the Council as follows :

Gentlemen of the Council,—On retiring from the office of President of the Medical Council, a position to which the most ambitious in the profession might well aspire, I desire to render a short account of my stewardship during the eventful year which is just closing.

I realized soon after I assumed the position in which you did me the honour of placing me that there was a considerable amount of dissatisfaction, and no little heart-burnings, among some members of the profession in different parts of the province. Unquestionably a good deal of this arose from the circumstance that till very recently many members of the profession had very inadequate and inaccurate knowledge of the sayings and doings of the Medical Council. Happily this condition of things no longer obtains. This is due, in a very great measure, to the arrangements made with the ONTARIO MEDICAL JOURNAL, whereby this publication reaches every registered medical practitioner in the province, and affords full information of the Council's proceedings. The members of the Council, I feel assured, must be fully satisfied that their expectations as to the benefits that would accrue from the establishment of this journal have been more than realized. I take the liberty of suggesting a continuation of the agreement between the Medical Council and the proprietors of this ably-conducted periodical.

Early in my year of office I deemed it a wise and proper proceeding to open a correspondence with the prominent members of the Defence Association, with a view to the promotion of that harmony which ought to exist in such a profession as ours. I was met by these gentlemen in a most friendly spirit, and arrangements were made and carried into effect for holding, in Toronto, a joint meeting of the members of the Legislation Committee of the Council and representatives of the Defence Association. At this meeting the matters in dispute were discussed and propositions were made by the Legislation Committee of the Council very similar to those adopted by the Special Committee of the Legislative Assembly of Ontario. Thus it was evinced that the Legislation Committee of the Medical Council was animated by a spirit of fairness, harmony and justice, while at the same time zealously guarding the interests of the Medical Council and the profession at large. It is greatly to be regretted that the Defence Association did not accept the terms offered at this conference, which were of such a nature as to render the agitation subsequently kept up and the appeal to the Legislature altogether unjustifiable. We are under great obligations to the chairman and members of this Committee, not only in this connection but also for their watchful care in respect to the bill introduced into the Legislative Assembly by Dr. Meacham. For these services, so cheerfully and efficiently rendered, I desire, on behalf of the Council, to tender hearty thanks.

It must be gratifying to one and all of us that the Legislature did not countenance the attempt which was made to effect radical changes in the Constitution of the Medical Council. Interests of a threefold character have existed since its inception in respect to representation, to wit, the Public, the Professional, and the Educational. The Universities fitly represent, and are in touch with, the public through their graduates, found mingling in every line of life. The territorial representatives, among whom I take the liberty of classing the Homœopaths as an important and influential factor, know fully the wants and aspirations of the profession at large. The educational representatives, elected by the teaching bodies, you will pardon me for saying, do and must form an essential part in carrying out, well and successfully, the work the Council has to do. So long as educational matters continue to play the important *role* which heretofore they have done in the Council's proceedings, these several interests are not, and should not, be antagonistic, but mutually dependent on and helpful to each other, severally attaining their greatest and best development and lustre when acting in perfect harmony.

In accordance with that portion of the report of the Education Committee, having reference to reciprocal registration with the other provinces of the Dominion, I proceeded to Ottawa on the first day of the session of the Dominion Medical Association. I found that Dr. Bray, the esteemed President of the Association, had, previous to my arrival, held an informal meeting with some gentlemen interested in the question of reciprocal registration. I soon ascertained that, under the present circumstances, reciprocity in registration with the Provinces of Quebec and Manitoba was impracticable. The apparent impossibility of assimilating the matriculation examinations, and the fact that the other provinces of the Dominion are not prepared to enforce a course of medical study extending over a period of five years, are obstacles in the way which obviously cannot soon be overcome.

Having been closely connected with the Examining Board of the Council for many years, and having acted as Chairman of the Board of Examiners on two occasions, I have had abundant opportunities of familiarizing myself with the system now adopted. I believe, and am sure, that as far as these examinations, which are conducted in a practical manner, are concerned, whether at the bedside, in the laboratory, or by other practical means, whether the examiners are teachers or non-teachers, there has been a great degree of efficiency reached, and that these examinations are eminently satisfactory and are exercising a most beneficial influence on the teaching at the medical schools. But in the case of the examinations of a non-practical character, in many cases there does not appear to be that harmony between the teachers and examiners which should exist. In my opinion the Council should instruct the examiners, more especially those who are not teachers, to keep themselves in touch with the didactic teaching of the medical schools, and mayhap aid in moulding it in the best form and direction for preparing students for the practical work which to-day is so essentially a characteristic of student life.

With reference to the mode of determining the results of the examinations, my experience as Chairman of the Board of Examiners leads me to suggest that the Council should instruct the examiners when they meet together for this purpose ; that they should not be guided in all cases by the cast-iron rule of passing all who attain a certain number of marks and rejecting all who do not. Following such a rule, in its strictness, is simply performing clerical work which does not require for its execution the solemn assembling of the Examining Board. Such work could be equally well done by the executive officers of the Council. I hold that the examiners should consider the marks obtained by the students as a whole and in certain cases recommend that the Council take cognizance of them. In justice to many students it must be remembered that success in passing examinations is often due, in a very great measure, to careful memorizing, and hence failures at the examining board often occur in these subjects which are not of a practical character, and among those students who, while inexpert at cramming, are otherwise well fitted to become able and successful practitioners. A careful consideration of such cases by the examiners, and their reference, if thought desirable, to the Council would, I feel confident, be eminently satisfactory to the students and remove all grounds for appeal against the decision of the examiners.

Moved by Dr. Harris, seconded by Dr. Bray, that Dr. Fowler do now leave the chair and that Dr. Campbell take the same. Carried.

Moved by Dr. Harris, seconded by Dr. Bray, that the Council tender Dr. Fowler their thanks for his able conduct of the affairs of the Council for the past year, and his interesting address just delivered. Carried unanimously.

Dr. Campbell presented the resolution to Dr. Fowler and left the chair.

Dr. Fowler replied in suitable terms, and resumed the chair and called for nominations.

Dr. MOORE—I have much pleasure, Mr. President, in proposing as President of the College of Physicians and Surgeons of Ontario for the ensuing year, Dr. Campbell, of London; and in nominating Dr. Campbell to the highest office in the gift of our Association I need offer no words of commendation, for every member is cognizant of his executive ability, honesty of purpose and keenness of perception, and I am satisfied he will discharge the duties devolving upon him with credit to himself, satisfaction to the Association and justice to the profession.

Dr. HARRIS—I beg to second the nomination of Dr. Campbell. Dr. Moore has certainly left nothing further for me to say, but I know, and I feel, and I believe, that each and every member of this Council must feel that Dr. Campbell will make a most excellent President.

On motion, Dr. Moore was asked to cast a ballot, there being no other nominations, and on the ballot being examined by the President he declared Dr. Campbell elected unanimously.

Amid applause Dr. Campbell was escorted to the President's chair by Drs. Moore and Harris, and addressed the Council as follows :—

Gentlemen of the Council,—I thank you very much for the honour you have conferred upon me in electing me to the office of President of this body. It must always be felt as an honour by any person to be placed for the time being at the head of his profession or calling; and when the selection comes, as it has in this case, unsolicited, of your own free will, without any canvassing, or log-rolling, or scheming of any kind by myself or by my friends, the honour is all the more appreciated. I thank you very much for it. I shall endeavour, to the best of my ability, to so perform the duties of the office that at the expiration of my term you shall have no cause to regret the action you have taken.

Dr. BERGIN—I move, seconded by Dr. Bray, that Dr. Philip, representing the Erie and Niagara division, be Vice-President for the ensuing year. I need scarcely say that Dr. Philip's merits are known to every member of the Council; he has been a long time a member of this body, and has filled a very important position to the great advantage of the Council—I refer to the chairmanship of the Finance Committee. He possesses all the qualifications necessary not only to fill this chair, but in due course of time the chair to which you, Mr. President, have now been elected with the unanimous voice of this Council.

Dr. BRAY—I have great pleasure in seconding that nomination. I have known Dr. Philip ever since he has been a member of this Council, and I am sure you will all agree with me that he has performed the duties pertaining to a representative, and particularly a territorial representative at anyrate, to the satisfaction of this Council, and I think to the satisfaction of the electorate in the constituency he represents; and am quite satisfied he will fill the position of Vice-President of this Council ably and well. And it therefore affords me very great pleasure to be granted the opportunity of seconding Dr. Philip's nomination.

On motion, Dr. Bergin was asked to cast a ballot, there being no further nominations, and on the bal'ot being examined by the President he declared Dr. Philip elected unanimously.

Dr. PHILIP—I feel very deeply indebted to the members of the Medical Council for the confidence which they have reposed in me in electing me to the high position of Vice-President of the Council. I do not think there is anything which a professional man will more desire, especially a medical man, than to know and to feel he enjoys the esteem and confidence of his fellow-practitioners; and it is very gratifying to my mind to be shown this mark of confidence and esteem by the members of this Council in electing me to the office of Vice-President, more especially as I have been upon the Finance Committee, thus expressing confidence in the chairman of that committee and the members of that committee. With Dr. Campbell, as President, in the chair, the duties of my office will be light no doubt; but such as they are I will endeavour to perform to the best of my ability. Gentlemen of the Council, I again thank you very heartily for this high honour you have now conferred upon me.

Dr. Bray moved, seconded by Dr. Bergin, that Dr. Pyne be re-appointed Registrar for the ensuing year.

The President put the motion, and there being no other nominations, declared Dr. Pyne unanimously elected Registrar.

Dr. Philip moved, seconded by Dr. Rogers, that Dr. Aikins be reappointed Treasurer for this Council for the ensuing year.

The President put the motion, and there being no other nominations, declared Dr. Aikins unanimously elected Treasurer.

Dr. Bray moved, seconded by Dr. Johnson, that Mr. B. B. Osler be reappointed Solicitor of this Council for the ensuing year.

The President put the motion, and their being no other nominations, declared Mr. Osler unanimously elected.

Dr. Bergin moved, seconded by Dr. Moore, that Alexander Downey, C. S. R., be reappointed Official Stenographer of this Council for the ensuing year.

The President put the motion, and there being no other nominations, declared Mr. Downey unanimously elected.

Dr. Henry moved, seconded by Dr. Orr, that Drs. Day, Thorburn, Bray, Williams, Johnson, Bergin, Harris and Logan be a committee to strike the standing committees for the ensuing year. Carried.

Dr. BERGIN—I might say to the Council, Mr. President, with your permission, that the Convocation of the Toronto University is to be held about this hour and that a very interesting address will be delivered by the Vice-Chancellor, Mr. Mulock, this afternoon, upon "Medical Science," and he will be very glad to see such members of the Council as can make it convenient to go to the Pavilion in the Horticultural Gardens.

Dr. Day moved, seconded by Dr. Ruttan, that the Council do now adjourn for ten minutes to wait the report of the Striking Committee. Carried.

On the Council resuming after adjournment, Dr. Henry presented the report of the Striking Committee, naming the various committees as follows:

Registration Committee—Dr. Rosebrugh (chairman), Dr. Johnson, Dr. Moore, Dr. Orr, Dr. Vernon.

Rules and Regulations—Dr. Day, Dr. Fowler, Dr. Luton, Dr. Thorburn, Dr. Miller.

Finance—Dr. Thorburn, Dr. Fulton, Dr. Henderson, Dr. Ruttan, Dr. Williams.

Printing—Dr. Johnson, Dr. Fenwick, Dr. Henry, Dr. Luton, Dr. Britton.

Committee on Complaints—Dr. Fowler, Dr. Johnson, Dr. Henderson, Dr. Miller, Dr. Henry.

Education—Dr. Harris (chairman), Dr. Bergin, Dr. Bray, Dr. Geikie, Dr. Logan, Dr. Moore, Dr. Rogers, Dr. Thorburn, Dr. Williams.

Property—Dr. Britton, Dr. Henry, Dr. Thorburn.

Executive—Dr. Campbell, Dr. Philip, Dr. Johnson.

Dr. Henry moved, seconded by Dr. Orr, that the report of the Committee be received and adopted.   Carried.

NOTICES OF MOTION.

No. 1.   Dr. Thorburn, to instruct the Education Committee to amend regulations by setting forth the qualifications necessary for lecturers in the various Schools of Medicine upon the various subjects.

No. 2.   Dr. Fowler, *re* the acceptance of graduates from the Military College as matriculates upon paying fees and proving identity.

No. 3.   Dr. Philip, *re* appointment of committee to consider advisability of establishing examination for the graduating of nurses.

No. 4.   Dr. Rogers, that he will move to change divisions Nos. 15, 16 and 17 in schedule passed in the Medical Act of 1893.

No. 5.   Dr. Harris, *re* instruction to Education Committee to define subjects, number of lectures, demonstration, etc., for summer session.

No. 6.   Dr. Bray, *re* the slanderous editorial appearing in the *Mail*, of 13th June, upon Medical Council of Ontario.

Communications and petitions were then read, received, and referred to a committee to report upon same :

From J. D. Fontaine, B. L. Bradly, Wm. Ewing, N. J. Bricknell, J. D. Smith, D. Macnee, E. W. Tonkin, O. C. Edwards, and the Editor of the *Lancet* and of the *Practitioner*.

Referred to Finance Committee.

From J. P. Hubbard, S. H. Large, W. E. Brown, E. W. Goode, J. A. McNaughton, L. Lapp, J. B. Ferguson, W. J. Arnott, D. J. Dunn, R. T. Corbett, A. B. Parlow, A. B. McCallum.

Referred to Committee on Complaints.

From Sir Oliver Mowat, Hon. R. Harcourt and Dr. P. H. Bryce.

Referred to Committee on Rules and Regulations.

From Thomas Bradley, W. F. Cunningham, H. B. Small, T. J. Coldwel, J. J. Davis, A. C. Halter, C. S. Proctor, George D. Porter, C. O. Fairbairn, Dr. Waugh, A. A. Metcalfe, A. G. Fletcher, W. A. McIntosh, Duncan McCallum, D. Jamieson, H. G. Williams, W. J. Beatty, A. Johnston, H. H. Millbee, J. R. McRae, F. McKinnon, J. A. Brown, M. Haight.

Dr. Rogers inquires why names of A. G. Allen and T. M. Macfarlane, members of the College of Physicians and Surgeons of Ontario, do not appear upon the Ontario Medical Register for 1892,

Referred to Registrar for reply.

Dr. Henry asks who was responsible for the gerrymandering of the constituencies by the new Medical bill, and is referred by the President to the Chairman of the Legislative Committee for reply.

Dr. WILLIAMS—Unfortunately the Legislative Committee do not know very much about it. The members of the Council are aware the bills were introduced into the Ontario Legislature without the sanction of the Legislative Committee, and attached to those, or at least one of those, was a schedule which proposed a rearrangement of a large share of the constituencies. That matter was brought up before the committee to which that bill was referred in the House and was dealt with by that committee. We had friends, of course, in that committee who endeavoured to see that the arrangement would be as equitable as possible, but unfortunately our friends were not able to get all their own way, and things were carried in that committee that were not sanctioned either by our friends nor would they have been sanctioned by any of our selves had we had a voice in the matter, but as a matter of fact we had no voice and they were not able to control the matter as they would like to have done. I have no doubt at all that they endeavoured to secure the best possible arrangement they could under the circumstances.

The report for the year of the Prosecutor of the College was read, and also the Prosecutor's report as to members of the College who were charged with unprofessional conduct. The report, on motion, was referred to the Committee on Discipline.

On motion of Dr. Harris, the Council adjourned to meet again at 10 o'clock a.m. on Wednesday, 14th June.

SECOND DAY.

WEDNESDAY, *June 14th*, 1893,

10 o'clock a.m.

Medical Council met in accordance with motion for adjournment.

The President in the chair called the Council to order.

The Registrar called the roll. All present except Sir James Grant.

Minutes of last meeting read and confirmed.

MOTIONS OF WHICH NOTICE HAS BEEN, GIVEN AT A PREVIOUS MEETING.

Dr. Fowler moved, seconded by Dr. Moore, that graduates of the Royal Military College be accepted as matriculants of the College of Physicians and Surgeons on proving their identity and paying the usual fees.

Dr. FOWLER—In moving this resolution I think it is probably not desirable for me to make any remarks upon this matter to any extent, as I think it will be well to refer it to the committee either on Registration or Education. I would just say I feel convinced, from a long connection with medical education, that it is not so much the special subjects which are passed upon that are of importance, but the fact that the student has had mental training ; and it seems to be conceded that the mental training gained in the Royal Military College must be fully equal to the requirements for those who commence the study of medicine, and I therefore propose this motion.

Referred to Education Committee.

Dr. Philip moves, seconded by Dr. Henry, that a committee be appointed by the President to inquire into the advisability, or otherwise, of the Medical Council taking under its charge the examination and granting certificates to the graduating nurses of the various hospitals in the Province and send in a report during the present session of the Council.

Dr. PHILIP—As it is at present we have a good many hospitals throughout the provinces, in some of the smaller cities and towns, that have their own training schools attached to them, and they grant, on an examination by the Local Board, certificates to nurses. The object of my motion is to inquire whether it is advisable, or whether it is feasible, or whether the Council have power to grant under proper provisions, which would be inquired into, a certificate in order to make the certificate held by the nurses of more value than a certificate from the local hospitals. At the present time there are a good many—I know in Brantford we have an hospital, and a pretty large hospital too, and we graduate some nurses there every year, and a good many of our nurses have gone to Buffalo, Detroit, and other places, and if nurses in thus going out had a Provincial certificate with the " hall mark," so to speak, of the Council upon it, it would be a great advantage to them, instead of merely obtaining the certificates, as they do now, from the various hospitals. This might be done, I thin, without any expense to the Council. Of course this scheme would have to be elaborated upon by the committee to which it may be referred. I do not think it would cost a single cent to appoint the gentlemen who now compose the Local Board of Examining Physicians. I noticed a little paragraph in a newspaper, to the effect that legislation would be asked in connection with the Kingston Hospital, from the Government, to permit the issue of trained nurses' certificates by hospitals having one hundred or more beds, to nurses trained in such hospitals. The Committee can inquire into this, and I would like the President to appoint a committee ; and if the scheme is not feasible to carry out at present session of the Council I might alter my notice of motion to read, that the Committee report at the next meeting of the Council, but for the present I will leave the motion as it is.

Dr. BRITTON—Have any overtures been made by any of. the hospital authorities regarding this matter? I ask this because if we were to take the initiative it might possibly appear to some of the hospitals that we were rather exceeding our duties. I should be most pleased to fall into line with this motion, provided we were sure that the hospital boards were inclined in the same direction and had said anything concerning it, because otherwise they might construe such an action on our part as a reflection upon the certificates which they have already granted.

Dr. PHILIP—The authorities of our hospital in Brantford have spoken about it, and there is also this paragraph I have referred to in the newspaper about the Kingston Hospital.

Dr. BRITTON—Might I suggest that the motion be worded differently—that a committee be appointed to confer with the directorate of the different hospitals to see whether or not they approve of such a scheme, and if they thought it would be any advantage to them; the endorsation of their certificates being a benefit to their nurses; in that event I should be only too glad to give it support.

Dr. WILLIAMS—I think in the meantime our acts of parliament do not give us any such power. And if we had any thought of taking such action, one of the first things we should have to do would be to go to the Legislature and seek for power to deal with it. I think at the present time we have quite enough to do to deal with matters that come under our own acts and that we have full control of. We certainly have not any control, or right, or power under those acts to interfere in any way whatever; and that being the case, the only way we could get it would be by seeking fresh legislation, which I think at the present time would not be a very advisable course to pursue.

Dr. ROGERS—I was about to make the same remark, that under the Medical Act we, as a Council, have no power whatever to grant certificates to nurses; there is no section, or part of a section, or word in the Act which would allow us to do so; and, as Dr. Williams has said, before we could undertake this task we should have to go to the Legislature and get power; and while personally I quite agree with all Dr. Philip has said as to the necessity of putting nurses on one footing, as it were, still it seems to me this Council have about all they can do if they attend to the affairs of the medical profession, and I think myself that we have no power to do this work, and it seems to me the motion is of no avail.

Dr. LOGAN—In order to avoid general discussion upon this matter at the present time, it strikes me that it would be better, and it would give consideration to Dr. Philip's idea, to refer the matter to some of our committees, such as Education or Registration.

The PRESIDENT—The motion is simply the appointment of a committee to inquire; it does not commit the Council to anything whatever.

Dr. Rogers moves to have this motion referred to the Education Committee.

Dr. MOORE—The Education Committee has enough to do.

Dr. HARRIS—The Education Committee will have a great deal of work to do, and I think perhaps Dr. Philip's suggestion to refer it to a small special committee, say of three, to consider and report this session. I must say I am heartily in accord with Dr. Britton's remarks on this subject, that I think it would be well to have the suggestion come from the Board of Directors of one or more of the different hospitals in the province. I think Dr. Philip said it had come from the Board of Directors of the John H. Stratford Hospital, at Brantford.

Dr. PHILIP—They spoke to me about it. They did not send any official communication.

Dr. HARRIS—But I think Dr. Philip's motion can be referred to a small committee, which would be the most proper thing to do.

On the motion being put by the President, he declared it carried.

The President then appointed as a committee, Drs. Philip, Henry, Day, Luton and Willliams, to consider the motion and report.

Dr. Harris moved, seconded by Dr. Ruttan, that the matter referred to by the mover of this resolution at last session, *re* summer session course, be sent to Education Committee for consideration.

Referred to Education Committee.

Dr. PYNE—In reply to an inquiry of Dr. Rogers, as to why the names of Drs. A. G. Allan and T. M. Macfarlane do not appear on the register, I wish to state I have looked the matter up, and I find the name A. G. Allan did not appear on the register for 1892, as he had been reported to me as dead, and I have marked him in my register as dead, and therefore dropped him out of the new register. The name of T. M. Macfarlane does not appear on the register. I think what is intended by Dr. Rogers is the name of Matthew Thomas Macfarlane, who formerly lived at Ridgetown and now lives at Fitzroy Harbour. His name does appear in the present register; it is a mistake in the initials; but he appears as living at Ridgetown, instead of Fitzroy Harbour, to which latter place he moved since the publication.

Dr. ROGERS—He wrote to me that he could not find his name in the book.

Dr. GEIKIE—With permission of the Council, I wish to give notice of motion, seconded by Dr. Britton, that every candidate for the final examination of this Council will be required to present, with his lecture tickets, a certificate of having undergone and passed an examination of the Medical College or school he has attended at the close of his third winter session on medical and surgical anatomy, general pathology and bacteriology, medical jurisprudence, including toxicology and mental diseases, principles of medicine, principles of surgery and sanitary science. This examination shall not in any way interfere with those required by the Council.

Dr. BRITTON—That he will move that therapeutics be embraced in the final examination. instead of the intermediate examination.

Dr. Orr moved, seconded by Dr. Henry, that the list of names of the Finance Committee be amended by striking out the name of the mover, Dr. Orr, and substituting therefor the name of Dr. Williams. Carried.

Moved by Dr. Harris that the Council adjourn till 2 o'clock p.m. Carried.

AFTERNOON SESSION.

WEDNESDAY, *June* 14*th*, 1893.

The Council met at 2 p.m., in accordance with motion for adjournment.

The President in the chair.

The Registrar called the roll. All were present except Sir James Grant.

The minutes of last meeting were read and confirmed.

Communications were read from W. O'Connor, M.A., M.D., and M. Embree, and referred to the Education Committee ; and from Messrs. Eastmure and Lightbourn, which was referred to the Finance Committee.

Dr. Thorburn moved, seconded by Dr. Moore, that inasmuch as the foot note on page 12 of the annual announcement of 1879-80 has been inoperative for thirteen years, it is declared by this Council now as rescinded, in order that no doubts may remain in reference to it.

Dr. BERGIN—I would like to ask before rescinding that order, if it is retained as a rule of the Council whether it will affect any teacher anywhere.

Dr. THORBURN—It will affect and has affected. It has been a dead letter inasmuch as we have been accepting certificates from McGill, and there are numbers of certificates from the United States and from other countries which we have been accepting where the teacher has not ·been a registered practitioner in Ontario. The schools here, to a certain extent, have been in the same position. It would place us in a very awkward position if we refused to accept such certificates; for instance, it would rule out all outside provinces and countries. I think it is a bad principle to have a law that you do not or cannot enforce.

The PRESIDENT—That is not our law now. We are governed by the regulations in our last announcement.

Dr. THORBURN—Is it rescinded?

The PRESIDENT—It is practically rescinded.

Dr. THORBURN—I would like to move that it be rescinded, because there is some doubt existing in the mind of our Registrar; for instance, he didn't know how to act in this matter; it was for that purpose I wanted a decision of the Council in the matter. I have been talking it over with my friend, Dr. Moore, and others, and we thought the best way to settle the matter would be by a vote of the Council.

Dr. BERGIN—If we have not been acting on it for ten or twelve years, and have been accepting these certificates, we had better set ourselves right.

Dr. THORBURN—I think we ought not to have a law that we do not enforce.

Dr. BRAY—Isn't that already rescinded? Does not the announcement for each year rescind the announcement of the past year?

The PRESIDENT—That is what I should hold myself.

Dr. THORBURN—It is as well not to have anything on our statutes that is liable to future discussion.

Dr. MOORE—There can be no harm in voting on it anyway.

Dr. BRAY—Before that is put to a vote I think it should be thoroughly understood what it means, and what it is intended to cover; according to that, any man can teach in any of our schools whether he is a practitioner or not, and I do not think that is the intention of the Act. While I am not opposed principally to that, I think there would be an injustice done to the schools in Ontario if that was carried out; still at the same time I don't think you want it to go to the profession that anybody can teach in a school, whether they know anything about medicine or not; and I think myself that the words "registered practitioner" should not be there, but there might be something inserted to the effect, that the man should have a degree from some·recognized university. The law is indefinite as it is now; we can't compel anybody in the United States, in the University of Michigan or elsewhere, or even in McGill, to come here and register before acting as a teacher, and it is imperative as far as that goes, but we can say that every man who teaches shall have a degree in medicine from some recognized university.

Dr. BERGIN—Yes.

Dr. MOORE—No. This has been a dead letter; and it is simply brought forward now to remove a doubt that existed in the mind ot the Registrar, and probably one or two others. It has been inoperative for thirteen years. It is a measure that we never could make operative, and quite properly has it remained inoperative and ineffective, and it is only to just clear up the doubt that we propose the motion that is now before you.

Dr. BERGIN—It strikes me at this moment, Mr. President, there is a case where I canwell understand if this rule were to be enforced it would bring about a very great friction between the schools and educational institutions in the Province of Quebec and our College. I understand that Professor Adami, who teaches pathology in McGill University, does not hold a degree in medicine, and are we to refuse to accept his certificates simply because he does not happen to hold a degree in medicine? Are we to prevent students from McGill coming here and registering, if they pass an examination, because this gentleman does not happen to be a registered practitioner in the Province of Ontario? Then take the professor of surgery and the professor of anatomy in McGill, who are not registered practitioners of any Medical College, are not registered practitioners in Ontario, and if this rule were to be enforced we could not accept the certificates of these gentlemen.

Dr. BRAY—You have been doing it right along.

Dr. BERGIN—Then make it plain. We should not keep on our books a law that is not enforced.

Dr. BRITTON—I might mention that not only is there one instance of that character in McGill, that of Professor Adami, but there are also Dr. Roddick, professor of ophthalmology ; Dr. Sheppard, professor of anatomy; Dr. Brown, professor of clinical medicine ; Dr. Laflure, professor of clinical medicine ; Professor Robert Craik, Dean of McGill ; Dr. Cameron, professor of obstetrics—men that we think a great deal of and men who are a credit to their College, all are minus that plume which they might perhaps with credit to themselves have, that is the license from our own College of Surgeons. But at any rate, to cut the matter short, there are only three professors in McGill University, I believe, who are members of the College of Physicians and Surgeons of Ontario ; and unless this rule be rescinded and that rescinding placed in so definite a form that the Registrar will have no doubt in his mind, it is quite certain there will be a conflict between ourselves and the schools, which we don't desire. At present there is sufficient competition among the different schools to insure they will at least try to keep up a fair standard ; there is a necessity on their part that they keep up to the standard laid down by us, and that very feeling of emulation that exists between the schools will lead them to seek for and select the best men they can, either inside or outside the profession. Professor Ramsay Wright, lecturer on physiology and bacteriology in the Toronto School of Medicine, whose ability I think nobody here will question, is not honoured with a license from this license granting body ; and I don't know that any one of us would wish to see a rule retained which would say that Professor Ramsay Wright is not qualified to grant a certificate that a student has attended a certain number of lectures pro-·erly delivered on physiology. I am very much in favour of the Council making it a plain statement that the rule which has been virtually out of existence for twelve years is rescinded. It has never, that I know of, been definitely so stated in the Council.

Dr. ROGERS—I think there is a lot of misunderstanding. I have just now read the rule, and I think the rule says "certificates from teachers in Ontario " ; the plain ruling of the foot note does not refer to teachers outside of the Province of Ontario ; it may, it is true, refer to Professor Ramsay Wright ; I don't know whether he is a doctor of medicine or not.

Dr. THORBURN—It is not Ontario, or any other place ; it is merely a rule that is not enforced.

Dr. ROGERS—While undoubtedly the rule should be that a man teaching any branch of the profession of medicine in Ontario should be a registered practitioner of Ontario ; that rule does not apply, as I read it, to teachers outside of this Province.

Dr. BRITTON—It applies to anybody.

Dr. THORBURN—It does not refer to Ontario or Canada or anywhere.

Dr. BRITTON—It refers to anybody from whom a certificate is received.

The PRESIDENT—If you adopt this resolution you leave it uncertain whether any of the old rules that appear in the old announcements might not still be force ; you are undertaking by this resolution to repeal a law which has been repealed long ago ; the curriculum for each year is practically repealed when you adopt a new curriculum. I rule that that rule is not a rule of the Council and has not been since 1879-80 ; and my ruling will be the opinion of the Council unless it is appealed from and overruled.

Dr. BERGIN—I do not agree with you in that the announcement of this year will repeal all former announcements, because there is embodied in these by-laws a large amount of material that is not new this year.

The PRESIDENT—All that is not embodied in our regular laws, but any foot notes or regulations in the announcement are necessarily repealed when you adopt a new one.

Dr. BERGIN— It may be so, but I do not think so.

Dr. THORBURN—Your decision, Mr. President, of course will be recorded.

The PRESIDENT—That will be recorded and will serve the purpose without raising new doubt.

Dr. Bray moved, seconded by Dr. Philip, that this Council desires to express their surprise at, and disapproval of, the disgraceful and slanderous article which appeared in the columns of the Toronto Daily *Mail* under date of June 13th, 1893, and at the same time brand it as false, malicious and misleading, reflecting as it does not only on the Medical Council but also on the Government of Ontario, and more particularly on the medical members of the Legislature.

Dr. BRAY—In introducing this motion I did it with the view of this Council giving expression to its views upon this article and other similar articles that have appeared from time to time in the secular press as editorials and communications. While it has been stated to me that the best way to treat these things is with silent contempt, I think that we have been a long-suffering Council; I think we have been treating them in that way too long. As far as the Council, or the individual members of the Council, are concerned, it matters not to us, because we know the inwardness of, and where these things spring from and the reasons that give rise to these articles. But this is not so with the public and the general profession; and if we allow these things to go on any longer, the public and the profession who do not know will naturally believe them—a great many will believe them unless there is some contradiction or some expression of opinion given by this Council, the authorized representative of the profession—and I think that while some of those things might be treated with contempt, an article of this kind should not be; and I move this resolution for the purpose of giving every member of this Council an opportunity of expressing his opinion, and to have those opinions published broadcast.

Dr. FOWLER—I quite agree with Dr. Bray in saying that we should not treat the matter with silent contempt, but I think we should use expressions of a less forcible character. I think we should speak in a manner to express those views without using such very strong language. The language, in my opinion, is altogether too strong, and we can express our views in a much more temperate way.

Dr. HARRIS—For my part I am entirely in accord with Dr. Bray. I do not think he has made his motion too strong. I do not think it could be made too strong. We have been very badly treated, as a Council, by the *Mail* newspaper—this very paper that has published the article referred to,—and I think it is high time this Council should rise up and defend itself in some way against false accusations of that kind. I think the resolution is the proper thing; I think it is properly worded, and not at all too strong.

Dr. BRITTON—I do not know that I should stand up to say a word regarding this were it not that there is a direct and personal charge, something more than bare insinuation, made against the members of the Legislative Committee of this Council; that the Legislative Committee last year wasted the funds of this Council and the funds of the profession. I was not a member of the Legislative Committee last year excepting by invitation; when the Committee met and approached the Legislature they asked my friends, Dr. Johnson and Dr. Geikie, and myself to join in with them and to use what influence we could; and therefore I personally hold myself quite as much responsible as I would hold any member of that committee as appointed by this Council; therefore, indirectly, I was a member of the Legislative Committee of last year, and directly by appointment I was a member of the Committee of this year. For a whole year we have been deluged with entire columns of insinuations, and I must say there were a good many prevarications and a few infernal untruths in those communications that came to the daily *Mail*. Some of us took time to read them; some of us could not find time to wade through the mass of rubbish. Now here we have before us a direct charge that not only have we conducted ourselves in an unseemly manner, but we have gone so far as to give a very expensive champagne lunch to several members of the Local Legislature, and the insinuation is that it was done for a set purpose. All I have to say is, that although I am not extremely fond of champagne, I am very sorry that it was done behind my back, for I do not know anything about it.

Dr. DAY—Do you admit it was done?

Dr. BRITTON—No. The gentlemen who were associated with me on the Legislative Committee were perfect gentlemen.

Dr. DAY—Your language would infer that it was done.

Dr. BRITTON—Had you awaited the completion of my sentence you would have inferred differently. I do not think any member of the Committee is low enough, degraded enough, bar-room frequenter enough, to give a champagne supper or any other kind of supper to members of the Local Legislature for the purpose of securing their influence on the side of this Council. I might say I had a conversation with one of the legal fraternity to-day and this matter casually

2

came up (he had read this editorial) and he called it an infamous thing; he was astonished the *Mail* had ever introduced it. I said, "what do you think about it from a legal standpoint?" He said, "considering everything, I think the Council has a very strong ground for legal action against the *Mail* newspaper." (Hear, hear.) And personally, unless a most ample apology is made for the insertion of that editorial, and in as public a part of the paper as that in which the editorial appeared, so that the profession at large and the public will know we are gentlemen and not blackguards, I would favor going as far as possible towards securing a conviction for criminal libel against the *Mail* newspaper for the course it has taken.

Dr. PHILIP—I would just say, as the seconder of Dr. Bray's resolution, that I quite agree with the resolution as it is worded. I speak as Chairman of the Finance Committee, and I can say for the members of the Finance Committee that when the matter of passing the accounts of the Legislative Committee came before us, we investigated every single account brought before us; and we gave, according to the regulations of the Council, the usual per diem allowance to the members of that committee, and nothing more, and nothing of the kind referred to in this article came out; and if it had, I am sure every member of the Council would have opposed the passing of any such item in the accounts. I can speak in strong language on this. I, myself, think Dr. Bray's resolution is not at all too strong; the article is an infamous one, written without any just cause whatever, and I think if the *Mail* is a wise newspaper it will withdraw it, because the facts are entirely against it; and in saying this, I speak as the chairman of the committee who investigated the accounts.

Dr. MOORE—I have the honour of being a member of that committee, and I brand this article as being a lie, and one manufactured out of whole cloth. No champagne supper was given, nor was any other kind of a supper given, nor was any undue influence of any kind used upon the part of this committee with the members of the Local Legislature. I do not think we can denounce this article in too strong language. We are charged with not only misappropriating the funds of this Council, but are charged with stealing; for the article says, if I remember right, that some person pocketed a certain amount of this $614; and if I remember right, it also says there were mutual recriminations between members of this Council regarding this, which I brand as another falsehood. Any influence we have used with the members of the Local Legislature was of the fairest and most honourable kind, and not one penny of the funds of this Council was paid out, that I know of (and I think I know of every dollar and cent that was paid out), towards intimidating, treating or influencing that body in any shape, manner or form; and I think it is disgraceful that this paper should not only charge this Council and the committee, as they have done, but also the members of the Local Legislature, with being influenced by a champagne supper. I want to put myself on record in this matter, and I will go this far, I heard a lawyer say to-day that he thought we had good grounds and very good grounds, for an action ; and I agree with Dr. Britton, that so far as I am personally concerned, I will go as far as I can towards securing a conviction against the paper that has published such an infamous article as this is.

Dr. THORBURN—Last year, in 1891-92, I had the honour of being Chairman of the Legislative Committee, and therefore ought to know everything that was done in connection with those committees, and I can only characterize the statement published in the *Mail* newspaper as a gross fabrication from beginning to end ; there is no truth whatever in it. As to taking action, that is an open question; I do not know whether it would be a wise thing.

Dr. BRITTON—Unless we get a full and ample apology.

Dr. THORBURN—It is a question whether it would be worth our while to fight in court, stirring up mud and dirt.

Dr. MOORE—There is none to stir up.

Dr. BRAY—We may stir up some, but it won't stick to us.

Dr. DAY—You are not so sure of that, it sticks sometimes where it should not.

Dr. THORBURN—That is an open question. I can only characterize the statement as utterly untrue.

Dr. ROGERS—Mr. President, in rising to speak to this motion, I confess, at the outset, it meets with my hearty approval. I was a member of the Legislative Committee for 1891, and with others I came to Toronto to endeavour to get the Medical Act amended in the way which we considered was in the interests of the whole profession of medicine. In getting legislation of any kind surely any person with common sense can see that it costs some little money; if, for instance, the municipality of London, Ontario, wished any part of their Act amended it would be necessary for that body to send a deputation— a legislative committee, if you like—consisting of the mayor and two or three aldermen and the solicitor, to Toronto, in order to get such legislation ; and it is not conceivable that that could be done without cost ; and just as that would cost some money, so it would cost a certain amount of money to get legislation on the part of any municipal body, as it does on the part of this body. It must be remembered that the idea the Council had in seeking the legislation they did in 1891 was, first, they sought to get the Act amended so that they could control matriculation examinations; in the second place, they sought legislation that they might be able to collect the outstanding dues without the great cost and expense and disgrace of going into the Division Court. At that time there were thousands of dollars of outstanding dues owing to the Council, and we could not collect them, unless we got some means the way we did in the legislation of 1891. Surely the object of the Council then in seeking that was to make the profession of medicine better in the Province of Ontario. But ever since we got the legislation which suspended a number for non-payment of dues, we have met with calumny and with the greatest amoumt of abuse from certain quarters, from quarters which we might have expected it from ; that is, from men like some of those who formed the Defence Association, men who refused to pay their annual and honest dues ; and it is to be regretted, and very bitterly regretted, I think, that a great newspaper like the *Mail*, a paper which undoubtedly wields an enormous influence in the Province of Ontario, should become the gutter for the vile stuff which has been poured into it for the last number of years against the Medical Council, against the executive body of the great profession of medicine of this province. This paper has been nothing less than the gutter in which that stuff has fallen ; and when we come together this year, on the first and opening day of our meeting, we find an editorial in this paper, directed against the executive body, elected by the medical profession, and sent here to do their work. If the medical profession have any fault to find with us it will be only a short time till they can turn us out, and surely we might have been left alone, instead of being trampled on and insulted in this way. I can speak only as far as I know in regard to this matter from the members of the profession in my own division, and I can truly say this, that the whole course which the *Mail* newspaper and Defence Association have adopted, has not been with the approval of the profession in my division. We admit that we have faults, but the medical profession, while admitting that we have faults and are only human, say we are quite capable of correcting these faults within ourselves. It seems to me the idea put forth by some of the members in speaking, is correct ; I think this way of treating a newspaper like the *Mail*, with silent contempt, is not correct ; I think the time has passed when silent contempt is correct. If this article is anything it is libellous ; if it is not libellous, then it is not possible for a newspaper to publish an article which is libellous ; if it is libellous, and we stand by tamely, like so many chickens, and allow our personal honour (because that is involved in that article), to be insulted, then, I say, we cannot expect to have the respect of the profession of medicine throughout this province ; and I maintain we ought to put this matter before our solicitor, and if he gives us the advice that it is libellous, to start and go ahead, and make them apologize and retract what they have stated. I brand as false, in every sense of the word, that there was any money spent for champagne or otherwise, by the Legislative Committee, in 1891, in getting the Medical Act amended. I brand as false that there was any undue influence used. I state emphatically that the doctors in the House on that occasion were in favour, almost to a man, of giving us the legislation we got. I state emphatically there was nothing done in any way, shape, manner or form, but what was fair and above board and honest in getting that legislation. I state also that the legislation was asked for for the benefit of the whole profession of medicine of Ontario. We asked for nothing that was wrong; nor would the doctors in the House, or the Premier of Ontario, or the members of the Legislative Assembly, have given us any legislation which could be in any way approached under the category which is indicated in this article. I wish to state this because the time is close at hand when there will necessarily be an election in the profession of medicine for the members of this Council. These statements going out will be read by many members of the profession, and they have already gained a certain amount of prejudice against this Council, owing to the unwarranted and unworthy statements made from time to time by the *Mail*, and I am very sorry and regret very bitterly to see a paper which we all like to respect stooping to such a level as to have become the gutter for all the rubbish which has been poured into it against this Council for the last number of years.

Dr. BERGIN—I have just read the article hurriedly and hastily, and I find it is so full of misstatements, not to say falsehoods, that I think it perhaps affords its own best refutation (hear, hear). The extravagance of the article shows that after all it is a mere exhibition of weak rage on the part of some one belonging to the so-called Defence Association, because that Association failed in accomplishing any of its objects, and because it obtained from the Legislature a portion only of that which the Legislative Committee of this Council offered to them in September last. As this article will show they aimed at the utter destruction of the Council. In this exhibition of rage the writer is so carried away as to say the Legislature had sounded the death note of the Council; he charges us with having instituted 1184 Division Court suits, before the legislation of which they com-plain, namely, the legislation which was devised to compel dishonest men to pay their debts; and the only way in which we could compel them, because they disregarded the judgments got against them in the Court; and we thought too highly of the honour of our profession to bring them before the judges upon the judgment summons. And that very charge that he brings against us, if it were true, which it is not, would justify the Council in asking for that legislation which, not only Osgoode Hall and the College of Pharmacy and other public institutions have, but which all clubs have of compelling men who do not pay their dues to leave their club. This is all that we ask. It is that to which no honest man will object; and no honest man ought to object nor ought any man claim to be a member of a body whose annual dues he refuses to pay. He ought, if he has any self respect, and I contend these men had no self respect (hear, hear), when they instituted the slanders that they have for three or four years past been circulating through the country, slanders which never would have been uttered by these men had we not put upon the statute book a law which compelled them to pay their debts; and these men, in making these charges against the Council, forgot that during all the years they had been supporting the Council, they had been casting their votes for the members who represent the profession in this Council, they had been a party consenting to everything the Council did and never an objection; and yet how can these men claim to have done their duty by the profession if during all these years they allowed us to perpetrate all the rascalities with which they charge us. I cannot imagine what sort of a mind the man has who penned this article; it is not the writing of a man inspired by a good motive, not the writing of a man who loves his fellowmen or of a man who holds high the honour of his profession. Men ought to stand by their own order; this man does not; he vilifies it (whoever he is), and he does not hesitate to state as truths things which he knows to be untrue; for instance, he charges this Council with having excluded reporters from its meetings; and yet this Council, so far from having excluded reporters, two or three years ago, in order that the profession outside might be fully informed as to what is being done here in this Council, although it involved a large amount of expenditure, did not hesitate to employ a shorthand writer and give the proceedings to the profession at large; and it continues that. Only yesterday we re-elected our official stenographer to give the work of this Council to the public that they might know who does the work in this Council, and the reason why the work is being done. He charges us with having improperly influenced members of the Legislature; that is a broad and general charge. We as broadly and as widely brand that as a falsehood. He charges this Council with having expended large sums of money belonging to the Council in champagne suppers; this same charge has been made previously to this; and we were charged at other sessions with junketting and spending large sums of money belonging to the Council; if he confined himself to that I do not suppose the members of this Council would care very much, because the very fact that the charge is made refutes it. We are a body of gentlemen. We have been a great many years here in this Council and our proceedings are well known. I believe the majority of us are known to a large number of the citizens of Toronto, and if we spent our time in rioting and drinking, the public press would have been filled with it long ago, but there is nothing of the kind; and the public know that it can't be true. It might be said that we ought to take criminal proceedings because of this; well, I do not think that we require to go that far; consider what this gentleman has said over his own signature, because, no doubt, it is said by the same man who has been writing long letters in the *Mail*. There can be no doubt in my mind that a jury asked to give a verdict that would consign the proprietors of the *Mail* to prison would not convict; I think you would fail; and to fail would be to do us a great deal of harm; it would injure the Council very much. It would be said that out of revenge because five territorial members are being added to the Council we brought a criminal action against Mr. Bunting. Whilst quite satisfied, as Dr. Bray says to the Council, that this article is libellous, I do not think—I may be wrong—that we stand in so poor a position before the public of this country that we ought to ask for a criminal conviction of the proprietor of this journal.

Dr. BRAY—The remarks of Dr. Bergin might apply were this not an editorial; if it were a communication it would be only expressing the views of one individual, but this is a different thing; it is a leading article in one of the leading papers of this country; and it is supposed to reflect the views of the managers and leaders of that journal, therefore I do not think the Council, in justice to itself and its constituents, ought to allow this to pass unnoticed. I do not think we are going to take an action; my object in bringing it up was that the Council might express their views on it, and express their disapprobation. It will be published (perhaps not in the *Mail*) before the public. But if we were to allow this leading article to go before the country without contradiction, the people might believe it, and they would have reason to believe it, because it charges us directly with all kinds of fraud; I do not think it is necessary for us to go into a criminal prosecution, although I think we should, for possibly the paper could be made to retract. While we believe it is from the pen of the man who has written these articles, when he signed his name it was all right enough, but this reflects the opinion and the views of this paper, and this paper goes into thousands and thousands of homes in this country, I think we would be doing ourselves a great injustice not to stamp this as it should be stamped.

Dr. BERGIN—You misunderstand me, Dr. Bray; I concede that this resolution should be passed by the Council; that is an entirely different thing from engaging in a law suit. Whilst I think we were bound, in defence of our honour, to pass a resolution of some kind contradicting the article, it is another thing to bring an action against the paper.

Dr. DAY—Mr. President, while agreeing that the article is away beneath contempt, there is not, so far as I know, a solitary sentence of truth in it; that we all know, everybody knows that, I think that a merely denunciatory resolution by this Council would be all that is necessary. I have no objection to the wording of the resolution; you cannot make the wording too strong to be truthful, because there is no possible foundation for any one charge that is made there, not the slightest. I was on that Legislative Committee myself. I have been asked to state some of the items that made up that account, but I am not in a position to do that; Dr. Pyne has given those items to the Council, and they have been audited, and anybody that wants to see them can see them, I presume. I think merely a denunciatory resolution would be all that is necessary; I have not the slightest fear of any one in the section which I represent, and I do not claim that they are any more intelligent than in any other place. The thing, as Dr. Bergin says, carries its refutation on its own face; it is too absurd to be believed by any man whose opinion is worth asking or having at all, and I think a mere denunciatory resolution is all that is necessary. When you talk, fight and fire, and blood and thunder, it is all nonsense; we do not want anything of the kind. I think we would be demeaning ourselves to go into anything of the kind.

Dr. MILLER—I must say that I heartily agree with the resolution which has been proposed by Dr. Bray, but I must at the same time say I do not agree with many of the sentiments which have been expressed during this debate, because we have been quietly and silently submitting for a length of time to a series of abusive articles, which in the main were entirely without foundation, but which obtained and had force as against this Council in the minds of many of the profession, as well as the people generally, simply because of our silence. The question has been frequently asked me, why, if you have a good defence, have you not published it; why have you not given your side of the question; it may be you are all right enough, but why do you not speak? I have been asked respecting certain matters, and after hearing the defence which I had to offer, it has been said, we have no doubt about the correctness of that, but why not give that to the public, why not give your side of the case? And I am quite satisfied, Mr President, that we would have been in a very much better position before the Legislature had these slanders and untruthful articles been answered from time to time. I am very glad to hear the members of the Legislative Committee, one after another, rise and denounce as untruthful these statements with reference to their transactions. If they are incorrect, as undoubtedly they are, because we have the testimony of the Chairman of the Legislative Committee, who certainly ought to have known of the proceedings of his committee; and we have the testimony of the

Chairman of the Finance Committee, who certainly should know as to the truth or otherwise of- the item of that account ; and we have the statement of the other members of this committee ; and they will now go forth to the profession and the public, and I think that while we have been very derelict in the past in our duty to ourselves in allowing these statements to go uncontradicted, we dare not submit any longer in silence after the publication of that article in which were contained the very serious charge that we had obtained this legislation, of which some of the members of the profession complain, by disreputable means ; that we had reached the intellects of the members of Parliament through their stomachs. But bad as that is, the other charge, that a portion of the six hundred odd dollars, which were expended by that committee, the remainder of that money not spent upon champagne, was misappropriated by the members of the committee, and that ·they then wrangled over the plunder, I think no resolution could be framed in terms too strong to meet a case of this description. After making the charges which this gentleman does, he probably has become a little afraid of his work ; he thinks he has gone a little too far ; he then begins to hedge, as you will see by reading the article, and he says, perhaps rumour has distorted some of these facts. But he was not so careful of the truth, not so careful of his own integrity before he made the most censurable part of the charges. Then he asks and expects that the members of the Council will purge themselves of this charge as speedily as possible, .arid in open Council. Now, that has been done, and I think that the next thing in order is that after that has been so thoroughly done that the person who wrote that article in the paper—of course we may entertain each his own opinion as to the authorship of the article, but it appears in the editorial columns of the paper, and as such the paper endorses it, that the paper which has endorsed that article now after we have complied with their suggestion, that the members of the Legislative Committee and the Council should purge themselves of this charge, should now apologize, and should give us a most ample apology. And in future I would suggest that it be the duty of some committee of this Council to meet false and calumnious statements that are made. I think· that it is quite time now that each side of the question should be presented to the public, in order .that the antidote and the bane may come together. I quite approve of the resolution, and I will vote for it cordially.

Dr. WILLIAMS—Mr. President, I would not feel much like saying anything on this question had it not been that as during the last year we have had a Legislation Committee of which I happened to be a member, and the chairman of that committee, I would fear that it might be supposed that this was the committee to which reference was made ; I·am glad to know that the insinuations thus far have not been made against our Committee, and the insinuations, or worse, are made against the Committee of 1891. Now, I was not a member of that committee, but I have a very great deal of confidence in the gentlemen who were members; and they have made their statements here to-day completely denying the statements that have been made against them, and I believe the statements of that committee to be true; I believe them to be true because, so far as the financial part of it is concerned, we have heard the Chairman of Finance, who has gone over the accounts, endorsing that statement, and saying that no charges for any such purposes went through. In looking over this article, I find several, what I would call, strong misrepresenta- tions, misrepresentations so strong that they ought not to go unchal- lenged. One of the statements seem to be, in fact is, that this Committee deceived the Government. It plainly points out here that in the last session of the Legislature the Government might reasonably have been expected to interfere and prevent dire calamity coming to this Council, but they were excused from doing so upon the ground that this Legislative Committee of the year before, acting on behalf of the Council had deceived the Government. Now I think that so far as any knowledge has come to the members of this Council, outside of that Committee, that there was no deception practiced either upon members of the Legislature or upon members of the Government. Then again, it says, that the influence of the majority of the medical men in the House was secured by means which may be the subject of an investigation under the Government. . Could there be a meaner slander cast upon the medical men in that House than to say that they had been secured by means that might require an investigation by the Government? I fancy there could not be a meaner thing.

So far as I know, the medical men in that House are above suspicion in that particular. (Hear, hear.) And those men are men that can be classed as gentlemen, and not as tools to be bought or bribed or got over in any such scheming way by a committee, even though that committee might have felt so disposed. On behalf, then, of these medical men in the House, I, for one, want to repudiate in the strongest terms that there is a single medical man in the House that would be guilty of receiving, directly or indirectly, anything to influ- ence his views in the matter; and when those gentlemen gave their influence to the Medical Council in securing what they believed to be wise legislation, they did it because it was their own conviction that it was in the interests of the profession at large.

I notice that they also make the statement that reporters have been excluded from the meetings of the Medical Council; and they intimate it was rather unwisely done; and they insinuate it was done because there were charges bandied about here, apparently by our members, against each other; and the insinuation is then thrown out that some person had pocketed portions of this money that didn't go for the champagne. I do not think there is a member of the Council, and I question if there is a reporter on any of the newspapers in Toronto, that does not know that the whole statement is most positively untrue. There never was a time, since I have had a knowledge of this Council, when there was a request or anything else to the reporters that they should not be present at the meetings, and that they should not make a full report and give the public all the information that might be considered interesting to the public, in the fullest and freest possible way. And yet we have this statement made by a paper that might have had reporters here, if it had been so disposed, to publish that reporters had been excluded. I do not think a statement of that kind could be characterized too strongly. It seems to me that you could not use terms strong enough to make it clear to the public that such a statement was wholly and completely unfounded. The statement has been made in this article also that the Council have taken steps in some way to prevent the public and the Legislature from getting the full amount of information upon the different points connected with it; and it throws out the statement that it may be necessary to have a government inquiry on the subject. Now, in the place of that being true, it will be recollected that something about two years ago, I think, or a year ago, the President of this Council reported that information had been sought for, and that without the sanction of this Council he had taken upon himself to ask the Treasurer to have a return of the receipts and expenditure of this Council, made from its first organization, and brought down and laid upon the Council table at this meeting; and that was done that the public and the profession and the Legislature, whoever saw fit, might become possessed of that information. The President, after having asked this information to be brought down, then asked the sanction of the Council, and the sanction of the Council was readily granted and he was sustained in the position he had taken in asking for full information to be laid on the table. Now, I understand that at the last session of the Legislature a return was asked for in the House with reference to certain expenditures in connection with the Medical Council; I am informed, and I believe it to be true, that the Treasurer of this Council furnished the exact items that were asked for by that Legislature. (Hear, hear.) Was it to be expected he was to rake all over his books and hunt up something, if it were in those books, that would gratify some particular persons that perhaps had an ill-feeling against this Council; was he not to assume that what they asked for was what they wanted, and was he not to furnish that in exact particular, just as they asked for it? Gentlemen, that is what was done; if I understand it correctly, they got all the information they asked for; they got every bit of it, and it was laid before them in the fullest and freest manner. Then, gentlemen, are they in a position to say information has been withheld? I think not, for one.

Our friend, Dr. Miller, has said he thought it was a mistake on the part of the Council that steps had not been taken to meet some of the slanderous statements that were being made through the public press. I grant quite freely that I do think the Council has made a mistake in the past in not taking steps to acquaint the profession with the proceedings of the Council; as I stated on previous occasions, it was not reasonable to expect the public press engaged in secular matters should give very full reports of the proceedings of the Council. Medical journals, from causes best known to themselves, did not think it wise to do so; and the Council made no special effort to get this information before the members of the profession; and the result was the profession was not well informed upon what was going on in the Council. It was a mistake; there is no question about it; and last year steps were taken to remedy that by giving a subsidy to a journal, and by having that journal circulated and sent to each member of the medical profession. That is a step, as I take it, in the right direction; we have a means by which every member of the profession throughout the entire Province may become acquainted, and acquainted from a stenographic report with what has been done in the Council. Now I have had members in the profession, who have paid nothing since the organization of the College, speak to me on this very thing, and they say, that is the first step to their mind the Council has ever taken in the right direction, and they were only too willing to adopt means of finding an easy way to get into harmony with the Council. The statement has been made in this article that the Council have not been able or have not from some cause made any defence to the article that was published by the Defence Association unless, as they say, that milk and water article which appeared in the ONTARIO MEDICAL JOURNAL may be considered a defense.

Mr. President and gentlemen, if there is any single article that has been published by any writer upon this subject of the Medical Council in the last three or four years that is a strong article, an article honestly put, an article carrying right in its substance the very grain of truth from first to last, strong and well and ably put, that is the article in the ONTARIO MEDICAL JOURNAL. (Hear, hear.) And we do not need to hunt for any other refutation than you find right in that very article; and it is because it stings, and stings home and hard, that the gentleman made the remark that it was a "milk and water article." I did not have anything to do specially with that article, and that is why I can express my honest conviction of the article in terms as strongly as I do. Another remark made by Dr. Miller, which would seem to be worthy of consideration is this, there are appearing from time to time in the public press letters against the Council, and it is no person's particular duty, no member of the Council can feel himself particularly called upon to become the champion of the Council, and write up articles in opposition to these. During the time when I was president, I felt that there was some considerable weight in that. Letters appeared in the paper, but I did not feel, as president, that I was perhaps justified in assuming to myself the right to undertake to defend the Council; and yet at the instigation of some members of the Council I did answer some of the letters; but I felt then, and I have still since felt, that if there was some person whose special duty it was recognized to be to meet calumnious statements of that kind it might be something worth while. I think now that possibly that may not be as necessary as it was in the past, because we now have a JOURNAL in which the full reports of the Council can be published; and it is not necessary for members of the profession to be in ignorance of what is going on. When that is done and the members of the profession throughout the country have read those minutes through, as most of them will, I do not think letters of the kind that have been published attacking the Council can have the same evil effect that they have had in the past, so that I think it possibly may not be necessary to appoint anybody whose special business it should be to act in that role. I fully agree with Dr. Bergin that while this newspaper article has a good many statements in it that are as far from the fact as they well could be, and that are calculated to call the Council into as much disrepute and ill favour as they could be if they were believed, yet I believe the bulk of the profession will not believe them; and even though there may be some who may believe them, yet I still think that it would be a very unwise course for this Council to rush into court and seek to punish a public company by entering an action for libel.

Dr. GEIKIE—I have taken the *Mail* for a great many years, and I think a great deal of it; I think it is an ably and well conducted journal; there may be but one opinion in regard to that. But I am very sorry indeed that the *Mail* saw fit to allow the paper to be used in that way, making statements that were baseless. However, it is very comforting to us, and that is why I agree with Dr. Williams, and some others, that it is foolish to talk about, and much more foolish to enter upon, a law suit in regard to the matter, that the statements are so devoid of truth. Our "death warrant has been signed," forsooth; I think I can see in the future a longer and a better life than the Council has ever had. And it has not been very short. And it has not had a life that people need be ashamed of in the past. With regard to a good many of the statements in that paper that have been referred to so ably and so well, it would be just taking up the Council's time needlessly for me to go over the same ground again. But there is one point, one insinuation, and a strong one, which has been made in that article, and it is against college representatives specially; for instance, they are spoken of as men who have interfered here and there, and who have been busying themselves in matters in the territories, and all that sort of thing. I need not say how baseless that is; the whole contention of the Defence Association would represent that there has been collision without end between the territerial and collegiate or university representatives. I need not say how utterly foundationless that sort of thing is. Everybody knows that the territorial men and the representatives of the educational institutes have worked hand in hand without the slightest jealousy one with the other; everybody knows that not a single school, or college or university man (a member of this Council) and any representative member had a single favour to ask from the Council, or a single desire to carry anything that was not in the interests of the general profession; and if no single member had, it is needless to say that the united body had nothing of the kind to do, so that, instead of our deserving a rap on the knuckles, as I think is the phraseology of this article, and instead of having received a very good one from the Legislature, I feel we have received no rap on the knuckles at all; in fact when an attempt was made to do away with all the educational representatives, it met with a unanimous "no." What more could the educational representatives desire from the Legislature than that? It was an emphatic "No," and I doubt very much if there was one member who, I am not aware of any, except perhaps the mover of the bill; and, on second thought, I doubt even whether he would be willing to reduce the number of representatives from teaching institutions even by one. With regard to the future, we shall be very glad to see the territorial representatives here who come in increased numbers.

I do not think this article is going to do any harm; I think it will do good, because when persons have to have recourse to untruthfulness and misrepresentation, I think it indicates a very very weak cause, and a cause from which we have nothing to fear. I do not allude to that unutterable meanness, contained in the references to jollifications, and that sort of thing, further than to say the first news that there had been such a thing, even in anybody's mind, including the mind of the writer of that article—that I had was from reading the article itself. I predict for the Council, and I am not a prophet and have no pretensions to be such, instead of a stormy, short and dishonourable career, a calm, long and honourable one; and before very long the profession, instead of being arrayed onehalf against us, will be united in support of the Council, which, after all is said and done, has done a great deal of good to. the profession and public in Ontario. I do not know that I owe anything to the Council; I do not think I do; at the same time I have always stood up strongly in its favour, because I knew, between the Council to regulate education, on the one hand, and unlimited, unlicensed quackery, on the other, there was nothing to choose between; and the Council had done unquestionable benefit to the profession, and was, and is, and will be worthy of the hearty support of the profession.

Dr. FULTON—I desire to make a few remarks on this question; I will not detain you long. It has been very ably discussed by the leading members of the Council, but it seems to me that the defence, if it is not placed in the hands of the courts should be carried a little further than the ONTARIO MEDICAL JOURNAL; we have a very strong exponent—a very strong arm ready to strike a blow in our defence in the ONTARIO MEDICAL JOURNAL; we have one that is very effective and very satisfactory, but that reaches the medical profession only, and I do not think it is to our credit to allow it to be said to the public uncontradicted, we are capable of holding champagne suppers to influence the Ontario Legislature. I do not think articles like this should be allowed to be placed in the hands of the Ontario Legislature unchallenged, for it must have its effect upon them. When we go to Parliament requiring some legislation, it seems to me their opinion of this body will not be very much after reading an article such as this which has appeared in the *Mail* unchallenged. I think in addition to the ONTARIO MEDICAL JOURNAL, there should be a committee appointed by this body to give our most emphatic denial to all such erroneous and false statements as have appeared in those papers from time to time; and to sound at the same time a note of warning as to the consequence of those statements being published in such a manner as this has been. I do not approve of going any further than having a resolution of denial passed by this body at the present time; but I think we should go further and have a committee appointed to meet all such cases as this, and if it is repeated let the Council deal with them in a legal manner later on.

Dr. ORR—I think the discussion has continued quite long enough. I wish to correct a statement made by some of the speakers present; some one said the Defence Association consisted of nearly one-half of the medical profession. I will call the attention, Mr. President, and gentlemen of this Council, to this, that the Secretary of the Defence Association, Dr. Sangster, issued a circular to the medical men of this province in connection with that matter, also issued a postal card upon which was printed a series of questions to be answered by the medical profession. The intention of Dr. Sangster at that time, without doubt, was to produce those answers to the questions that he had issued to every medical practitioner in this province before the Local Legislature of this province when in session during the last few months. I ask you, and I ask the Chairman of the Legislative Committee, did Dr. Sangster produce those postal cards; did he produce any of the returns he received from any of the medical profession? No; he did not produce the answers he received. If he had produced before the Legislature the answers he had received from the medical men of this province from one end to the other, the Legislative Committee would have found themselves endorsed from the documents at that time in the hands of the Secretary of the Medical Defence Association. (Hear, hear.) I arose simply to make this correction in reference to the statement that half, or nearly half, of the medical profession in this province belonged to the Defence Association. I do not think they had ever more than three or four hundred men enrolled upon their pages—at the utmost they had not more than four hundred men.

Dr. ROGERS—They had not that nor half that.

Dr. BERGIN—And the greater proportion of them have repudiated.

Dr. CAMPBELL—Before the motion is put, the Council will probably pardon me for speaking without leaving the chair, for I do not intend to take part in the debate. This letter, while it does not make any direct charge, makes a great many insinuations; and it insinuates that these items of improper expense could not be got at by anybody; information was asked for and was refused. And it refers to a motion by Mr. Waters, in the Legislature, requiring the Treasurer to give the Legislature certain returns of expense. I think the fact ought to be emphasized that this Council was never asked for any such information. No man can say the Council refused to give any such information, because it was never asked for it. The Defence Association, I think, asked Dr. Fowler, the President, during the recess of the Council, and they asked Dr. Aikins, the Treasurer, I presume, but this Council was never asked, and this Council never refused, to give any information in the shape of this detailed return that was called for. The Treasurer, I think very properly, there may be a difference of opinion on that point, but he thought very properly, at all events he was not authorized to give any return except he was ordered by the body whose servant he was, and therefore he refused to give these returns but to the Council. The fact should be emphasized that the Council never refused the returns that were asked for by the Legislature, so it was not necessary to go to the Legislature and ask for the return at all. If the people who were dissatisfied had waited till the Council met, and asked for it, they would have had it; the Council never refused to give anything, has never hidden anything, has always been ready to make the thing public.

The President here put the motion and declared it carried unanimously.

The President here announced that Hon. George Kirkpatrick, Lieutenant-Governor of Ontario, has requested the pleasure of the company of the President and members of the Ontario Medical Council to an "At Home" at the Government House, to be held from 4 to 6.30 o'clock this p.m.

Dr. Bergin moved, seconded by Dr. Thorburn, that the invitation of the Lieutenant-Governor of Ontario be accepted with great pleasure. Carried.

Dr. Aikins, the Treasurer, here read his report, as follows :—

TREASURER'S REPORT.

TORONTO, *June 14th*, 1893.

To the President and Members of the Council of the College of Physicians and Surgeons of Ontario :—

GENTLEMEN,—Herein I beg to submit a statement of the receipts and disbursements for the twelve months which have just expired.

The receipts have been :—

1892, June 15th.

To balance as audited	$371	47
Registration Fees	3,321	00
Assessment Dues	2,278	00
Fines on persons illegally practising	655	00
Fees for Professional Exams. in Fall $1,450 00		
Fees for Professional Exams. in Spring 9,410 00	10,860	00
Interest on current bank account	8	25
New building revenue (rents)	3,618	21
And refund	3	00
Temporary loans	11,907	25
Council meeting expenses—refund	85	05
Total	$33,107	23

The disbursements have been :—

Council meeting expenses	$2,185	90
Treasurer's salary	400	00
Registrar's salary	1,800	00
Official Prosecutor's salary	408	33
Expense of holding Professional Exams. in Fall	886	18

3*

Expense of holding Professional Exams. in
    Spring $2,389 80
Fines paid to former Prosecutor 145 00
Fine refunded 25 00
Committee *re* Legislation 586 85
Committee *re* Discipline 1,019 03
Fees returned to candidates 100 00
Permanent appar. for Exams 9 60
Registrar's office supplies and expenses 680 02
Treasurer's   "   " 27 65
Temporary loans returned 12,595 75
Interest 3,209 70
Printing 1,181 25
Legal and other expenses prosecuting illegal
    practitioners 1,055 47
Legal services *re* Discipline Committee 313 68
   "   "   *re* Elevator 24 24
   "   "   *re* Com. on Legislation 20 00
   "   "   General account 11 00
Grant to ONTARIO MEDICAL JOURNAL for
    Printing, etc., etc 500 00
New Building maintenance :—
    Caretaker.................... $530 00
    Elevator man 265 00
    Commission on rents 181 34
    Fuel 745 76
    Water 359 94
    Gas 168 32
    Insurance 70 00
    Taxes....................... 621 00
    Repairs, supplies, etc 549 00
                ——— 3,490 36
Balance in Imperial Bank 42 42

    Total $33,107 23

All of which is respectfully submitted.
        (Sgd.)   W. T. AIKINS, *Treasurer.*

Dr. Thorburn asks whether the actual expenses were more than the receipts?

Dr. AIKINS—No. We are less in debt now than we were last year. We have reduced our indebtedness.

Dr. BRITTON—To what extent?

Dr. AIKINS—I could not answer that. Before the students' fees came in in the spring of 1891 we owed the bank about $13,000. This time last year it appears we owed the bank $1,000; and to-day we owe the bank $300 on a note we discounted yesterday.

Dr. ROGERS—Is there a sinking fund at all to pay the debt on this building?

Dr. AIKINS—No; there is no sinking fund. At one time we owed not only the $60,000, but we owed about $12,000 of a floating debt; that floating debt is all paid off, and we owe nothing to-day except the $300 in the bank and the amount to the Canada Life Insurance Company.

Dr. THORBURN—What interest do we pay the Canada Life?

Dr. AIKINS—Five per cent. half yearly. The accounts are all ready for submission to the Finance Committee at any time.

Dr. HENRY—What amount has been paid by the profession during the last year?

Dr. AIKINS—$2,278. Dr. Pyne will tell you the amount now due from them.

Dr. Pyne states that he has not a statement of this ready.

Dr. Rosebrugh moves that the statement handed in by the Treasurer be received and printed and placed in the hands of the members to-morrow for use at this session.

Dr. PHILIP—It will be printed in our finance report.

Dr. BERGIN—It will be embodied in our announcement.

Dr. Campbell suggests that perhaps it could be typewritten by the stenographer more cheaply than printed.

Dr. ROSEBRUGH—I would alter my motion to the effect that the report be received and that typewritten copies be supplied to the members of the Council as soon as possible.

Dr. ROGERS—I second that motion. Carried.

Dr. BRITTON—There is a motion, of which I gave notice this morning, in reference to the subject of therapeutics. The object of the motion is to attach a little more importance to a subject of so much moment. At the present time, you will notice, on page 17 of the announcement of 1892-3, in the provisions that are made for examination, in sub-section C, general pathology, therapeutics and bacteriology are combined; and the consequence is, the examiner has not the opportunity to give the same attention to each one of these branches as if he had not the three to attend to. I would move that, instead of therapeutics being conjoined with general pathology and bacteriology, it be put under a sub-section L, following "diseases of women."

For practitioners of medicine there is perhaps no subject that requires more careful attention, and perhaps there is no subject less known by licentiates when they go out to practice. The practice of medicine .should be as free as can be from empiricism, and should rest on a rational and scientific basis; therefore, it is in the interests of the profession and of the students that the subject of therapeutics should be emphasized as much as possible; and I would therefore move that the word therapeutics, under the line C, be struck out and line L therapeutics be added following the words, " diseases of women."

Dr. MOORE—I will second that motion.

Dr. BERGIN—I quite agree with Dr. Britton, that therapeutics ought not perhaps to be in the position it is here in the announcement, bracketed with pathology and bacteriology; but I do not see any reason why we should change the usual practice of the Council because of this subject at this moment. I think we ought to follow the old rule and refer it to the Education Committee for their report. (Hear, hear.)

Dr. BRITTON—I would have no objection to that, provided therapeutics should not be relegated back to the primary examination, as it used to be. After a man has had a couple of years training in primary branches only, and, therefore, is without any knowledge of the practice of medicine, he has no more ability to learn therapeutics than an inhabitant of Hong Kong.

Referred to Education Committee.

Dr. Geikie moved, seconded by Dr. Britton, that every candidate for the final examination of this Council will be required to present with his lecture tickets a certificate of having undergone and passed an examination of the medical college or school he has attended at the close of his third winter session on medical and surgical anatomy, general pathology and bacteriology, medical jurisprudence, including toxicology and mental diseases, principles of medicine, principles of surgery and sanitary science. This examination shall not in any way interfere with those required by the Council.

Dr. GEIKIE—The idea was simply to give the students knowledge that at the end of the third year they had an examination to undergo and to make them do better in the way of work than they otherwise would, the examination costing the Council nothing.

Referred to Education Committee.

Dr. Day presented the report of the Discipline Committee, and moved, seconded by Dr. Harris, that the report of the Committee on Discipline, just presented, be received by the Council and referred to Committee of the Whole. Carried.

Dr. Fowler presented and read the report of the Board of Examiners, and moved, seconded by Dr. Philip, that the report be received and referred to the Education Committee. Carried.

.: Dr. Miller asks that Mr. J. A. Sangster's letter to the President, which was brought before the Board of Examiners, be read.

Dr. Fowler reads letter dated 14th July, 1892, as follows :—

EXHIBIT I.

183 ST. PATRICK ST.,

Toronto, 14, 7, '92.

Dr. Fife Fowler:

DEAR SIR,—I am labouring under a gross injustice done me at the hands of the examiners of the Medical Council of Ontario, and although I have appealed to them to have my wrongs righted, yet I have good reason for believing that they have paid little or no attention to my complaint, which I handed the Registrar, substantially as follows :

Toronto, 1, 6, '92.

DEAR SIR,—I beg leave to place in your hands my application to have my answers to the late Primary Examination held by the Council of the College of Physicians and Surgeons of Ontario, re-read, and especially my marks obtained at the Primary Oral Examination reconsidered.

I would take oath that the following five statements respecting the Oral Examination are correct:

1. I correctly tested for and recognized both salts in chemistry, for Dr. Acheson told me so, and that was all that was required of us in that subject.

2. I answered all his questions in toxicology, and he seemed very well pleased indeed, for he told me " that is all" long before the time was up.

3. I answered correctly every question in materia medica and pharmacy, even to complicated doses.

4. I did fail to answer one question in physiology, but Dr. Fraser, who also presided over the histological specimens, told me that I had recognized the specimen. " That's right," he said; and lastly,

5. I did fail to answer only two or three questions of the twelve or fifteen in anatomy.

Thus I am forced to believe, sir, that even if I obtained less than the required marks in one or two subjects in the written papers, yet I feel certain that I have more than made up the required percentage in that subject, or subjects, when the marks of the oral and written examinations are added together.

This is my second Primary Examination and I would feel too keenly its loss through injustice or mistakes, for I am convinced that there has been either :

1. Gross injustice done me, either wilfully or unintentionally, by the presiding examiners, or

2. Some mistake in transferring the marks.

In either case, sir, I trust that the error will be erased, and that the injustice done me will be promptly rectified.

I am, etc., etc.

I waited for an answer to the above for four weeks, and then wrote the Registrar as to the result of my appeal, which I was beginning to fear had either found the waste basket upon its arrival at the office or was beginning to blue-mould in his pigeon holes. He replied at once, "I beg leave to inform you that the Medical Council decided as follows : That they have very carefully examined your appeal and cannot see any reason for changing the decision of the examiners." I immediately replied that, as I still felt that there was a " snake in the grass," for I could swear that I had done very well indeed at my oral examination, I ask permission to see my examination papers and also to have access to the marks for the oral examination. This he partially granted a few days ago.

I appeal to you, sir, before I carry out my determination to expose the fraud, if necessary, by other means, in order that you may insist upon a thorough investigation that the injustice done me will be promptly rectified.

From the examination of my papers and marks I am led to believe that

1. They have not been re-read, indeed the bare figure on the back of my physiology paper would lead me to think that that paper had not even been read, although I was told that they would be re-read. The Registrar also informed me that there had not been a single change made in rereading my papers, or even those of any other, a very unlikely thing unless the examiners preconceived the defeat of all appeals. Then again, I hold that no examiner, however expert, could reread, even a few minutes later, six or seven sheets, as a whole, and give the second time the same number of marks, unless guided by the former figure.

2. What has evidently been the safest plan of causing my failure has been adopted, viz.: low marking at the oral examination. Dr. Pyne has told me that the oral questions are gone forever, such it seems has been considered ; but I was wise enough to keep a list of the oral questions asked me, and will take oath as to their correct-ness and also as to the manner of answering, if necessary, and, contrary to what he said when I first intimated my intention to appeal, tells me now that the oral marks cannot be reconsidered.

3. That if the examiner in anatomy can make a change during the first reading of a question, he is certainly not incapable of doing so

during a second reading; yet Dr. Pyne emphatically wishes me to understand that there never are any changes made. However this may be, he was forced to acknowledge that there had been a change made during the first reading in my second answer in anatomy, the figures for which being written 12, which, when I asked the Registrar the meaning, said that the 12 had been changed to 14.

4. Had the papers been re-read, it would not have been necessary to call upon the Registrar for an answer to my appeal.

5. The practice of deducing the marks for a wrong answer, that is the loss of twice the number of marks for that question, is unjustifiable. The Registrar could give me no information as to the authority the examiner had for such a method, but I don't think it necessary to discuss either the injustice or want of authority for such a course pursued by them in this connection, as it must be plain to all.

6. As the examiner in anatomy and physiology has not even given the Registrar the values for the several complete answers, they have purposely left me in the dark as to the number of marks which have been deduced in each question.

7. It is just possible that the examiners have deducted marks for other just as absurd reasons as for spelling, writing, etc., etc.

I have the honour to be, sir, your obedient servant,

J. A. SANGSTER.

Dr. THORBURN—I know something about that letter, and the young gentleman who wrote it. In July last year I received a communication from the Registrar asking me to come down and be present at a conversation with an applicant, who complained he had not been treated fairly at the examinations. I came here not knowing exactly what to do. Dr. Pyne told me he would like me to be present to hear a conversation between himself and the complainant; there was no particular reason for having me present except he (Sangster) had been formerly a pupil in the Toronto School of Medicine, in which I was a lecturer, and that I knew him and his father, and that in justice to himself, as much as anything else, he (Dr. Pyne) would like me to be present at the interview. The Registrar produced the papers and answers, and presented them to Sangster, and he acknowledged them to be his answers. We discussed the matter very fully and freely with him, and pointed out wherein he had failed; and in fact in one case he had given an unusual dose of a very active medicine; and we showed him the unreasonableness of his complaints; this was altogether a gratuitous thing on behalf of Dr. Pyne. I maintain that this applicant had no right to come and demand a reconsideration from him, but out of his usual good nature, and that there might not be any even pretence of an unjust act, he was listened to; and we went over this matter very carefully and thoroughly; and I think if ever a man deserved to be rejected, Mr. Sangster stands pretty well among that rejected class. And that his statements are just intended to annoy and interfere with the success of the Council more than anything else. He seems to be a chip of the old block, and equal to him in many respects. There seems to be some crookedness, if I may use the word, or as if things were all going the wrong way, and he is determined to oppose. I can only say that I fully concurred in the decision of the examiners. He seemed determined not to be satisfied He was determined to have a grievance, although it could be pointed out to him he had nothing to stand on, for not only were his answers incorrect, but if carried into action, they would be highly dangerous. He not only did not know the questions or how to answer them, but when he attempted to do so he fell into mȯst eggregious errors, and he well deserved to be passed by.

Dr. PYNE—I just want to make a few remarks. This candidate wrote to me and said he had been unfairly and unjustly treated, as Dr. Thorburn has just told you. He said : "Why can't I see my papers? I think you have given some other candidate's papers for mine, and there has been a mistake, and I would like to see them." To satisfy him, and as I knew there was nothing of the kind had happened, I replied : "You can see the papers to show you there has been no mistake.'' And I asked Dr. Thorburn to be present, as he was the representative of the Toronto School of Medicine at which this gentleman studied. Sangster identified each paper as his, and read it over. In the subject of anatomy he had made twenty per cent. on the oral ; he made fifty-five on the written. On that paper, he complains the examiner made changes. There was a change made, but by that change he was benefited. In regard to the physiology paper, he says he is prepared to make oath he answered every question but one while on the oral examination ; yet the examiner only awards him ten out of one hundred. On the materia medica paper—on which he claims he did not make a mistake—the examiner gave him forty-five marks, and then looked over the paper again evidently, and says, "minus 4=41 ; he gives two to five grains of cocaine for a dose—very poor paper " ; this is the examiner's own writing. He identified these papers as his— and the whole system of examination was explained to Mr. Sangster, showing him that it was impossible for the examiners to know his papers, as they were all under a number, and a number was used instead of candidate's name at the oral examination.

I made a memorandum of the interview referred to by Dr. Thorburn ; it was on Saturday, July 9th, at 2.30 p.m. :

" J. Thorburn met me this day in my office, as did also J. A. Sangster, who appealed from examiner's decision. His papers were shown him, and his marks ; and he appeared satisfied that everything was all correct. Dr. Thorburn and myself asked him questions, and explained to Mr. J. A. Sangster any matter he desired to know in connection with the examinations, after which Mr. Sangster withdrew. Correct."

(Signed)   J. THORBURN.
R. A. PYNE.

Dr. ROGERS—Does he write this long letter since?

Dr. PYNE—Yes.

Report of the Board of Examiners referred to Education Committee.

NOTICES OF MOTION.

Dr. ORR—That at the next meeting of the Council he will move that any medical man applying for registration, who has been in practice over five years, and who has passed an examination in some college or university, with a standard of examination as high as that of this Council, may be placed upon the Register by order of the Council of this College.

Dr. WILLIAMS—That he will move at the next session of the Council that the Education Committee be instructed to take into consideration the advisability of requiring all graduates of the college to sign the roll of membership personally, and also the propriety of having prepared and placed in the hands of each graduate an epitome of the Medical Acts by which the College of Physicians and Surgeons of Ontario is governed, and the duties and obligations of members thereto.

Moved by Dr. Harris that the Council be now adjourned till ten o'clock, a.m., on Thursday, 15th June. Carried.

THIRD DAY.

THURSDAY, June 15th, 1893.

The Council met at 10 a.m., according to motion for adjournment.

The President, Dr. Campbell, in the chair.

All the members were present excepting Sir James Grant.

The minutes of the preceding meeting were read by the Registrar and confirmed.

NOTICES OF MOTION.

1. Dr. Day—That when this Council assembles on Friday, the 16th inst., at two p.m., he will move that immediately after the reading of the minutes, the rules be suspended so as to consider the report of the Committee on Discipline.

2. Dr. Harris—That he will move to introduce a by-law to appoint a Discipline Committee at next session of this Council.

3. Dr. Fulton—That he will move, seconded by Dr. Henry, that the method of appointing. examiners for the College of Physicians and Surgeons of Ontario from the territorial divisions be changed. Believing that there are medical men in each division equally qualified and capable of becoming examiners for this Council, in order to insure them this privilege, to which they are entitled, the examiners from those divisions should be appointed in regular succession, one eastern and a western man, either alternately or together.

The Registrar then read a communication from the *Lancet* and from the *Practitioner*, opposing the giving of a subsidy by the College to any one journal. Referred to the Education Committee.

Dr. MILLER—Might I ask you to procure copies of the recently amended medical bill that passed the Legislature at its last session?

The REGISTRAR—I enquired of the Clerk, and he said he had not got any yet. I looked in the *Ontario Gazette* yesterday, and I see the bill is there numbered but not yet printed, along with several others. It is correct as it appears in the JOURNAL.

There being no other business, on motion of Dr. Bergin, the meeting adjourned until two p.m.

AFTERNOON SESSION.

THURSDAY, *June 15th*, 1893.

The Council resumed at two o'clock.

The President, Dr. Campbell, in the chair, called the Council to order.

The Registrar called the roll. All present except Sir James Grant.

Minutes of preceding meeting were read and confirmed.

NOTICE OF MOTION.

Dr. Miller gave notice that at the next session of this Council he will move a resolution respecting the redistribution of the constituencies for territorial representation at the Council Board.

The Registrar read a communication from Dr. R. Ovens, of Forest, in the nature of a complaint. Referred to Committee on Complaints.

Also a communication from Messrs. E. D. Hucheson, C. O. Fairbairn and William Cunningham, asking to be registered as matriculates.

Also a communication from Adam H. Wright, editor of the *Practitioner*, and John L. Davison, editor of the *Canada Lancet*, regarding the publication of proceedings of the Council. Referred to Committee on Finance.

Also a communication from Mr. Masten, of Messrs. Watson, Thorne & Smoke, regarding an application for registration. Referred to Registration Committee.

DR. HARRIS—I gave notice of motion this morning, Mr. President, that leave be granted to introduce a by-law to carry out the provisions of the Act passed in 1887, entitled, "An Act to Amend the Ontario Medical Act," and that the said by-law be now introduced and read for a first time. I do not think it would be desirable to go into a committee of the whole ; the present Committee on Discipline has not reported yet, and if we appoint a committee now and there should be any change, it might clash. There is no hurry about the second reading, I presume.

The by-law was then read the first time.

Dr. Williams moved, seconded by Dr. Orr, that the Education Committee be instructed to take into consideration the advisability of requiring the graduates of the College to sign the roll of membership personally, and also the propriety of having prepared and placing in the hands of each graduate an epitome of the Medical Acts by which the College of Physicians and Surgeons is governed, and the duties and obligations of members thereto.

Referred to Education Committee.

Moved by Dr. Fulton, seconded by Dr. Henry, that the method of appointing examiners for the College of Physicians and Surgeons of Ontario from the territorial divisions be changed; believing that there are medical men in each division equally qualified and capable of becoming examiners for this Council ; in order to insure them this privilege, to which they are entitled, the examiners from those divisions should be appointed in regular succession, an eastern or a western man either alternately or together.

Speaking to the motion, Dr. Fulton said : Some divisions have never been represented on this Board, I believe, at all, and the insinuation would naturally follow that there are no men in such divisions qualified for such a position. That I would consider unjust. I believe that it would be the opinion of all of you that there is no territorial division but what has men capable of filling the position of examiner, one territorial division quite as well as another. These appointments have been made before by the recommendation of some of the Education Committee. The way I have suggested will differ very little from that. The territorial district from which the examiners are to be selected will probably make some recommendation and allow the Council to select from such recommendations. Practically, the mode of selecting examiners will differ very little from what it has been in the past. It is impossible for every member of the Education Committee to know the qualifications or capabilities of the gentlemen whose names are proposed as examiners. They have got to rely, to a very great extent, on their recommendation by the representative of that district. Knowing that to be the case, the new mode makes but very little difference in the selection of examiners, while I think it is only just to all the representatives of the territorial divisions to allow them to have an opportunity of having a representative on the Board from time to time. The reason I suggest having members selected from the Eastern and Western Divisions was that I consider that would be probably better than having too many members from neighbouring territorial divisions. My plan of arranging that would be, if two examiners were required for the coming term, to select one from No. 1 Division in the west, or from No. 17 in the east, and proceed in regular succession through the rest of the division, as the examiners were required. The next appointment would be from No. 2 and No. 16, and so on. It would make it absolutely fair, in my opinion, and I do not see why, as stated before, there should be any difficulty in our securing as good a Board of Examiners as we have had in the past.

Dr. HENRY—I think the motion is a move in the right direction and will do away with difficulties against which we have had to contend. If we are not on the Education Committee we have to see our friends and put forth the claims and ability of the doctor we wish appointed. If we fix it that one man must be from the west and the other from the east, it will do away with the anxiety and effort of the intermediate representative to get a man on, and they can wait—their turn will come.

Dr. BERGIN—So will the millennium.

Dr. HENRY—I really believe that this motion will do away with the members going around and canvassing for the man they wish to see on the Board.

Dr. BRAY—I take it that this motion is not intended to dismiss any examiner. If I understand it right, it is only when vacancies occur that they are to be filled in the way proposed. I think it might do away with some ill-feeling that has heretofore been exhibited by some men who have not been on the Examining Board, and think their claims have been overlooked. I think perhaps it will be just as well for this motion to be referred to the Education Committee and let them bring in a report. I will move that the motion be now referred to the Education Committee.

There being no objection, the motion was referred to the Education Committee.

Dr. Johnson read the report of the Printing Committee, as follows :—

To the President and Members of the Medical Council of the College of Physicians and Surgeons of Ontario :

GENTLEMEN,—Your Committee on Printing beg leave to report, that owing to the arrangement entered into with the " Ontario Medical Publishing Co.," who printed the annual announcement of the College, it was not necessary to ask for tenders for printing as usual.

All of which is respectfully submitted.

(Sgd.)   ARTHUR JUKES JOHNSON,
Chairman of Printing Committee.

Dr. PHILIP—As to the advisability of having an examination of the nurses conducted by this Council, we made inquiries yesterday and went up last evening to see Dr. O'Reilly at the General Hospital. The doctor went over the matter very carefully, and told us that he was very much in favour of it, but some of the members of the Board were not quite sure of it yet and that it would be as well to leave it over for another year. After discussing the matter, we came to the same conclusion. We have not time, at this meeting of the Council, to get the opinion of the Board of Governors of the other hospitals, and consequently have decided to let the matter stand.

Dr. CAMPBELL—Will you kindly put your report in writing and hand it in to the Registrar. We will consider that the Committee has reported.

Dr. HARRIS—I would like, as Chairman of the Education Committee, for the information of the members of that Committee, to have any correspondence that may be in the Registrar's possession, between himself, as Registrar, and Mr. J. A. Sangster. I might say that we have at the present time a letter from this gentleman, Mr. Sangster, and I am under the impression that the Registrar is possessed of perhaps one or two more letters.

Moved by Dr. Rosebrugh, seconded by Dr. Miller, that the meeting adjourn until 10 o'clock to-morrow morning.

Dr. MOORE—I would like to ask if any of the committees would be ready to report if we met again to night at 8 o'clock.

Dr. Harris states that the Education Committee could furnish a partial report.

Moved, in amendment, by Dr. Rogers, seconded by Dr. Moore, that the Council meet at 8 o'clock this evening.

The amendment was lost and the motion carried to adjourn to 10 o'clock on Friday morning.

FOURTH DAY.

FRIDAY, *June* 16th, 1893.

The Council met at 10 a.m., according to motion for adjournment, the President, Dr. Campbell, in the chair. All the members were present excepting Sir James Grant.

The minutes of the preceding meeting were read by the Registrar, and confirmed.

Moved by Dr. Rogers, seconded by Dr. Logan, and

Resolved,—That in the opinion of this Council, Schedule "A" of "The Ontario Medical Amendment Act, 1893," should be amended at the next session of the Ontario Legislature, as follows: By repealing Divisions 15, 16 and 17 of the said Schedule "A," and substituting therefor the following:

	No. of Physicians.
15. County of Addington	15
County of Frontenac	50
County of Leeds	48
Total	113
16. County of Carleton	69
County of Lanark	33
County of Renfrew	19
Total	121
17. County of Grenville	23
County of Dundas	23
County of Stormont	15
County of Glengarry	18
County of Prescott	13
County of Russell	15
Total	107

1. That there is a community of interest existing between the members in Leeds, Frontenac and Addington resulting from the contiguity of the position of these counties, and the different portions of the proposed division are united by the Brockville & Westport Ry., the Grand Trunk Ry. and the St. Lawrence River, thus making it easy of establishing and maintaining a Medical Association therein, as contemplated in Section 15 of the "Ontario Medical Act."

2. That there is now a community of interest established between the members residing in Carleton, Lanark and Renfrew counties

inasmuch as these counties formed the greater part of Division XI. under the Medical Act before it was changed, and an active Medical Association is established therein which holds two meetings yearly. Also, these counties are united by the Canadian Pacific Ry., Ottawa & Parry Sound Ry. and the Ottawa and Rideau rivers.

3. The counties of Grenville, Dundas, Stormont, Glengarry, Prescott and Russell naturally form one division, and under the name of the St. Lawrence and Eastern Division have been united as one division since the formation of the Medical Act in 1869. That having been associated together in one division the members in these counties will have their interests better served without change under the new Act.

4. That the arrangement of Divisions 15, 16, 17, as passed in Schedule " A," will break up and destroy old-established Medical Associations, will unite in one division counties without easy means of communication one with the other; and, finally, Division 16, as established, consisting of Leeds, Grenville and Dundas counties, will only contain at least 130 members, or one-third more, which indicates the injustice and inequality of the arrangement.

Therefore, for those and other reasons, this Council of the College of Physicians and Surgeons of Ontario protests against the said Divisions of 15, 16, 17 as passed in the said Act, and if for any reason it is thought advisable to make the said changes, then the County of Stormont should be taken from 17 and added to 16, thus making 16 to have 108 members and 17 to have 115 members. Finally, this Council protests against eastern Ontario being deprived of its proper representation, as the same is unjust.

Dr. ROGERS—In making this motion, I want to assure the members of this Council that there is not the slightest wish or desire on my part to go to the Legislature; I would oppose such a move, but I think it is only due and just to the members in eastern Ontario who, for many years, have stood loyally by this Council, that when these members have been gerrymandered as they have in this Schedule " A," we should at least take some notice of the injustice which has been done to them. I might point out, perhaps, some of the reasons why it seems to me this great change which has been made to the eastern counties was unnecessary. In the first place, Division No. 15, as it stands in the new Act, consists of Addington, Frontenac, Lanark and Renfrew. Addington and Frontenac have no interests in common with Lanark and Renfrew at all; in fact, it is almost impossible, without a great deal of trouble, to get from one part of the Division to another. Addington and Frontenac, lying along the river, are interested in common, while Renfrew and Lanark, being inland, have no interests in common with the other two counties; so that in Division No. 15 the natural boundaries which divide the Division

have been lost sight of. In Division No. 16, Leeds, Grenville and
Dundas form a very small division. They have only about ninety
members, and there is no reason, and there was no reason, why Stormont and Glengarry, or Stormont anyway, should not have been left
in that division. I do not know whether it was the intention, on the
part of the framers of that bill, to gerrymander those counties, and
gerrymander me, and gerrymander my friend, Dr. Bergin, out of this
Council; but be that as it may, the facts stand out that in those three
counties there is only the small number of ninety members, or about
ninety members; and in Division No. 17, which has been placed
right along side of it, there are one hundred and thirty-five members,
or fully one-third more. Taking the reasons why I ask this resolution
to be passed, among others are: The new Division of No. 15 will consist of Addington, Frontenac and Leeds, which all lie in close juxta-
position to one another. Leeds is united by the Grand Trunk with
these counties, and there are interests in common between them. I
know the county personally, because it forms part of my old division,
and all the members there, I am quite certain, would be well pleased
to be united with Frontenac, because there is a community of interests
between them. Division 16 would consist of Renfrew, Lanark and
Carleton; these three counties form the major part of the Bathurst
Division, which was composed of these three counties and South
Leeds; and Dr. Bergin's division was the St. Lawrence and Eastern.
In making the Divisions 16 and 17 in this way, I am doing so in
order to leave my old division and Dr. Bergin's in the same position
as they were before; that is to say, the Bathurst and Rideau Division
is left in precisely the same position as it was, and the St. Lawrence
is left in the same position as it was, less Leeds, which had been partly
taken from my division and partly from Dr. Bergin's division and
placed in a new division. I think that while there can be everything
said in favour of passing a resolution of this kind to show or to point
out to the Legislature in what way these counties should have been
or might have been placed in order that the divisions might be more
equitable and fair than they are now, yet I have only this idea to pass
a resolution, and, as it were, to protest against the injustice, and leave
the Attorney-General and the Government to take such steps as they
feel inclined. But I do not ask this Council to go to the Legislature.
That I would refuse to sanction. I have only to add this, that in
making this motion I am doing it in the interests—at least, I am com-
plying with the wish of the great majority of members in my old
division, Lanark, Renfrew and Carleton. In many parts they have
written strong letters protesting against this arrangement, as it is; they
say it is simply leaving them without a division at all; and I am
making this motion because of that, and to ask the Council to pass
some resolution protesting against such an injustice.

Dr. BERGIN—Whilst sympathizing very strongly with my friend, Dr. Rogers, in the protest he makes, and very properly makes, against the unjust division made by the Act passed the other day by the Ontario Legislature, the unjust division of territorial divisions which have existed since the establishment of this Council, I must take ground against our attempting to do that which we condemn in the Ontario Legislature. I feel very acutely that by the Act of the Ontario Legislature the distribution or readjustment, as someone called it, was made for the purpose of gerrymandering myself, Dr. Rogers, Dr. Day and Dr. Ruttan out of the Council. I have no doubt it was intentionally designed; and while I feel that tne divisions that have existed since the formation of the Council answered the purposes admirably and suited everyone, I must protest very strongly against their being interfered with at all. The same injustice that is practised in Carleton Division and Stormont Division has also been practised in the divisions represented by Dr. Day and Dr. Ruttan. I think we have the right to protest strongly against the injustice that has been practised upon us ; and we have a right I think, to call the attention of the Attorney-General to it, and to make him fully aware of the strong feeling there is in this Council against the unfairness which has been practised toward these different territorial divisions. I think it is well the Attorney-General should know how strongly we feel that he interfered with divisions without a complaint of any kind on the part of the men representing those divisions against their then formation. I have here in my hand a tabulated statement of the number of members in each territorial division, which was given to me by our colleague, Dr. Day, and which I shall not read to you because I think it would come more properly from him. It is a statement which shows that at present, with the exception of three divisions, the medical population of each territorial division is practically the same ; and it shows there was no necessity whatever for this change in the territorial divisions. I might point out to you that in two of them, at least, there is such a number of medical practitioners that the number necessary to make up the territorial representation might very properly have been added to them, and then we would have had all over the Province of Ontario that which every honest man says there ought to be, wherever representation is concerned, representation by population. No principle has been served in the distribution that was made by the Legislature the other day except one of destruction. There was no attempt to improve the representation, but, on the contrary, an attempt to drive out the oldest members of the Council that they may be replaced, forsooth, by someone representing the so-called Medical Defence Association, which has really no representation in the country, which has no strength whatever in the country, and who were set forth, by a species of fraud before the Legislature, as representing a majority of the profession

4*

of this country. They do not represent much more than a handful of the medical population of this country. True, when they first began their agitation, a large number of gentlemen signed their petitions ; but, when they became aware of the nature of the complaints these men were making, and of their falsity in the city of London, in my county, everywhere they withdrew their names ; and the Defence Association dared not go before the Legislature with the postal cards that were returned to them, and which would have proved that they have no status in the country at all. They are represented by a few loud-mouthed, blatant, unprincipled individuals ; and it is to suit them the Ontario Legislature, the other day, without proper inquiry, committed a great injustice, that of which we now complain.

Dr. Logan—As seconder of the resolution, it affords me pleasure to give Dr. Rogers an opportunity to bring this matter before the Council. I have very litte doubt in my own mind an injustice has been done in this case ; clearly enough that is so from the geographical distribution. Whether it was intended as a fraud or not, whether it was a matter of accident, I am not able to say, but in either case it amounts to a positive fraud, and I am thus glad to have an opportunity of assisting in bringing the matter before the Council. I understand from Dr. Rogers that he has had some conversation with our representative from Ottawa, Mr. Bronson, and that he promised he would have this matter attended to ; that being the case, I think it becomes the duty of this Council to give a full expression of opinion upon the matter, so as to assist in carrying out the object in view.

Dr. Day—I will make a suggestion, a suggestion that I think ought to carry, and that is, that this matter be not now dealt with by the Council, but be referred to a committee of whatever number of territorial men you like, to make a recommendation. I do not like the geographical position ; it does not go far enough. As to the geological side of it, I suppose geologically it was intended to get rid of Dr. Ruttan, Dr. Bergin and myself, as fossils. However, I will just say very shortly what I think would be a far better distribution than anything I have yet heard of. Dr. Rogers' plan is very good, but I do not think it equals what I advocated at the Legislature, and what I tried to get the Legislature to adopt ; in that I made simply one geographical change ; I simply took West and North Middlesex from No. 1 Division and gave it to No. 2. That is all the geographical change I made. I think the present territorial districts, having been so long worked in the shape they are, it would be much better and much more convenient for the members to continue to work them in the way they are now constituted. In that division, Dr. Bray now having one hundred and ninety-two, by taking the Middlesexes away it would leave him about one hundred and forty, and adding fifty to No. 2 Division, which now has two hundred and sixty, would make it three hundred ;

then giving **No. 2** Division two members would give them one hundred and fifty votes per member. Then by adding all the unexplored and unknown district to No. 3 (Dr. Henry's Division), which goes from Guelph, I believe, to the North Pole, by adding the unsurveyed district to that which now has three hundred and nine voters, would give about four hundred and fifty members, or about that—within a trifle of it; that would give them three representatives having one hundred and fifty votes per member. Then, No. 4, Dr. Williams' Division, has one hundred and twenty now; leave that as it is. No. 5 has one hundred and forty-five voters; leave that as it is. No. 6 has one hundred and forty-seven; leave that as it is. No. 7 (or the Toronto Division) we find has four hundred and forty-one members; you will see that by dividing that number by three you get one hundred and forty-seven; and the majority, or, at least, a great many, of these divisions, number one hundred and forty each, and that seems to be exactly the number that it should be. No. 8 has one hundred and thirty-three members. No. 9 has one hundred and thirty-eight members. No. 10 has one hundred and forty-four members. Dr. Rogers' Division has one hundred and seventy-nine, and Dr. Bergin's one hundred and forty-four; so that there could not possibly be any fairer distribution, so far as number is concerned, than the divisions I now propose; and that makes only one geographical change; it leaves everything else just as it is now; and I think it would be much more convenient for the members of the profession to work in the old divisions in which they have hitherto been working than to form new divisions and new associations and new connections in every way. I would strongly recommend, if any recommendation is made, or suggestion or protest to the House, against the late gerrymandering—I think it was done in a hurry and inadvertently; I have not the slightest idea the Government had any intention to do any injustice or harm to the members of this Council—that that distribution and arrangement as I think would be much better than anything we could do, if we went to take a map and form new districts. I would suggest that this be referred to a committee of a few territorial members.

Dr. BERGIN—Name your committee.

Dr. DAY—I would move that it be left to a special committee, consisting of Drs. Bray, Bergin, Rogers, Henry and Johnson.

Dr. BRAY—With the mover?

Dr. DAY—With the mover, if you like. To meet and report at the afternoon session.

Dr. FULTON—My Division and Dr. Williams' Division are affected also. There is no objection to our being on the Committee?

Dr. DAY—No.

Dr. ROGERS—I have great pleasure in seconding Dr. Day's motion.

Dr. BERGIN—Since the Division is so large I would move that all the territorial representatives be on the Committee.

Dr. BRAY—Yes, I would second that.

Dr. ROGERS—I went to a great deal of trouble in getting a list of all the members in those counties from Addington downwards, to be exact in my numbers, but I couldn't go over the whole of Ontario; had I had time to do so I would have done so, but I have taken this portion which I could in the time being, and I have tried to do what was fair and right and just to all parties concerned. The Attorney-General has stated that the divisions should not be composed of parts of counties —that is, some whole counties, and other counties divided; he objects, I understand, to that—and says he wants the divisions composed of the whole counties; and that is the reason why I suggested this. But I can quite see the force of what Dr. Day says in regard to the changes he has proposed. In regard to what Dr. Bergin says about Dr. Day's and Dr. Ruttan's divisions being treated unjustly, I wish to second every word he said in regard to that. I look upon those divisions as being treated very badly indeed. I want to say more than that; I do not think, notwithstanding all that may be said, that the Ontario Government are responsible for this Schedule "A," as passed in the last Act; I am fairly certain the Government had nothing to do with it; and I am also certain when their attention is called to any injustice they will be the first to ask to have it changed.

Dr. HENRY—I rise to protest against the re-distribution or gerrymander that has taken place. In my constituency, a very large one, as Dr. Day has said, and in which there is a large number of medical men, they have made two divisions, and I am placed in the extreme end of the Division they have made for me—the point of it, rather. While I am displeased at the formation of the Division as it is at present, I am pleased, of course, that we have got that increased representation we have been asking for from time to time, but I am of the opinion it would be better if they had left the old divisions as they were (hear, hear), and the larger ones had been given an increased representation; for instance, mine would have been entitled to three representatives. I think that would have been very much better. Then the profession from one end to the other would have an opportunity to give expression to their views and feelings by vote. The way the thing is at present—for instance, Simcoe and Grey and Dufferin should have been the county to place it in the right centre, and to give satisfaction to the medical men; but it is Bruce, Grey and Dufferin; Dufferin is the tail end; the large end of the wedge is above, and Dufferin is at the other end. Then out of my county they have taken the Waterloo and Wellingtons; the Wellingtons form a county. They have taken the County of Simcoe, District of Muskoka, Parry Sound, Nipissing, Manitoulin, and so on, and formed another. Dufferin, Grey and Wellington or Simcoe would have made a better division than this. However, I think the true principle would have been to have left that question to this Council to agree upon.

Dr. Day moved, seconded by Dr. Rogers, that this motion be referred to a special committee consisting of the territorial representatives. Carried.

Dr. Harris presents report No. 1 of the Education Committee, and moved, seconded by Dr. Logan, that report No. 1 of the Education Committee be now received. Report received.

Dr. Rosebrugh presented the report of the Registration Committee, and moved that it be received. Report received.

Dr. Fowler presented the report of the Committee on Complaints, and moved that the same be received. Report received.

Dr. Britton presented report of Committee on Reciprocity, and moved that it be received. Report received.

Dr. Thorburn presented report of Committee on Finance, and moved that it be received. Report received.

Dr. Williams presented report of Legislation Committee, and moved that the same be received. Report received.

Dr. Harris moved, seconded by Dr. Logan, that report No. 1 of the Education Committee be now read and referred to Committee of the Whole. Carried.

Council in Committee of the Whole. Dr. Day in the chair.

Dr. Harris moved that the report be read clause by clause. Carried. Report read clause by clause and adopted.

Dr. Harris moved that the report as amended be adopted. Carried.

Dr. Harris moved, seconded by Dr. Rogers, that the Committee rise and report.

The Committee rose. The President in the chair.

Dr. Harris moved, seconded by Dr. Bray, that the report of the Committee of the Whole on Report No. 1 of the Education Committee as amended be adopted. Carried.

EDUCATION COMMITTEE REPORT No. I.

June 16th, 1893.

To the President and Members of the Medical Council of the College of Physicians and Surgeons of Ontario:

GENTLEMEN,—Your Standing Committee on Education begs respectfully to submit the following report (No. 1) on various matters referred to said Committee :

I. In regard to communication of Thos. Bradley *re* Matriculation Examination. He says he failed in French, and asks may he complete this examination any time before October, 1893, and the time of graduation.

To be instructed that he must pass the entire Matriculation Examination required by this Council prior to registration as a medical student on its register.

II. Wm. F. Cunningham applies for liberty to be brought under the four years' course. He matriculated in everything but Latin. He was unaware that the time for registration had been extended to November, 1892 ; also that he would have had time to pass it in that time.

Mr. Cunningham is to be instructed that he must comply with the regulation of this Council.

III. Thos. J. Caldwell, of Shanty Bay, failed by eight marks, passed everything but Algebra, failed by a few marks in that subject in his Matriculation Examination in July, 1892.

Mr. Caldwell is required to carry out the instructions of this Council.

IV. J. J. Davis, of London, Ont., asks to be registered on his Second Class certificate as a matriculated student. He is a few marks short in Chemistry. He went up in July, 1892.

Mr. Davis' request should be granted.

V. Mr. Proctor, who applies to register as a medical student, to be informed that his Matriculation Examination is considered satisfactory to this Council, and entitles him to registration as a medical student.

VI. Geo. D. Porter, in his third year of medical study. He registered with the Council two years after he began his medical studies. He had his Matriculation in Toronto University (Arts) in good time to have registered before he began medicine.

Request of Mr. Porter granted.

VII. In regard to Dr. Waugh's resignation as an Examiner in Medical and Surgical Anatomy.

Registrar to acknowledge receipt of letter.

VIII. A. G. A. Fletcher applies for permission to go up for final examination without taking a summer session, and be allowed to complete his course on the curriculum as it stood when he registered in 1887.

Mr. Fletcher's request should be granted.

IX. W. A. McIntosh, Simcoe. Has passed all his Matriculation Examination but Latin. He has taken one session of medical lectures, and asks to be allowed to register when he passes in Latin, and to have his medical lectures counted.

Mr. McIntosh to be informed to comply with the regulations of the Council.

X. Duncan McCallum asks to be registered if he passes his Latin before going up for his primary examination. He holds a Second Class certificate covering all the rest of the Matriculation work. Has attended one course of medical lectures.

Mr. McCallum must comply with the regulations of the Council.

XI. D. Jamieson applies for registration. He asks to be allowed to take a four years' course, as he held in 1887 the qualifications to do so.

Mr. Jamieson's request should be granted.

XII. H. G. Williams asks whether, as he has certificates of having passed the preliminary examination required by the Royal College of Surgeons, England, and the Royal College of Physicians, England, and also the examination of these bodies in many primary subjects, to be allowed to be registered as a medical student, and also to be allowed to go up for his final examination.

As no documents have been submitted with the letter of Mr. Williams, his request cannot be entertained.

XIII. W. T. Beatty, Collingwood, has a Third Class certificate dated 1885, without Latin. He asks can he now register by passing Latin, and if he does so, can he be allowed to take a four years' course.

Mr. Beatty must comply with the regulation of the Council.

XIV. A. Johnston, Goderich, wishes, if he enters a Medical College in the fall of 1892, to be allowed to take a four years' course.

His request should not be granted.

XV. Mr. H. O. Milbee asks for registration based on marks got at Departmental Examination in 1892 in Barrie.

Mr. Milbee must comply with the regulation of the Council.

XVI. J. R. McRae, Goderich, applies for registration with the Council.

He must comply with the Council regulations.

XVII. John Kerr asks for registration as a medical student, he having only failed by a few marks on Latin and French.

To be directed to comply with the regulations of the Council.

XVIII. J. A. Brown, M.D., Sarnia, desires registration. Holds a Second Class certificate, 1888, with Science, and writes to know if he could complete his matriculation by accepting Arts Matriculation in Latin of McGill.

Dr. Brown to be referred to regulations of this Council, Section I., Clause 1, under the head of "Matriculation." Also to be informed that not having registered before November 1st, 1892, he will be required to take five years.

XIX. A. C. Halter asks for registration as a Matriculate in Law. He presents a certificate in this from Osgoode Hall.

Mr. Halter's request cannot be granted, as only one Matriculation

Examination is accepted by this Council, viz., the Departmental Arts Matriculation.

XX. Fred. McKinnon, Vankleek Hill, wishes to be registered as a Matriculate. Says he has one year's attendance in Arts at McGill.

Mr. McKinnon is to be told that he must comply with the regulation of the Council.

XXI. Chas. O. Fairbank, M.D., a graduate of Royal Military College, wishes, as such, to be registered as a matriculate.

Request should be granted.

XXII. "That, with their final tickets, candidates shall (except in cases of graduates in Arts) present a certificate of having passed at the close of their third session in the College or School they may have attended, an examination in such parts of Medicine, Surgery and Midwifery as may be thought advisable by the Faculties of the respective Colleges or Schools."

This Examination is not in any way to interfere with any of the examinations of this Council.

XXIII. M. Haight asks to take a Primary and Final Examination together.

Mr. Haight's request should be granted.

XXIV. E. G. Hodgson asks for registration as a matriculate as an Honor Graduate from the College of Pharmacy.

Mr. Hodgson must comply with the regulations of this Council, as the Council cannot waive its Matriculation Examination in such cases.

XXV. A. A. Metcalfe has a matriculation entitling to registration ; cannot afford to spend the five years now required, and wishes his matriculation (Arts in Queens) to be registered so as to bring him within the four-year curriculum.

Request should be granted.

XXVI. It is recommended by this Committee, upon information received by Dr. Fowler and the Principal of the Upper Canada College, and other sources, as to the requirements for graduation, that graduates of the Royal Military College, Kingston, Ontario, be entitled, on presentation of their diploma and identification of their graduation, to registration as matriculates in this Council.

XXVII. Report of Board of Examiners of the College of Physicians and Surgeons of Ontario, dated June 8th, was considered and adopted.

XXVIII. The case of a candidate who personated another candidate in Chemistry at the recent Primary Examination of the Council, George Kraussman and A. T. Jones being the names of the personator and the personated respectively, was considered.

· It was agreed to recommend, and it is recommended, that both parties should be debarred from further examination before this Council for the next five years from the present date.

XXIX. It is recommended that the subject of Therapeutics be given in connection with Practice of Medicine, a separate paper being set in each of these subjects by the Examiner.

XXX. The President's address has been carefully gone over and his suggestions noted.

XXXI.—Inasmuch as the Council has referred all correspondence between Mr. J. A. Sangster and the President and Registrar, as well as the interview, it is recommended that the correspondence should be published in the Announcement.

XXXII.—It is recommended in accordance with the resolution referred to this Committee by the Council, proposed by Dr. Williams, that the said resolution is approved of, and a sub-committee, consisting of Drs. Williams, Logan and Bergin, be appointed to prepare the epitome suggested and to report to the Council next year.

XXXIII.—Dr. Fulton's resolution was considered, and it was agreed that the principle of the resolution be recommended, and is hereby recommended for adoption by the Council. This resolution will appear in the Minutes.

WILLIAM T. HARRIS,
Chairman of Education Committee.

Dr. Britton presented the report of the Property Committee, and moved that it be received. Report received.

Dr. Britton moved that the Council go into Committee of the Whole on report of the Property Committee. Carried.

Council in Committee of the Whole. Dr. Bergin in the chair.

Dr. Britton read the report, and moved that it be adopted. Carried.

The Committee rose. The President in the chair.

Dr. Britton moved, seconded by Dr. Orr, that the report of the Committee of the Whole on the report of the Property Committee be adopted. Carried.

PROPERTY COMMITTEE REPORT.

To the President and Council of the College of Physicians and Surgeons of Ontario :

GENTLEMEN,—Your Property Committee beg leave to report that they have carefully inspected the College building from attic to cellar, and it appears to their instructed judgment that it has, on the whole, satisfactorily withstood the ravages of time. The wood and brickwork are in a good state of preservation, and considering the magnitude of the structure, the evidences of settling are very slight.

There are several items of renovation and repair which we would recommend to your consideration, were it not that there is a species of Anæmia in the Treasurer's department. Our College income this year will probably be less than last, consequently we recommend only such expenditure as is at the present imperative.

1st. The boilers should have the ends well scraped and painted with red lead in order to prevent leakage.

2nd. The brick arches of the same were initially built of common instead of fire brick, and the heat has largely destroyed them. They should be rebuilt, and of fire brick.

3rd. The pipes and attachments of the furnaces require repainting.

4th. The elevator and its enclosure should be rubbed down and painted.

5th. The main valve controlling the supply of water is inoperative, and a new one should be put in.

6th. The main staircase, from the ground floor to the top, together with the landings, are becoming unsightly, and we would recommend that they be kalsomined and the ornamented portions tinted. This we believe to be a durable and a cheap method of decoration.

7th. The ground floor requires oiling.

8th The urinal on the first floor should be thoroughly overhauled, the floor of the lavatory repainted and the woodwork varnished.

9th. We find that the main roof leaks in several places, and to such an extent that the ceiling and walls of the examination hall are being rapidly destroyed, and the architect should be consulted without delay as to what should be done. We think from the information supplied by the caretaker, that this repair will not entail much expense.

10th. The radiators are blackening the walls, and with a trifling outlay shields could be procured which would effectually prevent this.

11th. In both the front and side vestibules, the walls and ceilings should be kalsomined, the wainscotting rubbed down in oil, and the steps oiled.

12th. The Bay Street doors should be revarnished. If not attended to forthwith, the woodwork will be roughened beyond restoration.

13th. The matter of insurance is in the hands of the solicitor, and has not been settled as to the amount of the premium the College is to pay to the Canada Life Assurance Company.

14th. The elevator has been injured to some extent by sand in the water. This matter is also in the hands of the solicitor who is urging our claim against the city to repair the damage done. We have not had time or opportunity to make full inquiries as to the cost of repairs, but we suggest that in case any repairs are likely to cost more than twenty dollars, the Registrar be instructed to ask for tenders for the same. Attached are communications from the caretaker and from Mr. Robb, Boiler Inspector, but as the details have been considered in framing this report, they do not require to be read.

All of which is respectfully submitted.

W. BRITTON, *Chairman.*

———

TORONTO, *June 9th,* 1893.

R. A. Pyne, Esq., M.D., Registrar College of Physicians and Surgeons of Ontario:

DEAR SIR,—On the 6th inst. the steam boilers were fully examined, and found generally sound and tight. The following points should be attended to:

The safety valves need grinding, to make them fit their seats properly and without leakage. The dampers for checking the draught are connected together, so that both open and close together. They should be separated, so that each will act independently of the other, because there may be a very bright fire under one boiler, and a very dull fire, or no fire at all, under the other.

In order to preserve boilers from injury during summer, it would be well to paint the boiler heads with boiled oil with a little red lead in it. Then put ten pounds of soda in each boiler, make the hand hole joints perfectly tight, and fill the boilers entirely full of water.

The arches over furnace doors, the bridge walls, and other parts of the brickwork need repair. I would advise that for this you employ a man of practical experience in such work, and would say that Mr. Geo. W. Gore's work is found to give good satisfaction. He is an expert at furnace building, and you can depend upon getting a good job done. You can easily find one who will work much cheaper, but I am satisfied that in furnace building it is cheaper in the end to employ a specialist.

The steam gauges were tested and were adjusted by our Inspector.

Yours very truly,

GEO. C. ROBB, *Chief Engineer.*

———

TORONTO, *June 10th,* 1893.

To Dr. R. A. Pyne, Registrar College of Physicians and Surgeons of Ontario:

DEAR SIR,—I beg to lay before you my annual report on the building of the College of Physicians and Surgeons of Ontario.

The boilers in connection with the building have been inspected twice during the year, once before starting the fires, and the other after the fires were closed down. I have had all the soot removed from around the boilers and flues in each one; I emptied the water from each boiler; I then dissolved ten pounds of soda for each boiler which I have put in and have again filled the boilers up with water, so as to keep them from corroding during the summer months.

The boiler pipes and attachments want painting; also the boiler-room whitewashed.

As to the other repairs required, the boiler inspector will report to you, but I would draw your special attention to the quality of brick used in the boilers, during the winter the archways having come down; I have had the brick taken out of the pit at the back of the tubes, also from under the boiler, and find that they are only common brick instead of fire brick; I have them still in my possession.

The water valve for shutting the water off from the elevator is not in working order, and when Fensom's men were repairing the elevator they could not shut the water off by the valve, and I had to get the Waterworks Company to send a man to turn the water off in the street. Therefore, should anything go wrong with the elevator, before the water could be shut off, the building would become flooded.

The plumbing work in all the lavatories requires overhauling, also the lavatories require the floors and walls painted, as they are commencing to look very bad and smell considerable.

All the doors on Bay and Richmond streets require varnishing, as they are getting very bare and will get impoverished by the weather.

The walls and ceilings of all the halls, landings and stairways are in a very bad condition and require either to be kalsomined or painted, also the woodwork varnished and the first floor oiled, and the paint work on the elevator also requires renovating.

I would also call your attention to the want of lavatory accommodation; there are at present twelve ladies working in the building, and the only closet which they can use is the one attached to the council chamber; the accommodation in the basement is also too small, about fourteen gentlemen having to use the same closet; so you will perceive that it is very unpleasant for the ladies to have to use the same closet; my own family also have to use the same one.

Since taking the position of prosecutor for the college I have had a man in charge of the building who is just as capable as myself; also my own son, a young man who has studied engineering, attended to the boilers and elevator, besides my wife who sees that everything is right; so that, in fact, the building is attended to better than if I was always at home. The man and my son I have to pay out of my own salary.

Messrs. Mulholland & Sharpe wish to have a sink put into their office as they wash a great many bottles, which they have now to do in the lower lavatory, and it, therefore, keeps the place always wet and dirty.

I am sir, yours respectfully,

THOS. WASSON.

Dr. Rosebrugh moved, seconded by Dr. Orr, that the report of the Registration Committee be now read and referred to Committee of the Whole. Carried.

Council in Committee of the Whole. Dr. Bray in the chair.

Dr. Rosebrugh read report clause by clause, and moved that the report be adopted without amendment. Carried.

The Committee rose. The President in the chair.

Dr. Rosebrugh moved, seconded by Dr. Orr, that the report of the Committee of the Whole on report of the Registration Committee be adopted. Carried.

REGISTRATION COMMITTEE REPORT No. I.

To the President and Members of the Ontario Medical College :

GENTLEMEN,—Your Committee on Registration beg leave to submit the following report :

1. That in reference to the communication from Dr. Herod, of Guelph, requesting that the title, "Member College Physicians and Surgeons, Ontario," should appear after all names on the register,

Your Committee are of the opinion that in the interests of uniformity, it would be well to comply with this request, and recommend the Council to grant the same ; to be carried into effect at the issuing of the next register.

2. In reference to the petition of Jacob Zelinski and Peter Reid McMonagle, again requesting to be registered,

Your Committee find that the said Jacob Zelinski and the said Peter Reid McMonagle have not furnished any proof of having complied with the Medical Act, and therefore recommend that their petitions be refused.

All of which is respectfully submitted.

J. W. ROSEBRUGH, *Chairman.*

Dr. Fowler moved, seconded by Dr. Williams, that the report of the Committee on Complaints be read and referred to Committee of the Whole. Carried.

Council in Committee of the Whole. Dr. Logan in the chair.

First two clauses of report read and adopted.

Dr. WILLIAMS—I presume that the Committee, in looking after these matters, have borne in mind that a student has a right to appeal from the examiners to the Council, and this Committee should remember that right, and the report ought not to be couched in terms, that no action be taken. We must at least recognize that the students have a right, and to some extent, whatever extent I don't know, their request was granted, their papers were looked into. Because it is a right under the statute that they may appeal from the examiners; and our report must recognize that fact. As the report at present reads, it would imply we did not think the matter worthy of consideration at all.

Dr. BERGIN—I do not wish to be thought captious at all, but I think the Committee might very properly have reported to this Council the number of marks by which a gentleman, who has been rejected upon one subject only, has been rejected; for instance, if he has been rejected by only one mark upon a subject, I quite agree with the President in his address that he made to us the other day, that we ought to have some little consideration for a student who fails by only one mark on one subject, when you consider he has passed in every other subject. I think we ought to know that. And another consideration, I think, is this, that if we should not have in September, and I am afraid we shall not be able to have because of want of funds, another examination this year, then it is a great hardship and a wrong to put a man over for another year because he has missed only one mark in the whole list of subjects.

Dr. FOWLER—I think Dr. Williams and Dr. Bergin misunderstand the action of the Committee. There are several cases in which we re-read, or heard the papers re-read, and the marks, as a whole, were considered by the Committee; and the Committee came to the conclusion, not that they should take no action in the matter, but to recommend the Council not to take any action, after the Committee had carefully considered the question. As you will see afterwards in the report, we re-read the papers.

Dr. WILLIAMS—That is the objection I take, that while you re-read the papers, you should show in your report that they were re-read, and then ground for objection, on the part of students who have a right to appeal under the statute, is taken away.

Dr. FOWLER—In the after part of the report the re-reading comes in.

Dr. RUTTAN—It appears to me, at the last meeting of the Council there were instructions given that the decision of the examiners should be final, without appealing to this Council.

Dr. BERGIN—Yes; but we added to that a recommendation which amounted to an instruction to these gentlemen, that when they found a student failed only by one mark or two that they were to recommend these cases to the Council.

Dr. ROGERS—I quite agree with a great deal that has been said in this matter, but I do not agree with the idea of putting it forth from this Committee and from this Council, that when a man fails by one mark or any other part of his marks, he shall be passed. That would mean that if you make your standard fifty per cent., you have then a standard of forty-nine per cent. ; if he falls below forty-nine per cent., that is forty-eight per cent. ; and so on *ad infinitum.* It seems to me we should have a standard, and should maintain it and keep it ; and we should have confidence in our Board of Examiners. And I am very glad to see the Committee bring in the report that they have.

Dr. MILLER—I think it is very proper where a student fails by only one mark on one subject to consider his general standing. I may say, as a member of that Committee, that where the failure was remarkably small, to the extent of one or two, three or four marks, in many instances the standing on every other branch was exceedingly good ; and from the suggestions which have been made respecting the quotation of the standing of these students in the other branches, I think it is a very excellent idea, and I would be in favour of asking the report referred back to the Committee with instructions to report the standing of these students who claim they have been unfairly dealt with in the other branches ; and then the Council would be in a position to judge how they should deal with each case.

Dr. HENRY—Yet we most distinctly last year, or the year before, decided we should not give the marks of the students.

Dr. BERGIN—But that was to give the marks of all the students. What was understood was, we would not give the marks of the entire body that came up for examination only in those cases where they were referred to the Council for consideration beyond that given by the Committee.

Dr. GEIKIE—The Registrar could give you that in a minute.

Dr. MILLER—Perhaps the want of propriety of publishing the marks in each subject might be got over if the Registrar were requested by you to produce the schedule, which could be read to this Committee as a guide in dealing with each case.

Dr. ROSEBRUGH—I think we should remember these young men are gentlemen. They have put in a petition to be considered ; and it struck me as the Chairman of the Committee read the report that the answer was rather discourteous, "No action taken." If he would say, "The gentleman came very near passing, but we cannot recommend that we should depart from our standard," or something of that kind, it would be a more courteous answer to the young gentlemen.

Dr. BRAY—I think all this discussion might be avoided if the Chairman in reading his report would say these matters had been considered by that Committee, and they report that this Council take no action.

Dr. Fowler proceeds with the reading of the report, and, on motion, the report was adopted as read.

The Committee rose. President in the chair.

Dr. Bergin—Before the Chairman asks the Council to adopt that report, I would like to say to the Council that in the matter of Doctor McCallum, the Council is not responsible for any statement made by the *Ontario Medical Journal*, and should repudiate it.

Dr. Fowler moved, seconded by Dr. Bray, that the report of the Committee of the Whole on the report of the Committee on Complaints be adopted as follows.   Carried.

COMPLAINT COMMITTEE REPORT.

June 15th, 1893.

Your Committee on Complaints beg leave to report as follows :

In the case of J. P. Hubbard complaining against the Examiner in Medical and Surgical Anatomy for treating him in an ungentlemanly manner, and also appealing against the decision, after due consideration the Committee recommend that no action be taken.

In the case of S. H. Large, asking for a re-reading of his paper on Physiology ; of W. E. Brown, who failed on Medical and Surgical Anatomy ; also in the case of E. W. Goode, who failed in Operative Surgery ; also J. A. McNaughton, who failed in Operative Surgery, your Committee, having re-examined papers, recommend that no action be taken.

In the case of Lapp, it was decided to re-read his paper on Practice of Medicine. After this was done it was found that his paper was of such a character as did not entitle him to be passed ; we therefore recommend that no further action be taken in his case.

In the cases of J. B. Ferguson and A. B. Parlow, who asked for a re-reading of their papers, it was recommended, after carefully re-reading, that no action be taken.

The papers of W. J. Arnott, J. T. Dunn and R. T. Corbett, on Medical and Surgical Anatomy, were directed to be re-read, and being re-read by a competent person, the award of the Examiner was not changed, and we recommend that no further action be taken.

FIFE FOWLER, *Chairman.*

Dr. Rogers moved that the report of the Committee on Reciprocity by now read and referred to the Committee of the Whole.   Carried.

Council in Committee of the Whole.   Dr. Harris in the chair.

Dr. Rogers read the report, and moved that it be adopted as read. Carried.

On motion, the Committee rose.   The President in the chair.

Dr. Rogers moved that the report of the Committee of the Whole on the report of the Committee on Reciprocity be adopted as follows. Carried.

REPORT OF COMMITTEE ON RECIPROCITY.

The Committee appointed at the last session of this Council to meet delegates from the Medical Councils of the various provinces of the Dominion of Canada, to formulate a scheme of reciprocity in medical registration between the said provinces, beg leave to report as follows :

This Council at their last session in June appointed a committee of their body to meet delegates from the Medical Councils from other provinces, in Ottawa, on the 20th of September, and to discuss reciprocity in medical registration and report at the earliest possible date. The meeting consisted of Dr. Bray, Chatham, Ont. ; Sir James Grant, Ottawa ; Dr. Logan, Ottawa ; Dr. Ruttan, of Napanee ; Dr. Rogers, of Ottawa—who formed the committee 'from the Ontario Medical Council—and Dr. F. W. Campbell, of Montreal, and Drs. Gibson and Brosseau, delegates from the Quebec Medical Council. Dr. Edwards represented the North-West Territories, and Dr. Milne from British Columbia. Communications and suggestions were received from Manitoba, Nova Scotia, P. E. Island and New Brunswick.

The whole subject of reciprocity in medical registration between the provinces was fully and ably discussed, and all the delegates strongly favored the adoption, in each of the provinces, of a Medical Act on the lines of the Medical Act in Ontario which gives the Medical Council full control over both pre-medical and medical education, and indeed over all matters relating to the practice of medicine in Ontario.

Also, it was the unanimous opinion that there should be established in each Province at once a Central Examining Board, to examine all candidates for the license to practise, and further, when such examining boards were established in the provinces, the standard of matriculation and medical education should be raised to a uniform grade, following that of Ontario, and then reciprocity in medical registration between the provinces would result as a natural consequence.

The following resolution was carried unanimously, the Committee and delegates all voting for it :

Moved by Dr. Rogers, seconded by Dr. Gibson, and

Resolved,—That in the opinion of this Conference there should be established in each Province in Canada a Central Examining Board to examine all candidates for medical registration therein.

Resolved,—That as soon as a Central Examining Board is formed in each Province, a committee should be appointed from each Provincial Medical Council, in order to have established a uniform standard of matriculation and of medical education throughout Canada, and also reciprocity between the provinces in regard to medical registration.

The meeting then adjourned, and all the delegates were satisfied at the progress made in this great matter of medical reform.

Your Committee have just pleasure in reporting that the delegates

5*

from the Quebec Medical Council heartily endorsed the idea of each Province in Canada having a Medical Act strictly on the lines of the Ontario Medical Act, and each one agreed to do all in his power to secure such a Medical Act in the Province of Quebec.

Your Committee can also express the hope that the time is not far distant when the various provinces of Canada will each have a Central Examining Board, and reciprocity in medical registration between the provinces will be an accomplished fact.

All of which is respectfully submitted.

A. F. ROGERS, Secretary.

Toronto, Ont., *June 15th,* 1893.

Adopted in Committee of the Whole.

WILLIAM T. HARRIS, Chairman.

Dr. Williams moved, seconded by Dr. Orr, that the report of the Legislative Committee be read and adopted as follows. Report read.

LEGISLATION COMMITTEE REPORT.

To the President and Members of the Medical Council of the College of Physicians and Surgeons of Ontario :

GENTLEMEN,—Your Committee on Legislation held a meeting on the 29th of September, 1892, and in accordance with arrangement made with the President, had a conference with the members of the Defence Association.

After considerable discussion, your Committee requested the Association to make their propositions in writing, which they did, as follows :

1. That Article 41 A of the Ontario Medical Act be repealed.

2. That action in regard to the levying of the annual fees be held in suspense until the medical profession is properly represented in the Council.

3. That only each of the following universities be allowed to send a representative to the Council, to wit : Queen's, Toronto, Trinity and the Western.

4. That the territorial representatives number seventeen, and the homœopathic five.

Your Committee, after carefully considering these propositions, replied :

1st. We consent to 41 A remaining in abeyance until after the next election, and allowing the electorate to pronounce upon it.

2nd. We do not consent to suspend Section 27, but will still rely on the honour of the profession to pay the fee.

3rd. We will favour adding five additional territorial representatives.

4th. We will not object to institutions which neither teach nor grant degrees being deprived of representation.

5th. We are in favour of protested elections being referred to the Senior County Judge in the division in which the election took place.

Some time subsequently the Secretary of the Defence Association wrote the President of the Council that the offer would not be accepted, and that the agitation would be continued.

Your Committee met on the 12th of January, 1893, and 23rd of February, 1893, with a view to consolidating the Medical Acts, and making some minor amendments thereto, in accordance with your instructions. These are appended to this report. The Registrar forwarded a copy to each member of the Council.

These proposed amendments were presented to the Attorney-General, but he and his Government declined to make any further amendments to the Medical Act.

On May 15th, 1893, your Committee met and discussed the "Meacham Bill," which was then before the House, and had been referred by the Assembly to a special committee.

Your Committee appeared before the Special Committee on the 15th of May, when the matter was fully discussed, with the result, you are aware, the Meacham Bill was amended in some particulars, and finally, passed as appended to the end of this report.

All of which is respectfully submitted.

J. ARTHUR WILLIAMS,
Chairman Committee on Legislation.

———

This bill passed the House on Friday, May 26th. A portion of the Medical Act affected is herewith appended. The alterations and new matter are in italics :—

Section 6. *Thirdly.*—*Seventeen* members to be elected in the manner hereinafter provided from amongst, and by the registered Members of the Profession, other than those mentioned in the preceding subsections of this Section.

(2) The *seventeen* members to be elected as aforesaid shall be *and continue to be* residents of the several Territorial Divisions for which they are elected ; and one member shall be so elected from each of the Territorial Divisions mentioned in Schedule " A " to this Act, by the registered Practitioners of Medicine resident in such Division ; and the manner of holding such election shall, with respect to the time thereof and the taking the votes therefor, be determined by a by-law to be passed by the Council ; and in default of such by-law being made, then the Lieutenant-Governor shall prescribe the time and manner of holding such election. R. S. O., 1877, c. 142, s. 6 ; 50 V. c. 24, s. 1.

7. (1) The members of the Council shall be elected or appointed, as the case may be, for a period of *four* years ; but any member may resign his appointment at any time by letter addressed to the President or Registrar of the Council ; and upon the death or resignation of any member of the Council it shall be the duty of the Registrar forthwith to notify the college or body wherein the vacancy has occurred, of the death or resignation ; and such college or body shall have the power to nominate another duly-qualified person to fill the vacancy ; or, if the vacancy be caused by the death or resignation of any member elected from a Territorial Division, *or by his becoming disqualified owing to his having ceased to reside there*, the Registrar shall forthwith cause a new election to be held in such Territorial Division in such manner as may be provided for by by-law of the Council ; and the election shall be conducted in accordance with the By-laws and Regulations of the Council, but it shall be lawful for the Council during such vacancy to exercise the powers hereinafter mentioned.

Section 7 of the said Act is further amended by adding thereto the following as sub-sections (3) and (4) thereof :—

(3) The Registrar shall, not more than 60 nor less than 40 days before the time for receiving nominations for any election under this Act, notify, by letter or post card, every registered medical practitioner in the province of the date of receiving such nominations.

(4) A general election shall be held in the year 1894 in accordance with the provisions of the said Act as amended by this Act.

5. (1) *In case the validity of the election of any member of the council is contested, the same is to be tried by the senior or other officiating judge of the county court, or the judge of the district court of the district in which the person whose election is complained of resides, and the proceedings thereon shall "mutatis mutandis" be the same (as nearly as may be) as in the case of municipal elections under the sections of "The Consolidated Municipal Act, 1892," relating to controverted elections. But no security by the complainant shall be necessary.*

(2) *Any person qualified to vote at the election complained of may be the relator in proceedings under this section.*

(3) *The decision of the said judge shall be final.*

29. The Board of Examiners appointed under the preceding section shall be composed as follows : one member from each of the teaching bodies now existing, referred to in Section 6 of this Act, and one from every other School of Medicine which may be hereafter organized in connection with any University or College which is empowered by law to grant Medical or Surgical Diplomas ; and a number not *less than six* members to be chosen from among those members of the

College of Physicians and Surgeons of Ontario who are unconnected with any of the above teaching bodies. R.S.O., 1877, c. 142, s. 29.

7. *The fees to be paid by the members of the college towards the expenses of the college, and the means of collecting and enforcing the same are to be in the discretion of the elected members of the council; and section 27 of the said Act, and section 41a amending the same, enacted by the Act passed in the 54th year of Her Majesty's reign, chaptered 26, and entitled " An Act to Amend the Ontario Medical Act," are hereby suspended, and are to continue suspended unless and until after the elections of 1894 a by-law is passed by the council adopting the same or part thereof; and the said council, after the said elections, is to have power from time to time to adopt the same in whole or in part, or with any modifications as the council sees fit, and is to have power to afterwards repeal, or from time to time vary any such by-law, and to re-enact the same in whole or in part after repeating the, same, subject always to the limit prescribed by section 27 of the said Medical Act. But the only members of the council entitled to vote on any by-law under this section shall be elected members of the council, nine of whom at least must be present at the passing of the by-law.*

8. *Schedule "A" to the said Act is repealed, and the schedule to this Act substituted therefor.*

SCHEDULE.

1. Counties of Essex, Kent and Lambton.
2. Counties of Elgin, Norfolk and Oxford.
3. County of Middlesex.
4. Counties of Huron and Perth.
5. Counties of Waterloo and Wellington.
6. Counties of Bruce, Grey and Dufferin.
7. Counties of Wentworth, Halton and Peel.
8. Counties of Lincoln, Welland, Haldimand and Brant.
9. County of Simcoe, and the Districts of Muskoka, Parry Sound, Nipissing, Algoma, including Manitoulin, Thunder Bay and Rainy River.
10. That part of the city of Toronto lying east of Yonge Street.
11. That part of the city of Toronto lying west of Yonge Street.
12. Counties of Ontario, Victoria and York, exclusive of Toronto.
13. Counties of Northumberland, Peterborough, Durham and Haliburton.
14. Counties of Prince Edward, Hastings and Lennox.
15. Counties of Frontenac, Addington, Renfrew and Lanark.
16. Counties of Leeds, Grenville and Dundas.
17. Counties of Carleton, Russell, Prescott, Glengarry and Stormont.

The "Ontario Medical Act" is consolidated in the Medical Register of 1892, and it was proposed to amend the Act as follows :

Page 14, Section 7 : 1. After word "resignation" in the 11th line, " or voiding of the election."

2. After word "resignation" in 1st line, "or voiding of election."

Page 15, Section 10, to be repealed and the following substituted : "That in case of any doubt or dispute as to the legality of the election of any member of the Council, it shall be lawful for the Senior County Judge, in the territorial division where such doubt or dispute arises, to hold an enquiry and decide who is the legally elected member of the Council ; and the person whom he decides to have been, shall be, and be deemed to be, the legal member ; and if the election is found to have been illegal the Judge shall have power to order a new election.

Page 18, Section 17, Sub-section (3) : Omit all after word "Council" in 12th line.

Page 19, Section 22 : In 9th line after word "letter" add "and register same."

Page 21, Section 27 : Word "first" in the 6th line to read "last," and "December" to take place of "January" in 7th line.

Page 22, Section 29, to read after word "Diplomas" in the 7th line, and such others as may be necessary from "among," etc.

Page 27, Section 39 : Word "reasonable" to read "such reasonable."

Page 28, Section 41 (a) : After word "annually" in second line, to " on or before."

Page 28, Section 41 (a) Sub-section (3) : Add after last word, "paid as hereinafter provided."

Page 28 : After sub-section 6 a new sub-section is to appear as No. (7) as follows : "No assessment dues or fees shall be levied upon any member of the College residing out of the Province of Ontario. If the member so residing has given notice of his intention of leaving the province, or that he has left the province, the member's name shall not be erased while not practising therein."

Another sub-section is added, as follows :

No. (8) : "The Council shall have power to remit the annual fee or assessment to any member of the College, and shall have power when advisable to order the restoration of the name of any member of the College, which may have been erased for default in payment of fees."

———

Dr. ROSEBRUGH—Was it the Meacham Bill that was carried ? I understood the large committee met and the Government took it in hand and constructed a new bill, and that it was really not the Meacham Bill that passed.

Dr. WILLIAMS—It is really the framework of the Meacham Bill, but it was very materially modified in going through the Committee. I think you will find the name "Meacham" is still on the bill, as it received its third reading, so that it was not recognized as a new bill, though it was practically new in contents.

Dr. ROSEBRUGH—All of the Committee's recommendations were practically embodied in the bill.

Dr. WILLIAMS—Certainly, what the Committee consented to are embodied in the bill. I think there are only one or two minor points of alteration that the Committee had not consented to. There is one point, they wished to have no representatives from universities, on the ground they had no right to it, and were spending money ; a proposition was made by one of the members, and incorporated into this Act, that members who were representatives of colleges in that way would not vote on questions of taxation on the profession. That was put in as a compromise, because the Council, or members of the Council or Committee, objected to striking out university representatives. The other party wished them entirely struck out, and in order to get as near as they could to that, they decided those representatives should not vote on questions of taxation of the profession. Otherwise you will find the bill very much as we agreed to it. There is one change, and that is, the old rule was the term of office of the Council after an election should run for five years. The proposition of the Defence Association was it should be changed to three years, and a compromise was made at four years. It will be within the recollection of a good many members of this Council that the subject was brought up a few years ago, and the Council very nearly tied on the question of whether it should be reduced to three, or whether it should remain at five years ; so that the compromise will not be a very great hardship to the feelings of any member present.

Dr. MOORE—As I understand, the only difference between the college representatives and the territorial representatives under the present law is that the college representatives do not vote when fixing a tax upon the regular profession, but in every other respect they have full powers and full privileges, as I understand the Act.

Dr. LOGAN—I noticed a statement made by Dr. Orr here the other day, speaking in reference to the claim made by the Defence Association that they had rather more than half of the population of registered medical practitioners—that is something over 1,100 I think they claimed they had ; and he asserted that he had knowledge, where he got it I do not know, and it matters not, that in place of having 1,100, they had less than 400. I want to know from the Chairman if he was aware of that fact when they were going before the House, because it is a very important point ; if they knew that, it should have made a very great difference with the action of the Government.

Dr. WILLIAMS—I might say the Committee were not aware of that fact ; nor have they any evidence of it up to the present time. I went to see one of the medical men in the House who had exhibited to him by the Secretary of the Defence Association, the cards he received; and he had a very large pile of cards ; some of these were not as courteous to him as they might have been ; and I do not know whether in counting his 1,100 he counted all the cards he received or not. If he counted all the cards, it is possible they did reach to the 1,100, but just how he could stretch his imagination to consider that some of those were persons willing to belong to the Defence Association is hard to understand, for the language used towards him in some cases was rather strong.

Dr. ORR—With regard to Dr. Logan's question as to how I obtained the information that I gave to this Council the other day, I might state that that information was given from the knowledge I have obtained in connection with the *Ontario Medical Journal,* and from coming in contact with medical men, not only in this city, but in various parts of the Province, and from correspondence received from various gentlemen over the Province. Report adopted.

Dr. Thorburn moved, seconded by Dr. Rogers, that the report of the Committee on Finance be now read and referred to Committee of the Whole. Carried.

Council in Committee of the Whole. Dr. Miller in the chair. Report read.

Dr. ROGERS—This case of Dr. Edwards is certainly a very hard one. In the first place, he was out of Ontario almost ever since he first registered, and it is only within the last couple of years he came back. He was born in Ontario, got through here, and then went out of Ontario to Manitoba, and from there to the United States. When he came back, of course his dues had been charged against him all this time, and it seems rather a hardship that he should have to pay dues when he never got any advantage from membership in any way, and was not living in the Province.

Dr. BRAY—The statute has fixed all these things. I think that part of the report might be left out entirely. We cannot collect dues now until after the next election, according to the statute.

Dr. Bergin moved that the clause in question be expunged from the report.

Dr. WILLIAMS—There is a clause of a similar kind occurring a little earlier in the report. I would suggest that all similar clauses be left in abeyance.

Dr. DAY—Lest a false impression might go out—because I think it is a false impression—to the effect that we cannot collect any dues for two years, I wish to say that that impression is wrong. We cannot enforce the collection of dues by suspension, but we have, power to sue a man to collect dues. We must not let practitioners think we have no power for two years to collect dues. We have the common law remedy we always had, and we can sue any man if we find it necessary.

Dr. Bergin's motion, that the clause be expunged, was declared carried.

Dr. BRITTON—In reference to the recommendation regarding the *Ontario Medical Journal,* I wish to say that the motion is not carried unanimously. Personally, I have a great regard for the editor and manager of the *Ontario Medical Journal.* Last year I was one of the two who voted against entering into a contract with the *Journal.* I have still the same reasons that I had at that time, although, in many respects, approving of the style of work that has been done by the *Journal* during the past year. There are two strong reasons, to which I shall now refer, why I could not vote for a renewal of the contract. I think it no unimportant matter that already a complaint, or what has been construed as such, has come in from a professor in one of our colleges, that certain articles have appeared in the *Journal* which reflect very greatly upon his personal and professional standing. I do not want to enter into a discussion of the matter, for it will come up later on, but it is significant, for it leads up to this question, whether or not we could be held responsible, either legally or in a moral sense, for the utterances of the *Journal.* The relationship between the *Journal* and ourselves has been such that the profession at large will instinctively hold us responsible for its utterances. Had we complete and full control of its editorial columns, we would be in a very safe position, but it is far otherwise. As I said before, I cast no reflection upon my friend, the editor, in whom I have a great deal of confidence; but, at the same time, I would hesitate before accepting Dr. Orr's opinions in preference to the conclusions of this Council. Were he and the *Journal* infallible, and should some important question arise affecting the profession, it would be unnecessary to convene this Council, but quite sufficient to find out what Dr. Orr says, and leave the matter in his hands. During this next year we expect a very large number of affairs of vital importance to arise; there will be necessity, possibly, for a good deal to be said on behalf of this Council. Every sentiment expressed should be a true reflex of the Council's thought; and, as I said before, we have not that proper control that we should have over the editorials or the letters that may appear, and the paternity of which will fall on our shoulders. The other reason I would give is this : last year we received from the profession in the way of dues, I think, some two thousand odd dollars ; this year an association that professes such purity that mortal fingers dare not touch it lest its lily whiteness be contaminated, whispered into the

ears of legislators an *ex parte* story before there was an opportunity
for them to hear a fair and full discussion of medical matters in the
House, and secured from as many as possible a promise of support,
without satisfactory reasons to back it up, because one side of the
story only had been heard. More than one member of the Defence
Association boasted, in my hearing, that they would secure a guarantee from their representatives that they would support their contentions
before the Legislature. It would appear as though there was a certain amount of truth in the expressed intention, because I believe, as
a matter of fact, there were members of the Legislature who were
indisposed to vote against us, who had to acknowledge that the principles that we contended for were just and right, but who were bound
by pledges given in advance to support the other side of the question,
which the immaculate Defence Association had impressed upon them
as the cause of the down-trodden and oppressed. Last year we
received some two thousand odd dollars in the shape of dues ; through
the machinations of the Defence Association, we shall not receive
those dues this year.

Such a lessening of revenue means a more or less serious matter
when the College building already carries a heavy mortgage ; and in
the face of this I cannot see how we can wisely supply the profession
with a free journal, for by the enactment of the Legislature we shall
not receive a solitary cent in return. I have given what I think to be
strong grounds on which I decline to vote for a renewal of the contract ; at present I shall not longer delay the Council proceedings, but
may have something further to say later on.

Dr. ROGERS—Before the question is put, I wish to state one thing
only. I noticed a letter-head used by the *Ontario Medical Journal*
in which they have these words lithographed, " The Official Journal
of the Medical Profession of Ontario." I think these are the words.
I do not think that the *Ontario Medical Journal* is the official journal
of the medical profession of Ontario—of this Medical Council, at
least. I do not think they have ever been placed in that position, and
I wish simply to draw the attention of the Council to that, because,
while the *Journal* can make that statement to the profession at large
they will believe it is the official journal of this Council ; and it
may be a very serious matter in the future, especially in view of what
Dr. Britton has said in regard to the University of Toronto Therefore I trust that Dr. Orr will see the fairness of taking these words out
of his letter-heads. In the second place, I wish to state this, that the
Ontario Medical Journal is doing a good work ; and I believe it is a
journal that has been favourably received by the profession of medicine of Ontario ; and I think it would be a great mistake to withdraw
our arrangement with that journal for another year. They have done
good. We are giving them $600, and for that all our printing is done,

which before cost us nearly $600, and in addition every member of the profession is getting a copy practically from us for nothing. For that reason, although last year I opposed this, as you all know—though last year I sided with Dr. Britton—I thought then it would be a mistake—I am willing now to say in taking that stand I made a mistake ; and I would like to see the *Ontario Medical Journal* go on, for I think it is doing a good work.

Dr. MOORE—I am glad to know that Dr. Rogers has come to my way of thinking. I may say the objection he takes to the words in the letter-heading does not amount to very much, to my mind ; for this reason, the heading says it is "The Official Journal of the Medical Profession of Ontario"; it does not say it is the official journal of the Council of the College of Physicians and Surgeons of Ontario.

Dr. BERGIN—I would like to ask the Chairman of the Finance Committee to read to us the letters from the editors of the journals named —the *Lancet* and the *Practitioner*.

Dr. THORBURN—The proposition of the *Ontario Medical Journal* I have here. The proposition of the other journals was that they would be very happy to publish all the transactions of the Council, provided they were supplied with them. They do not make any other proposition.

Dr. Thorburn here reads communications from Dr. Adam Wright and Dr. Davison, and a communication and the proposition of the *Ontario Medical Journal* Publishing Company, as follows :

TORONTO, June 10th, 1893.

To the President and Members of the Council of the College of Physicians and Surgeons of Ontario :

GENTLEMEN,—We take the liberty of bringing to the notice of your honourable body the following considerations ·

1. *The Canada Lancet* and *The Canadian Practitioner* are two journals devoted to the promotion of medical science and of the medical profession in Ontario, the one being established twenty-five years, the other eighteen years.

2. That these two journals were established by private enterprise in times when the medical profession in Ontario was not so prosperous as it now is ; that very considerable capital has been expended in establishing them and putting them where they now are ; that they have loyally served the interests of the profession from their foundation until the present ; and that now they are reckoned the ablest journals of their kind published in Canada, and among the ablest published on the continent.

3. That from the beginning until the present they have favoured

every movement which they thought would be for the advantage of the profession, but that they have ever done this with due respect for the opinions of those who have thought differently from them ; that they have always held their columns open for the discussion of timely topics by medical men of every shade of opinion without let or favour; and that in this way they have been very instrumental in elevating the status of the profession and in promoting needful reform.

4. That they have together enjoyed the confidence of the best men of the profession in Canada ; that they have been the means of making known to the world the advancement in medical knowledge which the critical observers and original investigators in our profession have been successful in achieving ; that in this way they have been greatly instrumental in stimulating observation and research among the members of our profession generally ; and that they have thus been the means of gaining for the medical profession of Ontario and of Canada a respected reputation at home and an honoured name abroad.

5. That in their dealings with your honourable body, and with the College of Physicians and Surgeons generally, they have ever endeavoured to shew it that respect and consideration which so important an organization merits, but that they have done this in no servile way, either in hope of pecuniary gain or for fear of pecuniary loss ; that when they have approved your actions, they have done so because they have deemed them worthy of approval, and that when they have criticised them they have done so honestly, thinking them deserving of criticism.

But now when the Council of the College of Physicians and Surgeons have entered upon an agreement to grant a large sum of money as an annual bonus to a rival journal, we think it right to call your attention to what seems to us three substantial facts, viz. :

(1) That the granting of this bonus was unjust ;
(2) That it was unnecessary ;
(3) That it was unwise.

It was *unjust* from the fact that it gave to a new and untried journal, one that had neither service nor character to recommend it, a very substantial pecuniary aid, while the journals which we represent, with years of service and well-earned reputations behind them, were thus by your honourable body officially discountenanced and subjected to an unfair competition.

It was *unnecessary* from the fact that the only advantage which the Council was to gain from the agreement was the publication of your official proceedings ; which advantage to yourselves and to the profession generally, our respective journals have always been willing, and are now and always will be willing, to give, by the publication in their columns of these said proceedings as often and whenever your Council provides official reports of the same.

It was *unwise* from the fact that by the granting of this bonus you, unwittingly perhaps, but none the less surely, have aroused against you the criticism of those who, for other reasons, are opposed to the Council, and who, seeing the injustice and needlessness of this grant, will use the facts against you.

It was furthermore unwise from the fact that as the journal which you have bonused charges no subscription fee, its entire revenue beyond your bonus must come from advertisers ; and we need scarcely tell the members of your honourable body that no medical journal whose revenue so largely depends upon the goodwill of its advertisers can refrain from admitting to its columns statements and opinions which, written as they are in the interests of the advertisers, must be inconsistent with professional honour and dignity.

Furthermore, we would say that from the fact that the journal in question is distributed gratuitously among the members of the profession, it must necessarily be valued by them in a measure correspondingly cheap ; and that your honourable body cannot but be somewhat discredited when the alleged "official organ" of the Council is held in so little estimation that many of the members of the profession, looking at it as they do as a mere advertising sheet, and valuing it accordingly, do not even take the pains to take it from the post-office when it is sent to them.

And too, it cannot but be anomalous, and provocative of trouble and ill-feeling, when a journal which is represented and represents itself as your official organ, is managed and controlled by persons who are in no way responsible either to you or to the College whose officers you are, for it cannot but happen, as we believe it has already happened, that these irresponsible editors and publishers will from time to time use the columns of the journal which they control, but which your money supports, to advance opinions which are neither your opinions nor the opinions of the profession at large.

The only argument with a show of reason in it that we have ever heard made use of in support of the agreement against which we complain is this, that inasmuch as the British Medical Association and the American Medical Association have official journals, which are supplied gratuitously to all their members, therefore, the College of Physicians and Surgeons of Ontario ought to have a similar journal published in the interests of its members and supplied to them gratuitously. But we would call your attention to the radical difference between the present case and these alleged parallel cases. The College of Physicians and Surgeons of Ontario is a Provincial institution established by our Legislature, to which everyone lawfully Practising medicine in our province must necessarily belong. You are not the officers of a voluntary association but the trustees under the government of the rights and privileges of the profession at large. We submit, therefore, that you are not entitled to take money which belongs to the profession as a whole, and spend it in the interests of one portion of 'the profession and to the detriment of the interests of another portion. You may perhaps be *legally* entitled to spend this money in the way we complain of, since it may be put through your books as a matter of necessary expense for printing and advertising. But everyone knows that it is not a necessary expense; that it is an interference with private enterprise, and an infringement of the vested rights of members of the profession in good standing whom it is your duty to protect in their rights rather than to hurt, and that the grant of this money by you is considered and rejoiced in by those who receive it as a *good business scheme* by which they have to that extent got the better of their competitors. We submit that it is not consistent with the honour and dignity of your honourable body to countenance such a scheme, although to the parties benefiting by it, it is, no doubt, good business for you to do so.

And lastly, even supposing there are reasons which are not apparent to us, but which may still lead you to think of continuing to grant this bonus, we would ask you to consider whether it would be wise or proper for the Council of the College of Physicians and Surgeons of Ontario, the highest medical body of our country, and the one upon which the greatest responsibility lies to do everything that it can to promote the well-being and efficiency of the profession, we would ask you, we say, whether it would be wise or proper for you to do so much to discourage and interfere with independent medical journalism, as you assuredly are bound to do if you continue this bonus.

We, for the present, are prepared to leave the matter entirely in your hands, believing thoroughly that you will fully recognize the unwisdom of continuing the bonus, and, therefore, decide to do away with it.

We remain, Mr. President and gentlemen,

Your obedient servants,

JOHN L. DAVISON, Editor *Canada Lancet.*
ADAM H. WRIGHT, Editor *Canadian Practitioner.*

Gentlemen of the Medical Council :

The *Ontario Medical Journal* Publishing Co. submit the following report :

They have published the annual Announcement of the College, as required by the agreement . They have inserted all advertisements of the College, and have endeavoured, through the *Journal*, to deal with all matters pertaining to your Council in such a manner as to be in the best interest of the profession, and have furnished as good a journal as any published in Canada.

The amount of money paid out by the Company for printing, etc., done for your Council is as follows :

Publishing annual Announcement $397.00
Stenographers' fees............................ 84.00
Advertisements inserted for the College........... 30.00

Total.............................$511.00

Thus the members of this College have been supplied with a journal at the magnificent sum of less than $89 to this College. The Company expect, that in view of the great expense they have incurred, that the contract will be renewed, and in the interest of the stockholders, would request that it be renewed for two years.

All of which is respectfully submitted.

NEIL McCRIMMON,
Secy. Board of Directors.

Dr. BERGIN—We have now before us the proposition of the publisher of the *Ontario Medical Journal*, and the proposition of the gentlemen representing the two other publications. I quite agree with Dr. Britton in his remarks as to the liability of the College in the case of articles that might possibly expose us to prosecution ; and I shall allude to them further on. I confess that whilst we have reason to complain that the medical journals have not in the past published a full, or a fairly full, or half adequate report—

Dr. MOORE—Or any.

Dr., BERGIN—Beyond an occasional paragraph, perhaps, of the proceedings of this Council, and have therefore not done much to facilitate the knowledge of the profession generally of what goes on in this Council, yet they have, on occasions where there have been differences in the Council, taken what I believe to be the side of the progressive members of the Council ; and they have advocated all the changes towards the advancement of the education of the profession, both parliamentary and professionally ; they have done that, and they have done it well ; and I desire to bear my testimony to the manner in which they have defended the Council when attacked on these occasions. But, at the same time, I must admit, we owe a duty to ourselves and to the Council, which, under the circumstances, no matter how strong our desire might be to see these publications get a share of the publications of the Council, would compel us, in our own interests, not to accept any of the propositions made by them. They offer to us, provided we give to them a report of our proceedings, to publish them without any charge. But they go no further. They do not offer to provide the stenographer, or to pay for him ; they do not offer to provide the necessary number of announcements (they offer to furnish one for each member of the medical profession throughout Ontario, but the extra number we require for gentlemen outside of the country they make no proposition as to), and, therefore, their proposition is not such that we can, if we have any regard for economy or the welfare of the Council, accept. I now come to the statement made by Dr. Britton that he objects to our having any connection with the *Ontario Medical Journal,* because we might be made liable at some time for the opinions of that journal.

Dr. BRITTON —Excuse me, I did not mean legally liable. I meant we were held responsible in the eyes of the profession.

Dr. BERGIN—That is almost the same thing. I would suggest that we prevent the likelihood of any such occurrence, by making it a part of our contract with the *Ontario Medical Journal,* that all the correspondence and all editorials be submitted to the Chairman of the Printing Committee and approved of by him before publication ; and I think the gentleman who represents the *Ontario Medical Journal,* as manager, will cheerfully consent to that, for his own protection as well as for the protection of the Medical Council ; and I would suggest that any arrangement entered into should contain that proviso.

Dr. RUTTAN—Why should it not be announced in the *Ontario Medical Journal* that the Council would not hold themselves responsible for any opinion expressed ?

Dr. BERGIN—That would not prevent the public outside, or the profession generally, from holding us responsible.

Dr. WILLIAMS—According to the agreement we had with that company last year, we were held free from any responsibility in that direction. I do not agree with Dr. Bergin that it would be wise to assume the responsibility, and have a committee to look over these different articles that are entering the *Journal* at all. My own conviction is that we pay the *Journal* so much money for doing a certain class of work, and we take no responsibility outside of the work which we employed them to do. We employ them to publish our announcement, we employ them to put certain advertisements in their paper, and we employ them to send a copy of that paper to each registered practitioner in the Province. Outside of that we have no responsibility whatever, and I think we should, either to this report or some other report, add a clause so as to make the matter thoroughly clear that we are responsible only for what we contract and pay for, and that the opinions of the *Journal* we have nothing to do with whatever. (Hear, hear.)

Dr. BERGIN—I would like to ask Dr. Williams one question, with the permission of the chairman. We agree to send to every medical practitioner a copy of the *Journal*, and when we send the *Journal* to them, does it not come from this Council?

Dr. ROSEBRUGH—No. If you subsidize them to this extent, they agree to send it to these parties.

Dr. BERGIN—And by making that contract we endorse everything in the *Journal*.

Dr. WILLIAMS—I do not think so. I do not think we could be held either legally or morally responsible. Our contract is, we pay so much money for so much work. I do not think we in any way endorse the sentiments of the *Journal*. We pay them so much money, and in addition to the printing they do, we ask them to furnish the *Journal* to each member, so that he shall become acquainted with our announcement and advertisements, and so on, so that it shall go in the hands of every man. Part of our contract is, they shall publish in the *Journal* a stenographic report of the proceedings of this Council. What we want is that the *Journal* shall go into the hands of every practitioner, so that he can become acquainted with the transactions of this Council. Outside of that, we do not assume any responsibility for the *Journal* in any shape or form.

Dr. BERGIN—You are held responsible all the same.

Dr. BRITTON—Whether we admit any responsibility or not, and whether or not it involves us in any legal responsibility, the fact that the *Journal* is subsidized by us to the extent of $600, and, according to our instructions, sent to the members of the profession—

Dr. WILLIAMS—It is paid for the work.

Dr. BRITTON—Certainly, it is paid for the work that is being done by it, but we must bear this fact in mind, and it is the most important one of all, that still in the eyes of the profession, and in the eyes of the different universities in the country, we are virtually held responsible for the utterances of the *Journal*. I am not speaking on theoretical grounds, but from what has already occurred. It is probably known to most of the members of the Council that in the early days of the *Journal* there was a certain amount of difference of opinion existing in the Senate of my own university—the University of Toronto—and in one number of the *Journal* one side was taken up, and taken up very vigorously. I asked that an explanation or apology be made, or that the statement that had already been made be withdrawn. The reply was given me, " In our next number we will make that all right." Sure enough, in the next number an apology was made for the personal references which had appeared in the first number, personal references directed to the members of the Senate of the University of Toronto. But then, to make the matter

6*

worse, they, after making the apology, went on to plead justification for having said what had formerly appeared—justification for an offence—and, in pleading justification, the old matter was reiterated and made three times worse. I do not think that will ever occur again, but because something else may occur for which, in the eyes of others, we will be held responsible, I do not see how we can maintain a close connection with a journal over which we have not direct control; and if the Council is determined to enter into another agreement with the *Journal*, I certainly would prefer that we have some committee or some person appointed—we have a committee—to whom these matters of correspondence would be submitted before appearing.

Dr. Rogers moved that a clause be added to the contract with the *Ontario Medical Journal* Company, which will state that this Council does not hold itself in any way responsible for editorial or other statements printed in the said journal.

Dr. BERGIN—That is like the railways saying they are not responsible for loss, damage or anything of the kind, but still they are.

Dr. BRITTON—That would only save us legally; it does not save us in the eyes of the profession and public.

Dr. THORBURN—There is further correspondence that I have not yet read, namely, a communication from Drs. Davison and Wright, giving their reasons why they object to the contract being renewed.

Dr. Britton asks for the correspondence.

Dr. DAY—I have served men with legal documents to appear here at two o'clock, and if you sit here till half-past one o'clock we cannot get back by two.

Dr. Harris moved, seconded by Dr. Ruttan, that the Committee rise and report progress, and ask leave to sit again. Carried.

Committee rose, reported progress, and asked leave to sit again. Leave granted.

Moved by Dr. Harris, that the Council adjourn, to meet again at two o'clock p.m.

AFTERNOON SESSION.

FRIDAY, 16*th June*, 1893.

The Medical Council met at two o'clock p.m., in accordance with motion of adjournment, the President in the chair.

The Registrar called the roll. All the members were present excepting Sir James Grant. Dr. S. E. McCully and Dr. William Anderson were present, in accordance with notice served upon them.

Dr. Day moved, seconded by Dr. Geikie, that the rules of this Council be now suspended, and that this Council do now go into Committee of the Whole to take into consideration the report of the Committee on Discipline. Carried.

Council in Committee of the Whole. Dr. Henry in the chair.

Dr. Day read the general report of the Discipline Committee clause by clause.

On motion, there being no objection, the report was adopted.

Dr. Day then read, clause by clause, the report specially dealing with Dr. S. E. McCully, and on motion, there being no objection, the report was adopted.

Dr. Day then read, clause by clause, the report of the Committee specially dealing with Dr. William Anderson, and on motion, there being no objection, the report was adopted.

Dr. Day moved, seconded by Dr. Rogers, that the Committee rise and report. Carried.

The Committee rose. President in the chair.

Dr. Anderson retired.

Dr. Day moved, seconded by Dr. Rosebrugh, that the report of the Committee of the Whole on the report of the Discipline Committee be adopted as follows. Carried.

DISCIPLINE COMMITTEE REPORT.

To the Council of the College of Physicians and Surgeons of Ontario :

Your Committee on Discipline beg to report that during the year they have had before them the case of William Anderson, and have held an investigation thereon, particulars of which are appended to the end of this report, together with the findings of your Committee thereon. There is also appended a copy of the evidence submitted and proceedings taken before your Committee.

Your Committee also report that the case of Samuel Edward McCully has occupied their attention ; and that (as in the case above referred to) a full account of the proceedings is hereto appended.

Your Committee also wish to call the attention of the Council most particularly to the efficient and effective services of Mr. Wasson in the above cases, and cannot too strongly commend him for his actions therein.

As to Mr. Wasson's request for a moderate sum of money to be placed from time to time at his disposal, your Committee beg to refer the matter to the consideration of your Committee on Finance.

Your Committee has also had referred to them by this Council several cases for investigation, upon which they have met and deliberated, and to which they will give their earliest attention, and will report upon the same to your honourable body.

All of which is respectfully submitted.

HENRY W. DAY, *Chairman.*

To the Council of the College of Physicians and Surgeons of Ontario:

Your Committee appointed to inquire into the facts, beg leave to report as follows :

Re William Anderson. For erasure from the register as a member and registered practitioner of the College of Physicians and Surgeons of Ontario.

Your Committee duly met after notice of the charges in the subject matter of the inquiry to be conducted had been given to the said William Anderson, who did not appear, either personally or by counsel, on Thursday, the 8th of December, 1892, and Friday, the 9th of December, 1892, when witnesses were examined in support of the petition, and when the letter hereto annexed, dated December 6th, 1892, from the said William Anderson to your Committee was read ; and after hearing the evidence, which herewith accompanies this report, your Committee arrived at the following conclusions :

1. That the said William Anderson has been guilty of infamous or disgraceful conduct in a professional respect, the particulars of which are as follows : By joining in a fraudulent conspiracy with one John Murray (alias H. Hales) to deceive the public in the Province of Ontario, and particularly all persons suffering from any disease or ailment, into the belief that an opportunity would be offered them to receive treatment for three months free of charge, by a staff of eminent physicians and surgeons, who were represented and alleged to be travelling from place to place in the Province of Ontario, whereas in fact no such persons were connected in any way with the said Anderson or Murray (alias Hales), nor did any registered practitioner for the Province of Ontario appear at any place named in any advertisement published by the said Anderson or Murray (alias Hales), except the said Anderson himself, and all persons calling at the places named in such advertisements were examined by the said Anderson or Murray (alias Hales), and were not treated without charge as represented in said advertisements, but were asked for and compelled to pay large sums of money for treatment.

2. That the said William Anderson has been guilty of infamous or disgraceful conduct in a professional respect, the particulars of which are as follows, that is to say : By joining with the said Murray (alias Hales), and by causing to be inserted in daily newspapers in the cities

of Ottawa, London, Hamilton and Toronto, and other places in the Province of Ontario, the advertisements, copies of which are hereunto attached and marked "A" and "B" respectively, and other advertisements to the same effect, containing similar statements, and naming various places at which the alleged staff of eminent physicians and surgeons could be consulted, and such advertisements have been frequently and continually inserted in said newspapers at various times from the month of November, 1891, up to the present time; whereas the persons intended by the said advertisements were not as described therein, but were only the said Anderson and Hales.

3. That the said William Anderson has been guilty of infamous or disgraceful conduct in a professional respect, the particulars of which are as follows, that is to say : By allowing his name to be used as a registered practitioner for the Province of Ontario to shield the said Murray (alias Hales) in carrying out a fraudulent scheme to evade the provisions of the Ontario Medical Act.

4. That the said William Anderson has been guilty of infamous or disgraceful conduct in a professional respect the particulars of which are as follows, that is to say : By representing to various patients who came to consult the alleged staff of physicians, that he, the said Anderson, was a member of said staff, and by representing and alleging that he could cure the diseases of such patients, and by guaranteeing to cure the same, whether he knew the same were incurable or not, and by taking money for such treatment after having made the representations aforesaid, and by issuing to patients coming for treatment aforesaid, certain checks, copies of which checks are hereunto attached and marked as exhibit " C."

5. That the said William Anderson has been guilty of infamous or disgraceful conduct in a professional respect, the particulars of which are as follows, that is to say : By alleging and by stating upon oath at the Police Court in the city of Toronto that he, the said Anderson, personally examined all patients applying for treatment to the said alleged staff of physicians and surgeons in the said city in order to save him, the said Murray (alias Hales) from conviction under the Ontario Medical Act, which said statements were false to the knowledge of the said Anderson.

6. As to charge No. 6, which alleges that "The said William Anderson has been guilty of infamous or disgraceful conduct in a professional respect, the particulars of which are as follows, that is to say : By representing to various persons, to wit, Mrs. Philip, Mr. Hopewood, Daniel Thomas, Mrs. Knight, Mrs. Wilkinson, John Train, Mr. and Mrs. Forgie, and Miss Hancock, that he was a member of the staff of eminent physicians and surgeons aforesaid, by guaranteeing to cure their ailments and accepting money therefor, and by obtaining from one Langman, a farmer in the county of Simcoe,

the sum of $200 upon a guarantee that he would cure him of his disease, which, as the said Anderson well knew, was incurable, and at the same time making the same Langman the various representations contained in the said advertisements as hereinbefore set forth," your Committee find on the evidence submitted as to the said Daniel Thomas that the portion of the charge relating to Daniel Thomas is proven ; and that as to the said Langman (as to whose case evidence was submitted), Mrs. Philip, Mr. Hopewood, Mrs. Knight, Mrs. Wilkinson, John Train, Mr. and Mrs. Forgie, and Miss Hancock (as to whose case evidence was submitted) that the charge is not proven.

7. That the said William Anderson has been guilty of infamous or disgraceful conduct in a professional respect, the particulars of which are as follows, that is to say : That the said William Anderson has not for a long time been engaged in the legitimate practice of his profession but has made his living by allowing his name to be used by unscrupulous and dishonest persons, and as a protection to them against the penalties provided by the Ontario Medical Act, and in order to allow such persons to practise medicine within the Province of Ontario contrary to the said Act, and to deceive and to defraud persons suffering from various ailments into paying money for treatment by ignorant and dishonest men.

Signed on behalf of the above Committee.

HENRY W. DAY, *Chairman of Committee.*

———

To the Council of the College of Physicians and Surgeons of Ontario :

Your Committee appointed to inquire into the facts beg leave to report as follows :

Re Dr. Samuel Edward McCully. For erasure from the register as a member and registered practitioner of the College of Physicians and Surgeons of Ontario.

Your Committee duly met after notice of the charges in the subject matter of the inquiry to be conducted had been given to the said Samuel Edward McCully, who appeared personally and by counsel on Friday, the 9th December, A.D. 1892, and Saturday, the 10th December, 1892, when witnesses were examined in support of the petition ; and at the conclusion of the case in support of the petition, Mr. Cassels, representing the said Samuel Edward McCully made the submission which was signed by the said Samuel Edward McCully, and which the Committee beg to report herewith, and which is hereto annexed and marked as Exhibit " I."

As to the facts so far as the petition is concerned, after hearing the evidence which herewith accompanies this report, your Committee arrived at the following conclusions :

1. That the said Samuel Edward McCully has been guilty of infamous or disgraceful conduct in a professional respect, the particulars of which are as follows, that is to say :

By causing to be printed and advertised in the newspapers published in the City of Toronto in the County of York, and generally in the public press of the Province of Ontario, and particularly in the Toronto *World* of the issue of March 26th, 1892, an advertisement of which a copy is herewith attached and marked Exhibit "A."

2. That the said Samuel Edward McCully has been guilty of infamous or disgraceful conduct in a professional respect, the particulars of which are as follows, that is it say :

By causing to be printed and advertised in the newspapers of the City of Toronto, and generally in the public press in the Province of Ontario, and particularly in the Toronto *Evening News* of the issue of March 26th, 1892, an advertisement of which a copy is hereto attached and marked Exhibit " B."

3. That the said Samuel Edward McCully has been guilty of infamous or disgraceful conduct in a professional respect, the particulars of which are as follows, that is to say :

By causing to be printed and advertised in the newspapers published in the said City of Toronto and generally in the public press of the Province of Ontario, an advertisement of which a copy is hereto attached and marked Exhibit " C."

4. That the said Samuel Edward McCully has been guilty of infamous or disgraceful conduct in a professional respect, the particulars of which are as follows, that is to say :

By causing to be printed the said advertisements marked " A," "B" and " C " respectively, or one or more of them or other similar advertisements in the public press of the Province of Ontario, and particularly in the *Evening Telegram* in the issue of December 7th, 1887, April 21st, 1888, May 5th, 1888, May 12th, 1888, and June 2nd, 1888.

5. That the said Samuel Edward McCully has been guilty of infamous or disgraceful conduct in a professional respect, the particulars of which are as follows, that is to say :

By advertising in the public press of the City of Toronto and Province of Ontario, the advertisements hereinbefore referred to, and other similar advertisements containing scandalous and defamatory statements regarding the medical profession and the various institutes connected therewith in the City of Toronto and Province of Ontario.

6. That the said Samuel Edward McCully has been guilty of infamous or disgraceful conduct in a professional respect, the particulars of which are as follows, that is to say :

By advertising in the public press from time to time, details of his professional practice, the names of his patients and the particulars of their diseases and statements regarding alleged cures by treatment.

7. That the said Samuel Edward McCully has been guilty of infamous or disgraceful conduct in a professional respect, the particulars of which are as follows, that is to say :

By advertising in the public press from time to time, in a glaring and conspicuous manner the symptoms; details and descriptions of the various diseases he professed to treat, thereby deluding and defrauding the public.

8. That the said Samuel Edward McCully has been guilty of infamous or disgraceful conduct in a professional respect, the particulars of which are as follows, that is to say :

By advertising in the public press from time to time, representing that he, the said McCully, was, and is better qualified for the practice of the medical profession than other registered practitioners, and that he had cured patients whom other registered practitioners had failed to cure.

9. That the said Samuel Edward McCully has been guilty of infamous or disgraceful conduct in a professional respect, the particulars of which are as follows, that is to say :

By instructing certain assistants employed by him, to wit, Dr. J. C. Burt, Dr. T. H. Brent and others, to make patients believe that they were curable, whether the ailments from which they were suffering were in fact curable or not, and if necessary to guarantee to cure and continue treatment of the patient whether curable or incurable, and by giving such assistants general instructions to deceive and defraud patients who might apply for treatment.

10. As to charge No. 10, which alleged that the said Samuel Edward McCully has been guilty of infamous or disgraceful conduct in a professional respect, the particulars of which are as follows, that is to say :

By undertaking and guaranteeing to cure a certain woman living in the City of London, suffering from tumour in the lower part of the abdomen, although incurable, and when she afterwards died in the house of the said McCully by refusing to give up her body to her husband until paid an amount of money, your Committee find that on the evidence submitted as to this charge the same is not proven.

11. That the said Samuel Edward McCully has been guilty of infamous or disgraceful conduct in a professional respect, the particulars of which are as follows, that is to say :

By representing to a man living in the neighbourhood of Whitby or Oshawa, suffering from paralysis or locomotor ataxia or nervous affection, that his disease was curable, and that he would cure him for a certain sum of money, although the said McCully well knew that such patient was absolutely incurable, and represented and guaranteed to the said patient that he could effect a cure simply in order to obtain money for treating the said patient.

12. That the said Samuel Edward McCully has been guilty of infamous or disgraceful conduct in a professional respect, the particulars of which are as follows, that is to say :

By representing and guaranteeing that he could cure one Mrs. White, who was suffering from a warty cancer, which the said McCully knew well to be incurable, and by treating the said Mrs. White for such ailment, and taking money therefor upon the said representation and guarantee, and afterwards by representing to the said patient that she was cured ; and by obtaining a photograph of the said Mrs. White and publishing the same and advertising in the Toronto *Evening News* in the issue published in the latter part of May, 1889, that the said Mrs. White had in fact been cured by him, whereas the said McCully well knew that the said Mrs. White was absolutely incurable, and had not in fact been cured by him.

13. As to charge No. 13, that the said Samuel Edward McCully has been guilty of infamous or disgraceful conduct in a professional respect, the particulars of which are as follows, that is to say :

By representing and guaranteeing that he could cure one Sarah Rachford, and by advertising that she had in fact been so cured by him and by accepting money in consideration of such cure as above alleged in paragraph six of this petition, whereas the said McCully well knew that the said Sarah Rachford was suffering from an incurable disease and had not in fact been so cured by him, your Committee report that evidence was not submitted in support of these charges, and therefore find the same not proven.

14. As to charge No. 14 which alleges that the said Samuel Edward McCully has been guilty of infamous or disgraceful conduct in a professional respect, the particulars of which are as follows, that is to say :

By representing and guaranteeing that he could cure one Thomas Percy, of the City of Toronto, and by accepting money from the said Percy in consideration of such cure, and by advertising that said Percy had, in fact, been cured by him, whereas the said McCully well knew that the said Percy was suffering from an incurable disease and was not in fact cured or benefited by the treatment of the said McCully, your Committee report that evidence was not submitted in support of these charges, and therefore find the same not proven.

15. That the said Samuel Edward McCully has been guilty of infamous or disgraceful conduct in a professional respect, the particulars of which are as follows, that is to say :

By representing and guaranteeing to cure one George Tuston, and by receiving the sum of $18 in consideration of such cure, whereas, in fact, the said George Tuston was suffering from an incurable disease and was not cured by the treatment of the said McCully.

16. That the said Samuel Edward McCully has been guilty of in-

famous or disgraceful conduct in a professional respect, the particulars of which are as follows, that is to say :

By practising his profession continually in a disgraceful manner, by guaranteeing to cure patients suffering from incurable ailments and by endeavouring to obtain weekly or monthly payments from them in consideration of treatment, and generally by fraud and deceit endeavouring to obtain money from persons suffering from various diseases regardless of his ability to relieve the same.

Signed in behalf of the above Committee,

HENRY W. DAY, *Chairman of Committee.*

Dr. Day moved, seconded by Dr. Rosebrugh, that Dr. S. E. McCully be now called upon to show cause why the Council should not proceed to deal with his case.   Carried.

The President then called upon Dr. S. E. McCully to show cause why the Council should not proceed to deal with his case.

Dr. S. E. McCULLY—Mr. President and Gentlemen, I have very little to say in this matter.   A part of the charges that are made against me were made before this Act had any existence, and part of the charges, of course, have not been proven, as you have heard. (He here refers to the report of the Committee).   After the case for the Council was closed, I was advised by my counsel to submit, and sign a paper, which is in the possession of this Council; and I believe there was an understanding if I ceased advertising altogether, and did business in the usual way that other medical men are doing, that the Committee would make a favourable report, and that the Council should allow me to continue practising in Ontario.   All I have to say is that after signing that paper not to advertise, I have endeavoured legitimately to live up to my promise, and have continued to do so, and have no intention of failing my promise.   I am not going into the legal aspect of the case.   My counsel advises me that the Committee are all-powerful in the case, and that they can pursue whatever course they like, either to take my name off the roll, or continue it on.   Of course, I am a man raising a family in Toronto, and I have to practise medicine to earn bread and butter, and keep my children comfortable ; under these circumstances it would be a little bit hard on me to take my name off the roll, but of course I must leave the matter with you ; you are the parties who must decide the matter ; I must leave it in your hands, and if you make a favourable decision in the matter, I shall be very much obliged to you, while if you decide the other way, I must submit, I can say no more.

Dr. DAY—I would suggest that the Council see the exhibits privately.

The President asks Dr. McCully to retire from the room while the Council is considering his case. Doctors McCully and Anderson both retire.

On the request of Dr. Day, the stenographer read Exhibit 1 to the Discipline Committee's report :

EXHIBIT 1 TO DISCIPLINE COMMITTEE'S REPORT.

" Mr. Cassels, for the defence, submits an admission and under-taking on behalf of his client, Dr. McCully, which is here copied in the minutes as follows :

" Dr. McCully, being called on for his defence, submits the follow-ing statement and undertaking to the Committee, and asked the Com-mittee to report the same to the Council when reporting hereon :

" ' I admit that the advertisements complained of herein, and any others of the like effect or nature, are unprofessional, and the publi-cation thereof by me constitutes infamous and disgraceful conduct in a professional respect within the meaning of the Ontario Medical Act.

" ' I submit myself to the action of the Council in the premises, and admit that I am liable, on the evidence, to have my name erased from the Medical Register.

" ' I undertake and agree not further to offend in the premises, and ask the Council to suspend action on the report of the Committee so long as I in good faith comply with the above undertaking.

" ' It is agreed that the charges, other than those which charge the advertisements to be a breach of the Act are to be considered as un-disposed of and untried.

" (Signed)   S. E. McCULLY,
" 12th December, 1892.   " (Signed)   WALTER CASSELS."

Dr. Bergin suggests that Dr. Day, who/has inquired into this matter, and who has made himself master of the matter, should give this Council his view as to what the Council should do in connection with this case.

Dr. DAY—I may say that after we had held our investigation, in consultation with Mr. Osler, his opinion was that after the complete submission which had been made that the Council would be in a better position by accepting that apology or submission, and putting Dr. McCully on his good behaviour ; first, for the reason that it would show the public and the law authorities that we were not inclined to act harshly or vindictively against any man. In fact, he said to me that the action we took in Dr. Washington's case, in suspending him on his good behaviour, had a very great deal to do with the decision of the judges in sustaining our final action ; and he thought we would be placed in a much better and a much stronger position by taking that course than we would by promptly, and no doubt properly, striking Dr. McCully's name from the roll. I have also had conversation with many of the medical men in Toronto—Dr. O'Reilly particularly, although I beg his pardon for mentioning his name, as he asked me not to. He said he thought the Council would be in a better position, and it would be better that the Council should leave him in abeyance; that he has not been since his submission (Exhibit 1 to report) conducting himself in an improper manner, and he thinks he is honestly endeavouring to live up to what he has there promised to do. This is the intimation I have had upon the subject; and I must say I quite agree myself with that opinion. And if afterwards we had to erase his name, and went to the courts, I think it would strengthen our case very much with the courts; that in fact it would make us impregnable in the courts.

Dr. THORBURN—How does this case come up, if he has not been misbehaving?

Dr. DAY—This is simply the report of the Committee. The Committee has no power to do anything further than investigate and report to the Council.

Dr. BRAY—The Committee's functions are merely to take the evidence as to the guilt or innocence of those parties, and make a report to this Council. There has been no opportunity to make a report since we held the investigation, and we now make this report; and according to the law, Dr. McCully had to be notified to appear here to show cause why the Council should not take action on the Committee's report. As to the other part of it, I quite agree with what Dr. Day has said, as a member of that committee. It was all discussed thoroughly with the solicitor; we followed his instructions to the letter in the matter, and he said, as in the case of Washington, he thought it would be better, it would give a better impression, and it would strengthen us to accept Dr. McCully's admissions and submission, and it would keep him, as it were, under suspended sentence. So long as he behaved himself, all right enough; if he did not, then we would be so much the stronger before the courts. That is my view of the case, and that is the way I would be pleased to see the matter disposed of.

Dr. HENRY—What guarantee does he give?

Dr. BERGIN—The guarantee that he will be struck off if he does not behave himself.

Dr. BRAY—We could not accept a guarantee. He admits in his letter that he might be struck of for his breach of the Act; and this does not take the case out of the Council—out of Court as it were—on the evidence submitted without taking further evidence; if he does not live up to his admission and submission, you have the power to strike him off the register at any time you see fit. To suspend sentence does not take any power away from this Council at all; it only gives him a chance to live up to what he professes and promises; and it strengthens this Council before the courts; and more than that it will show the profession and public that this Council is not a vindictive body, but that they want to do what is right between man and man; and so long as a man is willing to act honestly the Council is willing to accept his word; but the very moment he abuses the privileges this Council has granted him, then the Council has power to erase his name from the register.

Dr. MOORE—While not wishing to appear vindictive or show a spirit or desire to persecute anybody, we must remember that this man was an offender and a gross offender. We did the very same thing for Dr. Washington that is now proposed to be done for this man; and he kept his promise up to the time the Council held its session, or thereabouts, and then he broke loose and we could not afford to call a special meeting to deal with this man, and he went on until we did strike his name off; then he appealed his case, and the consequence was he practised until a short time ago—he is practising still. The courts disposed of him in a sense, but he has appealed, and I believe he is practising still; and if this man sees fit after to-morrow to begin his nefarious business again he can do so, and go on perhaps for two or three years. It is worth while considering whether we should do this, and whether it would be popular with the profession, for if there is one thing the profession give us credit for, and that they ought to give us credit for, it is that of putting down those offenders, and while it may look well and be charitable to put them down slowly and stealthily and with a hand well tempered with mercy, yet sometimes we may exceed the bounds of good sense and good judgment. So I think it is worth while for this Council to carefully consider whether it would not be better now to make an example of this man and strike his name off.

Dr. RUTTAN—You cannot punish a man, whether he is criminal or not, until he has perpetrated a crime, but Dr. McCully has been proved to have perpetrated a crime. We have found out that he is capable of doing what he has done. Many a man living his life through the world may be a thief, but we never can find out till he steals. When Dr. McCully does this, then we know what he is capable of doing, and his repentance here is simply the repentance of a fox with his foot in a trap; let him out, and he is a fox again—the same "two-and-six-pence." You may try that experiment as often as you like, and it will be the same thing. Take a man capable of stealing, and if he is let off quietly without a punishment, the public are exposed to his going on and practising the same thing afterwards.

You may put him in the penitentiary, and keep him there for a year or two, and when he comes out he is as bad as ever. That is my experience and observation in these matters. I do not think we are justified in letting him off now. The better way is for this Council to act promptly and decisively, so that there will be no equivocation about it. The next one will come around and say, "If I am hauled up before the Council I will make an apology to them, and then practise as much as I like afterwards. Even if erased from the register, he will go on and practise just as others have done who have been already erased from the register.

Dr. GEIKIE—I have listened with a great deal of interest to the report of the Committee, and to what has been said with regard to this case. I noticed at the time the Committee was sitting, or shortly afterwards, how very ably the thing had been conducted, and I think all credit is due to that Committee for the way in which the enquiry was conducted. The evidence was carefully brought forward, and the criminal, you may say, convicted so clearly that he promptly made his acknowledgment and submission. I agree, and I hold very strongly with the position Dr. Day takes, that Dr. McCully having stated distinctly that he had done what was not right, but that he would not do it again, pledged himself—that is the position he occupies now—and it is not for us to say what we think as to whether he will or will not keep his pledge. And in view of the result of the last case, I think, with Dr. Day, that our position as a Council would be quite impregnable before the courts in the event of our having to take action, should Dr. McCully break his engagement; and I think the plan of just holding him in the position of being under suspended sentence, as it were, on his good behaviour, just as Dr. Day expresses it, is the wisest one for this Council—

Dr. BERGIN—Hear, hear.

Dr. GEIKIE—And in the best interests of the profession. I am quite sure of that.

Dr. JOHNSON—It seems to me we should remember this is one of the first cases of this kind, cases where we have the power to take away the license of a practitioner. I cannot think that Dr. Ruttan exactly represents the case when he speaks of a fox being caught in a trap, and of Dr. McCully's repentance being of that kind. The trap is still upon the leg of the fox if we keep him in the position that he is in now; and that is a safe position; it is safe to the Council and safe to the profession at large. And I know, practising here in the same city where Dr. McCully has brought about all this trouble, and where every medical man in the place has suffered—we have all suffered keenly and severely from the advertisements he has from time to time published. They have been most rascally in every way, and they have brought down a shower of indignation upon me personally, because a member of the Council, and as the representative of this division I did not do more, and do it earlier, to take means by which he should be removed. At the same time, now that he is in a safe position, I do not think the Council has time or opportunity, or that it would be politic at present to do more. The Council has sufficient in its hands without going any further and being aggressive in this matter.

. Dr. ROSEBRUGH—Will your constituents be satisfied with this action?

Dr. JOHNSON—I think they will be satisfied if Dr. McCully is kept in his proper place. I do not think any man in this constituency, however keenly he may feel, however he may know the injustices that have existed through what Dr. McCully has said and done, I do not think any of those men would feel that they wished to remove from Dr. McCully that which he once held, and held honourably. He will always be under a cloud. We know he can never take the position in the profession he once held at one time ; at the same time I do not think that they wish to take away his license completely, and to refuse him the opportunity to make his living in this country, but they do feel that they have been slandered by him and that he should be quieted. And since he has been quieted I have had no complaints brought to me from any of my constituents.

Dr. FULTON—I would like to ask in case Dr. McCully breaks his pledges, would another examination of witnesses have to be gone through?

Dr. BRAY—No.

Dr. MOORE—You would have to call a meeting of the Council and go to that expense.

Dr. ORR—I quite endorse the remarks just made by the member for the Midland and York Division. I think it would be very unwise for us, at the present time, to deal with Dr. McCully's case too harshly. I think by placing him under suspended sentence at the present time we would be serving the interests of this Council and the interests of the profession in the city of Toronto, and the neighbourhood of the city of Toronto, in the best manner. We should remember at the time we secured the legislation that we are acting under at the present time, and I happened that time to be a member of the Legislative Committee, the course Dr. McCully pursued in the House when we appeared before the Attorney-General. He appeared there and spoke ; he will, without doubt, make use of that in case of our, at the present time, striking his name off the register. Dr. Moore objects upon the ground that if his name is erased from the register now he will have to discontinue practice ; such, I think, is not the case ; if his name is erased at the present time he will appeal to the Court, and will keep his case in the courts quite as long as Dr. Washington has done ; and, under the law, he may continue to practise for a long time. I think the interests of the medical men of the city of Toronto and of the profession will be best served by letting Dr. McCully remain for a time under suspended sentence ; and I think under the severe castigation he has received, and after his apology, he will live up to the promise he has made.

Dr. HENRY—I have no sympathy with offenders of this kind. We have had experience with Dr. Washington, who has put this Council to a great deal of expense totaling up to nearly $1,200 ; he has appealed, putting them to more expense ; and I believe to-day he is practising as usual. Then what guarantee have you got that this gentleman who has perpetrated the faults, which he himself admits, will not do the same again. He is an old offender, and I can remember the time a few years ago when medical gentlemen of the city of Toronto were horrified, disgusted and shocked with the writings and talk of this man. I have no sympathy with him—I think it is misplaced, and I think you should deal harshly with that man.

Dr. PHILIP—I would just say there is one point we ought to pay special regard to, and that is the recommendation of our solicitor, Mr. Osler, who knows how he wishes us to stand when we go before the Court. It is all very well for us to say, suspend, and this and that, but I think we ought most certainly to take the advice of our solicitor. I have been impressed with the words of Dr. Johnson, who has lived here, and who knows a great deal more about this matter than those who have not been here, and who knows about Dr. McCully's actions and all ; and I am quite satisfied when Dr. Johnson and the men in authority are willing to let Dr. McCully go under suspended sentence. If he offends again, let justice, although slow, be sure and far-reaching.

Dr. BRITTON—Dr. McCully has been a sinner above all sinners in the profession. He has been a disgrace, and a standing disgrace, in the city of Toronto. So far as I am concerned, he does not deserve one particle of sympathy from us ; and therefore it is for us to deal with him, not according as is best for him and his family, much as we may pity them, but according as is best for ourselves, and therefore I think the best plan for us to follow is to take the advice of the solicitor.

Dr. ROGERS—The solicitor does not advise us to erase Dr. Mc-Cully's name.

Dr. BRITTON—No. His advice, as I understand from the Chairman of the Committee, is to hold the matter in suspense.

Dr. THORBURN—Although he is a sinner of sinners, I maintain the decision of the Council is one of the most severe that can be inflicted. Who is there among us that would not rather know the result of a decision than to have a deferred decision, a suspension. He is then living with a sword hanging over his head; and that very fear or apprehension will be far worse—will be stronger far to control him than if he knew he was convicted or erased from the list of physicians.   I think the advice of our solicitor should be followed in this case, not from any sympathy, but I think he will feel it far worse than he would if his name were erased.

Cries of " Question," " Question."

Dr. BERGIN—The name of Dr. McCully for years past has been really a stench in the nostrils of the profession all over Ontario, and I rejoiced, as all other members of the College of Physicians and Surgeons did rejoice, when I found that the Discipline Committee of this Council had so thoroughly exposed and so unequivocally convicted him of infamous conduct.   And now when I see that man, in the decline of his life, coming before this Council, and admitting that he has been guilty of infamous conduct, and promising the Council, and the world at large, you may say, that he will no longer be guilty of these practices, that he will indulge in them no more, that he will endeavour to practise his profession as an honourable man ; and keeping in mind the case of Dr. Washington, and what this man might do if we passed a resolution to-day to strike him from the roll of the College, I think we can do no better than to treat him with some sort of merciful consideration ; and I think we should take the advice that our solicitor has given us, take the advice that the Chairman of the Discipline Committee has given to us, remembering always that justice should be tempered with mercy.   And when men who, like the representative of this division, and Dr. Britton, can forget all that has passed, and recommend to this Council to keep him under suspended sentence, with the sword of Damocles over his head, I think we have the best possible guarantee that this man will endeavour in the future to conduct himself as a member of this honourable profession should, but if he does not, the punishment will fall, not only upon him, but upon those who ought to be dearer to him than his life—his wife and his children.   And I think we ought to remember when we are inflicting punishment upon an offender, that the punishment does not fall upon him alone, and if we can possibly avoid it, we should not punish the innocent with the guilty.

Moved by Dr. Day, seconded by Dr. Rosebrugh,

Whereas, the Committee on Discipline reported to the Council in the case of Dr. Samuel Edward McCully as appears in the report of the proceedings of the Discipline Committee as the report in the case on file in possession of the Registrar ;

And whereas, the said Dr. Samuel Edward McCully has been called

7*

upon to show cause why the Council should not act upon the report
of the said Committee, as appears upon the notice served upon him;

And whereas, the said Dr. Samuel Edward McCully has appeared
upon the said notice in person, and the Council has been addressed by
the said Dr. Samuel Edward McCully showing cause to the said
notice;

And whereas the offences charged and reported as proved by the
said Committee are not within the premises contained in sub-section 2
of section 34 of the Ontario Medical Act as amended;

And whereas, as to the said facts stated in the said report of the
Committee on Discipline, the Council now resolve to act, and hereby
adopt the said facts and report as to the finding of the facts in the case
of the said Dr. Samuel Edward McCully; be it therefore

Resolved,—That upon the application therein, and upon the inquiry
herein before the said Discipline Committee, and upon the report of
the said Committee, and upon the facts herein found and adopted by
the Council:

That the name of Samuel Edward McCully, now appearing in the
register of the College of Physicians and Surgeons of Ontario, remain
upon the said register for the present in consideration of the submission and subjection thereto made by him, the said Samuel Edward
McCully, and that action thereon be suspended until this Council may
see fit to take further action thereon.

Carried unanimously.

CL. T. CAMPBELL, *President.*

Dr. McCully was then called into the room, and on his entering,
was addressed by the President as follows:

The Council has very carefully considered your case. You have
had a very fair and impartial trial before the Discipline Committee,
and on the evidence submitted to that committee, they have found
you guilty of the charges that were preferred against you, or very
many of them. In the justice of that conclusion you have yourself
coincided by the statement you have made to the Committee in the
document which you have submitted to them. The Council now
have power, without further delay, and without further action on its
part, to strike your name from the register, but in consideration of
the submission you have made, your confession of guilt and your
promise to refrain from any further offence of a like kind in the
future, the Council has seen fit more mercifully to defer action in your
case, so long as you faithfully and honestly abide by the promise
you have made. I think I can safely say you will be unmolested in
the discharge of your professional work. You have not, however,
been acquitted; the Council now has power to erase, and may at any
time in the future, should it find cause to do so, remove your name

from the register without further inquiry. That, I think, would be a sufficient warning if at any time you were tempted to forget your promise. I have no expectation, however, that you will be so tempted. I have no doubt your promise has been honestly made, and that it will be honestly kept.

Dr. McCully then retired.

Dr. Anderson was then called into the room, and on his entering, Dr. Day moved, seconded by Dr. Rosebrugh, that Dr. William Anderson be called upon to show cause why the Council should not proceed to deal with his case. Carried unanimously.

The PRESIDENT—Dr. Anderson, you are now called upon to show cause why the Council should not proceed to act upon the report of the Discipline Committee, which you have heard read, and to deal with your case.

Dr. ANDERSON—Would you be kind enough to furnish me with a copy of the charge?

The PRESIDENT—I presume copies of the charge were sent to you in the first place.

Dr. ANDERSON—Yes, I received a copy of the charge, but it has been mislaid or lost. We moved since then from London, and I was not able to put my hand on it.

The Registrar hands Dr. Anderson a copy of the charges.

Dr. ANDERSON—I see I stand charged here with joining with one John Murray to deceive the public (refers to charge No. 1). In regard to that charge, I may say there is no truth whatever in it. The man, John Murray, I never saw until a certain day, about eight or ten days previous to my coming to Toronto ; and he intimated to me on that occasion, at that interview, that he was in search of a doctor to open an office in Toronto. As I was aware it was too often the case that men who are specialists cheat the public under false pretences, I said: " Dr. Murray, if you want a man of that class, a man who will rope in victims, and promise cures in any and every case, I am not the man for you ; but if you want a man that will do honest work, and take such cases as he believes he can treat successfully, then it will be all right." He said that was just such a man as he wanted, and, accordingly, we entered into an agreement. The remuneration I was to receive was $100 a month. Regarding the advertising, I had nothing to do with it. My position was merely to stay in the office and attend the patients as they called. So much for that charge. The business went on in this city at No. 272 Jarvis Street. I think I was here some six weeks, or thereabouts. Certain rumours very unfavourable to Murray came to my ears—the chief one that came to my ears was that he went under two names. I took a good deal of trouble to search out in reference to that matter, and I found that it was true ; and, on the strength of that, as well as some other unfavourable rumours, I resigned. I went home again to London, and remained there for two weeks, when he and I patched up another arrangement; and I stayed in the office for him in London, from the 15th February until the 1st of May, when I came to Hamilton, and stayed there two months, or until the 1st July. On the 1st July, I went back to London, and I was to take charge of an office for him there for a year. And on or about the 16th July I was arrested in the office and brought here on a charge—I was charged with taking $200 from a man. That charge was as false as anything in the world ever was false. I freely admit the $200 was paid. The man Langman called at the office of 272 Jarvis Street about the 25th November—I came to Toronto on the morning of the 23rd November, and yet Mr. Langman swore in his information that he paid this money to me on the 16th, when I was in London.

Dr. DAY—I think perhaps this is irregular, and I wish to say right here that all these points in the evidence have been sworn to and the evidence has been taken down. You have had full notice of the trial going on, and you never came to contradict that evidence. I wish it distinctly understood that you are not here legally entitled to review anything that has been proven; you are here simply to make any statement you choose, but it certainly cannot have much effect on the sworn evidence taken, when you had notice that that sworn evidence was about to be taken, and then did not come to defend yourself. Of course you may make any statement you choose; I do not wish to curtail your statement.

Dr. ANDERSON—The man Langman swears he paid the money—

Dr. DAY—It is all taken down; the evidence is here in black and white, and it is quite impossible for you to go into the evidence of the case, because it has been tried, and you had notice of the trial and did not appear then to defend yourself.

Dr. ANDERSON—I supposed I was called upon here to give my version of the case.

Dr. DAY—You are called upon to show cause why the Council should not act upon the facts as proven. The facts have already been proven, and now you are called upon to show cause why the Council should not act upon those facts. They have been established to be facts. You are not here upon your defence.

Dr. ANDERSON—Am I to understand by that that if Langman swore he paid me certain money on a certain day, when I was not here, that that is to be recognized as a fact?

Dr. DAY—You are here to show cause why the Council, upon certain sworn facts, should not take action. You had ample opportunity to refute anything that Langman, or anyone else, might have said by appearing when the evidence was being taken, either in person or by counsel. That you failed to do, and therefore you are simply here to show cause why the Council, upon certain facts which have been proven, should not take action in the case.

The PRESIDENT—In order to save time I will explain to you the report of the Committee—probably you did not pay attention to it when it was being read—states that the charge as to Langman was not proven. As stated by the Chairman of the Discipline Committee, Dr. Day, you have been found guilty on certain charges, and you are now called upon to show cause why you should not be dealt with. But we shall not curtail you.

Dr. ANDERSON—In that case it is not necessary for me to say more. I will just leave my case with the Council to deal with it as they please. I did propose to go into it at length, but as it will be out of order it will therefore be useless for me to do so.

Dr. DAY—I say this that you are not here to review any evidence taken; you are here to show cause why the Council should not proceed upon that evidence. You can say as much as you like and speak as long as you like; we are not wishing to curtail you. But I simply want to put you right in the matter.

Dr. ANDERSON—I presume it would be useless for me to go on in the same line any further, therefore I refrain from making any further—

The PRESIDENT—Say all you wish to say.

Dr. ROSEBRUGH—Dr. Anderson is acting upon the assumption that he was found guilty on this Langman charge, which the Committee reports as not proven.

Dr. DAY—That is why I did not want him to spend time over it.

Dr. ANDERSON—There is another matter stated in the charge, that the advertisements Murray put forth said that three months' treatment free of charge would be given. That is not so. The advertisements that Murray put out were to the effect that all who applied before a certain time would receive services for the first three months free of charge. That was never intended to include medicine. I saw from some of the remarks of one of the gentlemen speaking on the subject to-day that they were labouring under the supposition that three months' treatment was promised free of charge, whereas to my knowledge no such thing was the case. So far as I am concerned all I would like in the matter would be that the real facts would be got out.

Dr. BERGIN—Then why did you not appear and defend yourself at the proper time and proper place?

Dr. ANDERSON—Perhaps it would not effect any good purpose if I would tell my reasons for not appearing at that time. I did not think

I would do any good by coming ; I thought I would be very likely to say and do things that would injure my case, and therefore I did not appear.

The PRESIDENT—Is that all you wish to say ?

Dr. ANDERSON—That is all.

Dr. Anderson, at the President's request, retires from the room, while the Council is considering his case.

Dr. FENWICK—I have received a letter from Dr. Anderson ; in that letter he says he has broken through the regular rules ; and I told him he had better come down and explain it, but he has taken another course. If you will allow me, I will read the letter to you.

Dr. BRAY—Is it to the Council, or is it a private letter ?

Dr. DAY—It is a letter to Dr. Fenwick, as a member of the Medical Council. It is not in evidence, but you may consider it.

Dr. FENWICK—He ends this by saying : " You can say to them, on my behalf, that I promise that I will not offend any more against the laws of the College of Physicians and Surgeons, and that I will endeavour to keep on the lines of the general profession in the future. I will hold myself in readiness to start for Toronto by the earliest conveyance on receipt of your answer to this letter." I answered the letter and told him to come down.

Dr. GEIKIE—What is the date of that letter ?

Dr. FENWICK—It is the 13th June. I do not read this on his behalf, for I have no desire to help him out ; but I certainly have a great desire on behalf of his family, whom I have attended in London when they have been sick. I do not excuse him in any way.

Dr. JOHNSON—I hope I am not uncharitable, but I cannot believe that that man is as simple as he wishes us to think he is. When a man at his age stands up as he has done and takes the most miserable side issue out of the question that he possibly can, and wishes to get out of answering or facing the question in any way, I think it is a pretty good guarantee that he knows what he is doing, and that we should deal with his case very carefully.

Dr. DAY—Dr. Anderson wrote some letters which Dr. Pyne has, I think, which are too long to waste time reading ; they were not only foolish, but they were defiant ; his letters are anything but what I think they should be ; and I think, perhaps, for the information of the Council, there are some portions of his letter of December 6th, 1892, that Dr. Pyne might read to give the Council an idea—

Dr. FENWICK—I have no sympathy with the man himself, but as to his family I have great sympathy. I think, moreover, that he will acknowledge that he has broken the laws, and that he will make a promise not to offend again.

Dr. Pyne reads letter of 6th December, 1892 (marked as Exhibit 2 to the evidence on the investigation of the charges against Dr. Anderson).

Dr. DAY—I think that letter shows the style of the man.

Dr. BRAY—In this letter to Dr. Fenwick he says: "I trust you will succeed, etc. . . . You can say to them, on my behalf, that I promise that I will not offend any more against the laws of the College of Physicians and Surgeons, and I will endeavour to keep on the lines of the general profession in the future." That is an instruction to Dr Fenwick to make that statement to the Council.

Dr. RUTTAN—Let him come in and state that.

The PRESIDENT—With the Council's permission I will ask Dr. Anderson if he wishes to come in, as Dr. Ruttan suggests, to make any further statement.

Dr. Anderson is here called into the room.

The PRESIDENT—I understand from a member of the Council that you may possibly have a further statement to make.

Dr. ANDERSON—Yes. On further consideration I find there is a point or two I would like to set before the Council. I freely admit that I have been guilty of stepping outside of the lines of professional ethics ; and I will give my promise to the Council, if I am allowed to go on in the practice of my profession, that I shall not be guilty of doing so any further.

Dr. ROSEBRUGH—Show him that letter, and ask him if he wishes to endorse it.

The PRESIDENT—Is this letter, dated at Otterville and addressed to Dr. Fenwick, your letter ?

Dr. ANDERSON—Yes (Letter marked Exhibit 1).

Dr. Fenwick: OTTERVILLE, *June 13th,* 1893.

DEAR DOCTOR,—As I am very busy and find it nearly impossible to go to Toronto, I write you to see if you would kindly send me a telegram (unpaid) as soon as you receive this in case you deem it very important that I should go down ; in that case I will go by first train after receiving the message.

Although we are here over two months we are unsettled yet, being delayed on account of repairs that are still being done to the house and store. I trust that you will succeed in my interests with the matter in which I am so much interested, and that the Council will not deal too harshly with me.

You can say to them on my behalf, that I promise that I will not offend any more against the laws of the College of Physicians and

Surgeons of Ontario, and that I will endeavour to keep on the lines of the general profession in the future.

I will hold myself in readiness to start for Toronto by the earliest train on receipt of your telegram requesting me to do so.

Yours very sincerely,

W. ANDERSON,

Otterville, P.O., Ont.

Dr. ROSEBRUGH—You acknowledge that as your letter?

Dr. ANDERSON—Yes.

Dr. Anderson again retires from the room.

Dr. DAY—I have no recommendation for the Council. You all know the case now as well as I do. I have here a resolution filled up down to the point where it is fish or flesh, and you can do just as you like with it.

Dr. ROGERS—I would ask the Chairman of the Discipline Committee if Mr. Osler is satisfied that this case is properly drawn out so that if Dr. Anderson goes to the Court we would have a good case to proceed with?

Dr. DAY—I have not consulted Mr. Osler as to the legal steps taken, but I think there is no doubt about the proof of guilt in the matter. He is guilty of what he is charged with. There is no doubt about that. The report of the Discipline Committee as to his guilt is amply borne out by the evidence recorded; there is no question about that at all.

Dr. HARRIS—He now admits himself that he is guilty.

Dr. FOWLER—I would like to know from the Discipline Committee what their views are as to this man compared with Dr. McCully. Of course the Council as a whole can have very little knowledge, comparatively little knowledge of these cases; and we act in a great measure upon the statements and views of the Discipline Committee. I would like to know whether the members of the Discipline Committee look upon this man as better or worse than Dr. McCully.

Dr. DAY—I have no hesitation at all in saying that Dr. McCully as a sinner is ten times worse than this man knew enough to be. McCully, as a transgressor of medical etiquette, is as much ahead of this man in iniquity and violence as he is ahead of him in intellect, and that is a long way. There is no question about McCully's case being worse than Anderson's than there is that Dr. Anderson's is worse than strict propriety.

Dr. FOWLER—I think under these circumstances we can do nothing else than keep him under suspended sentence, as in the case of Dr. McCully.

Dr. BRAY—I do not wish to be vindictive; and I am perfectly willing to give him a chance. The difference I see is what Dr. McCully did he did for himself; what this man did he did for somebody else who was not a member of the profession at all. He farmed out his license for the benefit of somebody else. While I am on this matter, although perhaps a little out of order, I wish to say that this Council may be called upon to act in regard to people who are going to do the same thing in connection with the gold cure; there are companies formed all over this country that are seeking to hire men at small amounts to conduct their business, not because it is necessary to have a medical man, but because there is a certain amount of medical treatment to people necessary; and they cannot give them treatment without transgressing the law unless they have a licensed practitioner in connection with their establishment, therefore they have to hire a medical man. Dr. Anderson was doing exactly the same thing with this Murray. I quite agree with Dr. Ray that Anderson did not transgress to the same extent or anything near the same extent as McCully did, and I think perhaps it would be well, and I would be quite willing to deal with him in the same way as with Dr. McCully.

Dr. ROGERS—Before you do that I think there is something more to be done. In the cases of McCully and Washington we were in a different position; when Dr. Washington came and asked us to suspend sentence, he did so upon writing a definite statement and a definite undertaking. Dr. McCully does the same thing; he admits he is guilty of disgraceful and unprofessional conduct. I contend until such time as we get something definite like that, something to fix the case afterwards, from Dr. Anderson, we had better go slow. The unfortunate part of this thing is this man comes before us without a solicitor; if he had a solicitor here I am quite certain the solicitor would help him out of the difficulty; he would write such a letter, and the Council would accept it. But this man appears without a solicitor. If he would undertake an agreement such as Dr. McCully did, I would say at once suspend sentence. And I think if he knew enough he would do so.

Dr. BERGIN—That man knows what he is about.

Dr. ROGERS—I would like to ask the Chairman of this Committee if it would be in order for any one member of the Council to write a letter?

Dr. DAY—I do not think so. I think it would be necessary for Dr. Anderson to tender a letter.

Dr. BERGIN—We would have nothing on record now were we to put him on suspended sentence.

Dr. ROSEBRUGH—Our stenographer took down his words; and Dr. Anderson might be requested by us to come in and sign a transcript of the stenographer's notes as his statement. While I am on my feet I wish to state I think we should not take up more time; we certainly cannot deal with this man any more severely than we have dealt with McCully; and I think myself in view of his acknowledgment, if he were brought in and severely reprimanded, and if he will promise, as he has done, that he will not offend in this manner again, we should accept his statement and let him go under suspended sentence, the same as the other.

Dr. HARRIS—I certainly cannot agree with Dr. Rosebrugh in this matter. I believe that we should just erase this man's name from the register.

Dr. ROGERS—Hear, hear. Take a stand now.

Dr. HARRIS—Take a stand. The man is guilty; he says he is guilty, and I have not one bit of confidence or faith in that man at all. I believe it will be the old story; I believe firmly that next year the chances are we will have to take Dr. McCully's name off and Dr. Anderson's name off, too.

Dr. HENRY—Dr. Anderson's sins are not as bad as Dr. McCully's.

Dr. HARRIS—I am willing to move a resolution to remove his name from the register.

Dr. LOGAN—As the opinion of the Special Committee has been asked for by one member of the Council, I trust you will pardon me if I make a statement. I did not wish to have anything to say upon it, because I think it is wiser, perhaps, for the Committee to have very little to say upon this matter, as we are acting as judges, so far, at all events, as to receive evidence. In my opinion, in reference to the heinousness of the offences of these two, I look upon Dr. Anderson's case more in the light of what he consented to do for others. He violated the Ontario Medical Act in trying to shield another. I might call him a rascal; he certainly showed that. The heinousness of his fault consists in what he attempted to do and did do for others. He shielded a rascal, and therefore he must partake of his sins. The distinction in the other case was, the man was open in his violation. He went right and left, and in all directions, and appeared to have no respect for anyone, or for the opinions of respectable men. But this man did it quietly, insinuatingly, and with the express purpose of putting money in his own pocket. He violated the Ontario Medical Act and the law of ethics in shielding a scoundrel.

Dr. BERGIN—I hold very much the view that Dr. Logan holds as to the comparative guilt of the two men. As Dr. Logan says, what Dr. McCully did he did openly and over his own name—he didn't do it in the dark; but this man hid himself away in an office, and did the villainous work he was asked to do, which, as he says himself, he told the man who employed him he was not the kind of man to do ; so that we have his own evidence that he knew the enormity of the crime he was about to commit, and that he attempted to shield himself by a form of words in the contract that he made with this man Murray. And when he found his fellow-partner in guilt was being prosecuted, he did not hesitate to go to the Court, and before high heavens, swear falsely that he himself examined all the patients, and he denies here to-day that he was guilty of that perjury ; and yet, on the record we have the sworn statement of the Crown-Attorney, that he was present when this man committed the perjury. And are we to say here to-day that a man who, for his own purposes, and not concealing his name or concealing the work he was about to do, is to be compared in guilt with the man who sold himself, with the man who committed perjury to shield his fellow-criminal in guilt ? I saў, not at all. These cases are not similar, and I would like to draw the attention of the Council to this fact, that we have no recommendation from the Committee or from our solicitor to avoid striking this man off the roll, to hold him in suspended sentence, as he advised us to do in the case of Dr. McCully, and I take it he did so for the reasons I have given, that the cases are not alike, that one man has been far more deeply criminal than the other. And they who think that this man Anderson does not know enough to commit as great crime as Dr. McCully does, are terribly deceived. I have not seen in a court at any time a man who gave greater evidence of acuteness than this man Anderson gave here to-day.

Dr. Rogers moved, seconded by Dr. Day, that the consideration of the case of William Anderson be taken up at the meeting of the Council this evening.

Dr. ROGERS—In making this motion, I wish to say I think if the matter is pushed on now, there is no alternative but to erase this man's name, unless you want to go over all the expense of giving evidence again, but I am satisfied if ʰe had a solicitor here to help him out a little, the man would—

Dr. BERGIN—Why should this Council get a solicitor to help a criminal out ?

Dr. ROGERS—He will do it himself.

Dr. BERGIN—You are suggesting it.

Dr. JOHNSON—If this man's name be struck off the register now, why should it not be replaced in a year or two years, if he behaved himself ?

The PRESIDENT—He can be replaced by order of the Court.

Dr. ROGERS—The Council has power to replace him.

Dr. FENWICK—I believe you have his own writing, and have his acknowledgment in the letter he wrote to me, and I think he will not commit the offence any more. I think it would be unfair to erase his name from the register. I do not make these remarks in his particular favour beyond this, that I think it would be justice, since you have let Dr. McCully off and Dr. Washington off, that you should give this man the same chance.

Dr. BERGIN—But I would say in reply to that, that we have the evidence alleging that this man is a perjurer, and that his word cannot be taken.

Dr. DAY—Your committee has not said so.

Dr. HENRY—I have no sympathy with either of those men, but I think this case is not any worse than the other, and I would certainly support dealing with him in the same manner as Dr. McCully was dealt with. The Committee do not recommend the erasure of this man's name, neither has his case been submitted to Mr. Osler, our solicitor; possibly if it had been, he would have given the same advice. As I said before, I have no sympathy with either, and I would at this moment go for striking both off, but as we have been lenient with Dr. McCully, I think we should deal just the same with this man as with the other one.

The President puts Dr. Rogers' motion to postpone, and declared it carried.

Dr. Miller moved, seconded by Dr. Moore, and resolved, that the President, Vice-President and Dr. Johnson do constitute the Executive Committee for the ensuing year, with authority to take proceedings on the part of or in defence of the proceedings of this Council in accordance with the duties of this committee, as defined by the rules and regulations of this Council. Carried.

Dr. Bergin moved, seconded by Dr. Rosebrugh, that the treasurer be instructed, in addition to making the annual report, to have printed and placed upon the table of this Council each year a tabulated and comparative statement, showing the receipts and expenditures of the College for each year from June, 1889, up to the close of the year for which he is making his annual report.

Dr. BERGIN—I think this will be found very useful to the Council. It will show at a glance the difference between the expenditures of each of the years under the proper headings, so you can know at once what has been spent on a certain account at any time. I may say this motion covers the period from the time we entered upon this Council, though we actually came in the year before—it was a broken year. And the cost will be very little, about ten or twelve dollars at the outside. Motion carried.

Dr. Miller, at the request of the Chairman of the Committee on Rules and Regulations, presented the report of that committee. Report received.

Dr. Thorburn moved, seconded by Dr. Rogers, that the Council go into Committee of the Whole on the report of the Finance Committee. Carried.

Council in Committee of the Whole. Dr. Miller in the chair.

Dr. THORBURN—When we adjourned, you will recollect that we had under consideration a recommendation of the Committee in reference to the paying of a certain sum of money to one of the journals for the publication of the proceedings of the Council, and for distribution among the profession. I read to you the applications of three different printing firms, and I was about to proceed to read a long communication from Drs. Wright and Davison, the respective editors of the *Canada Lancet* and *Practitioner*. This letter proceeds to give their reasons why we should not subsidize any particular journal.

These are the only communications we had received up to the consideration of the matter. We had gone over several items, and then came to a recommendation of granting a sum of money to the *Journal*.

Dr. Thorburn continues reading report.

FINANCE COMMITTEE REPORT.

June 16th, 1893.

To the President and Members of the Ontario Medical Council:

GENTLEMEN,—Your Committee on Finance beg leave to submit the following report :

We have examined the Treasurer's books, compared them with the vouchers, and find them to be correct.

The Registrar's books have also been examined and compared with the Treasurer's and found correct.

The financial state of the Council is much better than last year, as the annual dues are better paid than in former years. There are still a great many delinquents who are several years in arrears, which if promptly paid, would in a short time enable the Council to clear off the greater part of its indebtedness.

We regret to state that the change last year proposed in the method of conducting the examinations with a view of decreasing the expense has not resulted as we anticipated.

The balance to the credit of the Council in the Imperial Bank of Canada at present is $42.42.

The application of Mr. E. W. Tonkin for return of registration fees is not granted.

The request of Duncan McNae, of Perth, Ontario, not granted.

Dr. Smith, Mount Elgin, asking refund of assessment dues, not granted.

Dr. Wm. Ewing, of Hawkesbury, asking to be relieved of annual dues, deferred until after next election.

Dr. Bradley, of Grafton, asking to be relieved of fee while out of country, not granted.

No action in the case of Dr. N. Bicknell, of Camden East.

Dr. J. T. D. Fontaine, of Angers, Quebec, asking for refund of portion of examination fees, not granted.

Dr. O. C. Edward, of Ottawa, asking Council to relieve him from assessment dues while not living in the country, not granted.

In the matter of Insurance we have considered the proposition of the Citizens to insure in the Hartford, and recommend that it be accepted.

We also advise the continuance of the Boiler Insurance for one year.

Your Committee present the proposition of the *Ontario Medical Journal* Publishing Company, also a communication from the editors of the *Canada Lancet* and *Practitioner* for your consideration.

Financial Statement.

Building and Site	$100,000	00
Assessments Unpaid	5,000	00
Cash in Bank	42	42
	$105,042	42

Liabilities.

Mortgage on Building	$60,000	00
Note in Bank	300	00
Estimated Expenses of Council, 1893	2,200	00
	$62,500	00
Balance in favour of Council	$42,542	42

We also append Treasurer's report, also financial statement in regard to building.

JAMES THORBURN, *Chairman.*

Your Committee have carefully looked into the printing as done by the *Ontario Medical Journal* Publishing Company for the grant made to them by your honourable body at last session and find

That the Company furnished 2,600 copies of the
annual Announcement at a cost of............: $397 00

Stenographer for reports of Council proceedings..   84 00

Advertisements for College based on prices of
previous year.........................   30 00
_____

$511 00

The Announcement was made larger than the previous year by about forty pages. It is therefore safe to say that on former prices the cost would have been much above the $600 paid by you to that company, and the *Journal* was practically furnished to the profession free.

Your Committee find that your agreement with this company did not cover all the announcements required for the purposes of the profession, and the Registrar was obliged to procure another thousand at an expenditure of eighty-seven dollars.

The company has made a proposition to renew the contract for two years at the same rate, and to furnish the full complement of announcements required.

Your Committee have also had before them a communication from the editors of the *Canada Lancet* and *Practitioner*, in which they take strong grounds against the Council letting this work to the *Ontario Medical Journal* Publishing Company, and at the same time proposing that they will publish any reports prepared by the Council and given to them.

While your Committee fully appreciate the efforts of these medical journals in behalf of science, we cannot see that it would be in the interest of the profession to return to the former arrangement when no reports were furnished to the profession, nor do we think it wise to accept the proposition of these journals which would be much more expensive to the profession than the proposition of the *Ontario Medical Journal* Publishing Company.

Your Committee therefore advise that the proposition of this journal be accepted for one year.

Moved by Dr. Williams, seconded by Dr. Fowler: Your Committee would further recommend, that while the contract be given to this company for the performance of the work specified, the Council disowns any responsibility for either editorial or other matter therein contained.

Moved by Dr. Johnson, seconded by Dr. Bergin, that the opinion of the Solicitor of the Council be obtained as to the liability, if any, of the Council because of any article that may appear in the *Ontario Medical Journal*, and should that opinion be unfavourable to the Council, then that such addition or amendment be made to the contract as shall avoid all or any liability by the Council.

Passed in Committee of the Whole this 16th June, 1893.

THOMAS MILLER, *Chairman.*

TORONTO, *June 14th,* 1893.

*To the President and Members of the Council of the College of Physicians
and Surgeons of Ontario :*

GENTLEMEN,—Herein I beg to submit a statement of the receipts
and disbursements for the twelve months which have just expired.

RECEIPTS.

June 15, 1892.

To balance as audited..................	$371	47
" Registration fees....................	3,321	00
" Assessment dues....................	2,278	00
" Fines on persons illegally practising...	655	00
" Fees for Professional Exam- inations in Fall...........$1,450 00		
" Fees for Professional Exam- inations in Spring....... 9,410 00		
	10,860	00
" Interest on current bank account......	8	25
" New building revenue (rents).........	3,618	21
" Refund..........................	3	00
" Temporary loans...................	11,907	25
" Council meeting expenses—refund....	85	05
Total........................	$33,107	23

DISBURSEMENTS.

Council meeting expenses..............	$2,185	90
Treasurer's salary.....................	400	00
Registrar's salary.....................	1,800	00
Official prosecutor's salary.............	408	33
Expense of holding Prof. Exams. in Fall..	886	18
" " " Spring	2,389	80
Fines paid to former prosecutor..........	145	00
Fine refunded........................	25	00
Committee *re* Legislation..............	586	85
" " Discipline...............	1,019	03
Fees returned to candidates.............	100	00
Permanent appar. for Exams...........	9	60
Registrar's office supplies and expenses....	680	02
Treasurer's office supplies and expenses...	27	65
Temporary loans returned..............	12,595	75
Interest............................	3,209	70

DISBURSEMENTS—*Continued.*

Printing.............................	$1,181 25
Legal and other expenses — prosecuting illegal practitioners..................	1,055 47
Legal services *re* Discipline Committee....	313 68
" " " Elevator...............	24 24
" " " Committee on Legislation	20 00
" " ". General account........	11 00
Grant to *Ontario Medical Journal*........	500 00

NEW BUILDING MAINTENANCE.

Caretaker....................	$530 00	
Elevator man.................	265 00	
Commission on rents...........	181 34	
Fuel........................	745 76	
Water.......................	359 94	
Gas.........................	168 32	
Insurance....................	70 00	
Taxes	621 00	
Repairs, supplies, etc..........	549 00	
		3,490 36
Balance in Imperial Bank.............		42 42
Total............................		$33,107 23

All of which is respectfully submitted.

(Signed)   W. T. AIKINS, *Treasurer.*

—

Item No. 1.

Site cost	$13,000 00
New Building......................	75,046 54
Total........................	$88,046 54
Less material in old building...........	100 00
	$87,946 54

Item No. 2.

Paid on building and site up to June 13th, 1893........................	$28,146 54

Item No. 3.

Mortgage principal.. .... $60,000 00
Interest since 1st May, 1893 to 13th June,
    1893......................... 375 00
                                                           ————

Amount of principal and interest due this
    13th June, 1893 .... $60,375 00

Item No. 4.

Rent for 1888-89, from September to June $1,853 45
  "   1889-90, from June to June.....   3,888 91
  "   1890-91,   "   " 4,090 72
  "   1891-92,   "   " 4,097 34
  "   1892-93,   "   " 3,618 21

In this last statement the portion of the building used for college purposes is not taken into account. Upon the valuation of an estate broker he estimates the rental of portion occupied and used for college purposes at $2,000.

Approved of in Committee of the Whole this 13th June, 1893.

THOMAS MILLER, *Chairman.*

The PRESIDENT—I may say in justice to other parties, a communication was received this afternoon, and in hurriedly going over the order of business, it was omitted. I will now ask the Registrar to read that communication.

Dr. Pyne reads letter dated June 16th, 1893, from Drs. Wright and Davison, as follows :

TORONTO, *June 16th,* 1893.

The President and Members of the Council of the College of Physicians and Surgeons of Ontario :

GENTLEMEN,—In addition to our former offers, we desire to add that we are willing to pay for the official report of the proceedings of the meetings of the Council.

A. H. WRIGHT,
    For the *Canadian Practitioner.*
JOHN L. DAVISON,
    For the *Canada Lancet.*

Dr. ROSEBRUGH—I would suggest that this communication be added to the report.

Dr. BERGIN—I think before we declare that section carried, we ought to have the opinion of our solicitor as to whether we run any risk of being held responsible for anything that may appear in that journal during the time that we direct the publishers to furnish it to the profession at large.

Dr. BRITTON—I do not know that I have anything more to say on the subject than I said this morning. The letter sent in by the two editors contains quite a large number of arguments, and it is not necessary to go over these, or tire the members of the Council. For me to say anything more would be unnecessary reiteration.

Dr. THORBURN—The report recommends that means be taken to collect arrears. There is an impression that according to the last amended Act of the Ontario Medical Acts, we have not power to collect anything until some definite time in the future. As I read it, and as others read it, it does not interfere at all with the collection of old debts, or debts up to a certain time.

Dr. BRITTON—Would you add the words to that, " On instructions from the solicitor ? "

Dr. THORBURN—I think it would be advisable to get the solicitor's opinion.

Dr. WILLIAMS—I am pretty well satisfied that we have a perfect right to collect old debts in the Division Court as formerly, but the question in my mind would be whether or not that would not be looked upon as a breach of faith, seeing that clause 27 is suspended for the time being, and suspended until put in force after the new elections. Of course that suspension could only take place with reference to fees imposed for this year and succeeding years until that time. But there is the difficulty if you proceed to collect in the Division Court the old debts that are outstanding, you can only collect, at any rate, for six years back, while there is quite a considerable portion of it from a period previous to that ; and you would be practically throwing that away, while if you let that alone until after the election, and then section 41 A is put in force, you collect the whole amount. It strikes me it would have the appearance of attempting to override the suspension of that clause by the Legislature, and I would not like to see the Council do anything that would be questionable in character, and to my mind that would look questionable.

Dr. GEIKIE—There is a great deal in what Dr. Williams says. The impression abroad would be exactly as he has put it.

Dr. MOORE—I quite agree with what Dr. Williams has said, and I think it would be well to amend that portion of the report.

Dr. THORBURN—There has been an addendum, " under instructions from the solicitor.'

Dr. WILLIAMS—It is a question of whether the moral influence on the profession would not more than counterbalance any gain you would get from it.

Dr. ROGERS—It would certainly arouse a strong feeling. I would strongly oppose coercing the profession to pay their dues just now. I would move that that clause be struck out.

Dr. BRITTON—I would ask about what percentage the legal expenses formerly bore to the amounts collected.

Dr. THORBURN—When we had to collect the dollar subscriptions under the old law, it cost about seventy-five to eighty cents on the dollar.

Dr. PYNE—It was impracticable. It did not pay.

Dr. WILLIAMS—I think it is much better to leave that in suspension, because it is only a source of irritation in the meantime.

Dr. THORBURN—I think they ought to be notified—send the accounts as usual.

Dr. FULTON—We might add, "No legal means to be taken." We are in need of money, and it is necessary for the carrying on of the institution. If you leave it in abeyance, no dues will be paid.

The PRESIDENT—While it is quite true, perhaps, that an endeavour to collect those dues might not be very profitable, and while it might give rise to some ill-feeling, yet at the same time I think there should be something placed on record to show that those arrears are due. There are some men throughout the country who have an idea that this whole thing is under suspension until the next election. That is not the case. So far as the arrears up to December, 1892, are concerned, they are as much due to-day as they ever were. Those who are in arrears at all events should be notified to pay their dues to December, 1892, not to let them have the idea they can go without paying those dues. I am not disposed to say we should collect them by process of law, because I do not think it would pay.

Dr. BERGIN—I am as loath as any member of the Council to do anything which might irritate any member of the profession, but I do not think for a moment we ought to abandon our right to obtain from any member of the profession that which he owes to the College, and I think that we would be untrue to the College if we did not warn every man indebted to the College that he is still a debtor, and remove in that way the impression that is abroad that we have no power to collect, for I have no doubt that gentlemen like Mr. Sangster would give the impression everywhere, if they had the opportunity, that this College had no power to collect. You should remove that idea from their minds by directing the Registrar to call upon everyone who is indebted to the College to pay his dues. You send them the accounts, and the honest men amongst them will pay them; the dishonest men, of course, will not.

Dr. RUTTAN—The position the Council stands in should be such as to endeavour to secure fairness between the members of the profession. If one man pays, and another does not, who is to look after that—who is to enforce the law? It is very dishonourable, certainly, of those who do not pay towards those who do pay; and we are here to defend decent people, and so long as people refuse to pay, and quietly sit by and allow the remainder of the profession to pay the expenses of this Council, we must be held personally responsible for it.

Dr. ROGERS—I made a motion to strike out that part of the report altogether.

Dr. WILLIAMS—The suggestion of the President strikes me very favourably, that their attention should be called to the fact that they owe the fees previous to the time of suspension, and even though we do not try to make them pay in the Division Court, still, if we give them a knowledge that they are owing that part, and that the Act being suspended makes no difference so far as that part of their fees is concerned, we are doing no more than we should do.

Dr. THORBURN—There might be a tacit understanding with the Registrar that no legal proceedings should be taken.

Dr. BERGIN—If he is directed to notify them, that is all right.

Dr. THORBURN—I will alter the report to read, " That the Registrar notify all members of the College in arrears to December 31st, 1892, to pay all such arrears." That is all we can do.

Dr. BERGIN—That is not all we can do, but all we care to do just now.

Clause of report adopted.

Dr. Thorburn reads statement of financial condition, which, on motion, was adopted as read.

Dr. WILLIAMS—I do not wish to move an amendment, but I have a resolution I would like to get introduced into that report before the Committee rise, if the Committee are favourable to it. I will just read the resolution, and with the consent of the Committee, if they will refer back, insert it where they think it ought to go. This is supposed to follow the clause of the report dealing with the *Ontario Medical Journal* Publishing Co., which reads, " Your Committee will recommend that while the contract be given to this company," etc.

Dr. Williams moved, seconded by Dr. Fowler, the Council disclaim any responsibility for any editorial or other matter therein contained.

Dr. BERGIN—I think, in accordance with the chairman's ruling, that had better come up in Council after we leave Committee of the Whole.

Dr. THORBURN—Will a clause of that kind fortify us any better against any proceedings?

Dr. JOHNSON—I have a motion, " That the opinion of the solicitor of the Council be obtained as to the liability, if any, of the Council because of any article that may appear in the *Ontario Medical Journal,* and should that opinion be unfavourable to the Council, that then such addition or amendment be made to the contract as shall avoid all or any liability by the Council."

The CHAIRMAN—I see no reason why Dr. Johnson's motion might not be put as a substantive motion irrespective of the finance report altogether.

Dr. GEIKIE—I notice in a great many journals a condition similar to that made by Dr. Williams and Dr. Fowler, and it seems to me a legal disclaimer, that is to say, a disclaimer that holds good in the courts, and I do not see any objection to it here. It relieves us of legal responsibility, that is all.

Dr. BERGIN—It is doubtful whether it would relieve us from legal responsibility, and we do not want to make a contract that will take us before the law courts.

Dr. WILLIAMS—I will move that we refer back to that section dealing with the *Ontario Medical Journal* Publishing Co., and insert the following immediately thereafter : " Your Committee further recommend, that while the contract be given to this company for the performance of the work specified, the Council disclaims any responsibilty for either editorial or other matter contained."

Dr. ROGERS—In that case, if you had any authorized statements on the part of this Council, and the *Journal* happened to publish them, we would not be responsible for them.

Dr. WILLIAMS—Certainly not, unless we specify they are authorized.

Dr. JOHNSON—That does not cover the ground I take at all. The ground I take is this : we ought to ascertain from the solicitor whether there is any liability ; and if there is, no contract should be let, arranged in such a way that liability might be imposed on the Council for any articles that might get in the publication.

Dr. LOGAN—One objection to Dr. Johnson's motion is that in carrying it out, it cannot be done by the Council, unless you now ascertain the information you wish. Unless it were done now, it would have to be done by the Executive Committee, and that Committee does not constitute the Council.

Dr. ORR—The Company are willing and instruct me to state they are willing to make satisfactory arrangements with the solicitor of this Council to hold the Council free from all liability for any article that may appear in the *Journal.* Of course the instructions that the Company have received from their solicitor, and the instructions I received at the time the arrangement was made from the solicitor of the Council was that the Council is not in any way, under the contract made last year, responsible for anything that appears in the *Journal.* The Company were simply under an agreement with the Council to carry out the printing contract ; and the work they were to do for the Council in that journal they could do simply as they pleased. Holding the contract from the Council it was presumed the Company would serve the best interests of the Council and the best interests of the profession in the Province of Ontario.

Dr. JOHNSON—That is very well so far as it goes, and it may be far enough, but it must be understood by the profession not only that there is no legal liability, but that we have no hand in private matters which have from time to time crept into the *Journal* in the last year. Personally I have been blamed for many of the articles which have appeared in the *Journal,* and which I had nothing to do with, which I never saw before they were in print ; and I may say I never saw them after they were in print—many personal matters that were ventilated in the *Journal* that should not have been there undoubtedly ; and I wish the profession at large to know that either we have or have not supervision of that journal ; if we have not then I do not care ; if we have, then it is our duty to look after it.

Dr. WILLIAMS—My resolution is inserted for that special purpose, so that every member of the College of Physicians and Surgeons throughout the Province who reads our reports will see that we publicly disclaim any responsibility, so far as it is possible to put that in our report ; and that is the reason why I want that clause inserted, that we disclaim any liability in any sense whatever. Subsequently to that if the Council wish to get information of a higher legal authority, well and good, but I think we should make it clear so that every member of the profession would know we do not assume any responsibility for any article except what we authorize.

Dr. THORBURN—I have no objection to accepting Dr. William's motion as part of the report.

Dr. BERGIN—I object to it on the ground that although we may disclaim by a resolution of the Council any responsibility for anything that may appear in that journal, yet at the commencement or in the middle of the next month, notwithstanding our disclaiming any responsibility, we shall cause to be sent to every member of the profession throughout the country that journal ; then, because of that we would be made responsible. We ought to have some guarantee that this resolution would relieve us from all liability. I do not believe it would. We know that large commercial concerns, steamship and railway companies, and so forth, have on their bills of lading a clause of this kind, and we know that for years it was supposed that that freed them from any obligation. But the courts have held that was not a contract ; it was binding only upon one party and not binding upon everybody else. We know that railways have placed clauses and conditions upon the back of their tickets up to within a few years, disclaiming any responsibility, but the Court said men buying tickets at the window have not time to examine these conditions and do not know anything about them ; and the courts held that that was not law and that they could not make an arrangement of that kind where the other party had no time to understand it or to examine it, or perhaps did not know it was there at all. The same remarks will apply to telegraph messages. Do not let us jump into a law suit. Let us put a clause like that there, and then you can authorize the President and Secretary to make the contract, if it is found we incur no legal liability because of anything that may appear in the *Journal*. We may have that opinion before to-morrow, then why such haste? Pass that resolution, and it will not prevent the contract from being signed, because you can authorize the President and Secretary who are the proper parties to sign the contract to do so at any time.

Dr. WILLIAMS—I must press my motion ; and if it is thought advisable afterwards to adopt the suggestion of Dr. Johnson and obtain a legal opinion on it, I am not going to oppose that, but I must press my motion to see whether or not it is the will of the Council that it be inserted in the report. I believe it is to the interests of the Council and profession that they should understand that, and that our report should place it clearly upon its face, and then if subsequently a legal opinion is wished, I shall not object to it.

Dr. FULTON—I do not see why you should take up so much time discussing this matter ; it seems to me it is plain to everybody the solicitor should be present when this contract is signed ; and with such a resolution as Dr. Williams' before them stating what our requirements are, there is no danger of our becoming liable for anything.

Dr. THORBURN—Our solicitor draws up the agreement, and he will put in any clause that is necessary.

Dr. FULTON—My impression last year was, we are not liable for anything that appeared in the *Medical Journal* last year.

Dr. BERGIN—There was an omission of a clause that we directed to be inserted, and yet in that case it was left to our solicitor.

Dr. MOORE—I cannot see the slightest objection of passing both of these right here in committee. I am very much in favour of Dr. Williams' resolution ; I think it is very necessary we should show through our announcements to the profession at large that we disclaim any responsibility for this journal other than that which our agreement holds us to. I do not see any reason why we should not pass the other resolution also, and then probably this mistate will not be made. I hope it will not—that was made last year. In good faith we believed the clause was going to be inserted in the contract that this Council should not be held responsible for anything that appeared in that journal. I was under the impression that clause was in the contract until it was placed in my hands, and I could not find any trace of it. I do not think there will be any mistake in passing both resolutions, and then we will be quite certain that it will appear next time.

Report adopted as amended by the addition of Dr. Williams' and Dr. Johnson's respective motions.

On motion, the Committee rose. The President in the chair.

Dr. Thorburn moved, seconded by Dr. Rogers, that the report of the Committee of the Whole, recommending the adoption of the report of the Committee on Finance, be adopted. Carried.

Dr. Miller read the report of the Committee on Rules and Regulations, and moved, seconded by Dr. Henry, that the report be received and adopted by this Council. Carried.

REPORT OF COMMITTEE ON RULES AND REGULATIONS.

To the Council of the College of Physicians and Surgeons of Ontario :

Your Committee on Rules and Regulations beg leave to report that they met and organized, by electing Dr. Day, Chairman.

Your Committee have had referred to them the following papers, namely :

1st. A communication from Dr. Bryce, Secretary of the Provincial Board of Health, enclosing letters of invitation from the International Congress to be held in Rome, in September, 1893, to send delegates who will represent the College of Physicians and Surgeons of Ontario at the Congress.

2nd. A communication from S. T. Bastedo, enclosing a copy of invitation from Secretary-General Reid to College of Physicians and Surgeons, requesting that representatives be sent to the Pan-American Medical Congress to be held in Washington, in September, 1893.

Your Committee recommend that the receipt of the communications be thankfully acknowledged by the Registrar.

All of which is respectfully submitted.

HENRY W. DAY, *Chairman.*

On motion of Dr. Thorburn, the Council adjourned to meet at 8 p.m., on Friday, the 16th June, 1893.

EVENING SESSION.

FRIDAY, *June 16th,* 1893.

The Council met at 8 o'clock.

The President, Dr. Campbell, in the chair, called the Council to order.

The roll was called by the Registrar; all present éxcepting Sir Jas. Grant and Dr. Philip.

Minutes of the previous meeting were read, and, on motion, confirmed.

The PRESIDENT—I would suggest to the Council that as this is probably the last meeting, or is at all events drawing towards the end of the session, it would be well to suspend the order of business.

Dr. Bray moved, seconded by Dr. Johnson, that the order of business be suspended for the remaining meetings of the Council. Carried.

COMMUNICATIONS.

The Registrar read a communication from Mr. P. R. McMonagle, enclosing diplomas in support of his application for registration, which application was referred to the Registration Committee.

Referred to Registration Committee.

A communication from Messrs. Haverson & St. John *re* Dr. Nelson Washington, dated 15th June, 1893, asking that the name of Dr. Washington be reinstated on the register on a period of probation.

Dr. Day moved, seconded by Dr. Rogers, that the communication be laid on the table.   Carried.

Communication by telegram from Whitby, saying the appeal of Mason has been dismissed, and Mason ordered to pay the fine and costs of conviction.   The Registrar states that this was a case Mr. Wasson had the prosecution of in Port Perry, which was tried in Whitby; and the defendant appealed from the decision of the Court there, with the result as shown by this telegram that the conviction has been sustained.

Dr. Williams moved, seconded by Dr. Henry, and

Resolved,—That Mr. Thomas Wasson be reappointed prosecutor for the coming year, at the same salary and on the same conditions as last year.   And that the sum of $200 be placed to his credit, in order that he may carry out his work satisfactorily.

Dr. WILLIAMS—The object in placing the $200 to his credit is to avoid the necessity of his raising the money on his own personal credit to do the Council's work. It is thought advisable that he shall be provided with the requisite means in advance, with instructions, of course, to report at the end of each month. Carried.

Mr. H. M. Mowat here addressed the Council as counsel for and on behalf of Dr. Anderson, as follows:

Mr. President and Gentlemen of the Council,—On behalf of Dr. Anderson I am here to address you with regard to his case. From what I can learn, in the short instructions I have had since five o'clock this evening, Dr. Anderson has been singularly ill-advised, as it appears to me, in the manner in which he has treated the Council. On the complaint being laid against him, the details of which will be familiar to all the gentlemen present, Dr. Anderson, instead of acting in the way one might expect from not only a clever doctor, but a good business man, seems to have entirely neglected to look after his interests. As I am told that was due to a peculiar feeling, and I may say without disparaging the worthy doctor too much, with a certain amount of obstinacy on his part, so far as I can learn, the result being that when the case came to be deliberated upon by the Discipline Committee, Dr. Anderson was not present and his case was decided in his absence. But had he been here, from what I can learn, I can assure the Committee and the members of the Council that he could have shown without doubt that he was not guilty of the charge which was laid at his door. And shortly, to recapitulate what the charge was, and to look into it, Dr. Anderson would have been prepared to show conclusively, had he not suffered from this peculiar temperament of his, that at the time he was charged with the offence he was not in Toronto at all. He would also have shown that when this charge was laid against him and heard in the proper court in the city of Toronto, the case was dismissed without the defence being called upon. He would also have shown that, on the advice of eminent counsel, he took an action for malicious and false arrest against the parties who laid the complaint, but that, owing to his financial disability, he was unable to carry that to a conclusion, although the advice of his counsel was that he would have succeeded on a trial. Even this course of action by Dr. Anderson, in not carrying such a law suit or action to its conclusion, showed that wonderful lack of business ability which he seems to suffer from. But apart from that I am now here on behalf of Dr. Anderson to say to the Council, to bring before the Council, and to point out to the Council the fact that Dr. Anderson is now approaching that age at which a physician feels that, to a great extent, his practice has gone from him. He is now close on to sixty years of age, and unless a man becomes noted and able at that age and has got a firm footing in a community, it is difficult for him to make that living for his family which is expected of him. Dr. Anderson, having taken advice and having considered the matter carefully, instructs me to say that although his action in associating himself with a person who is considered, and probably rightly considered, improper in his conduct in the practice of medicine, and although he admits, and freely admits, and has instructed me to say he admits, that he committed a breach of medical ethics, he now asks the Council to consider his case with that benevolence which has characterized the Council in other cases, Dr. Anderson, while expressing this regret, has also instructed me to say that he will sin no more, if I may so express it; and if the Council will deal leniently and temperately with his case, and will not resort to the harsh, and to him, very severe measures of erasing his name from the register, that he will give such undertaking that the Council will have no further fault to find with him. To a large extent Dr. Anderson has given up the practice of his profession, and has contented himself with establishing a business of a mercantile character in the small town of Otterville, in the western part of Ontario, but he fears the result to him and his name ; and he fears the result to the credit of his family after him should it be handed down in the annals of the family that his name was erased for improper conduct from the register of the Medical Council for Ontario.

It is on these grounds that Dr. Anderson asks for the lenient consideration of the Council. And I ask the Council, with what feeling I can and with what force I can, that the Council, many of whom must have seen cases of this sort before, will deal leniently with him, and that they will not use the power which the law has given them to completely shut out a brother practitioner, who has sinned but who is now repentant, from further practising his profession ; and I venture to say if the Council does deal in this way with Dr. Anderson that the name of Dr. Anderson will from henceforth never be heard of except in an honourable manner. And I ask the Council, in consideration of the facts that I have stated, to give Dr. Anderson's case every consideration, and to deal with it in a benevolent and lenient spirit.

Dr. GEIKIE—May I ask in what form Dr. Anderson contemplates placing his undertaking, to which his solicitor has referred, in the hands of the Council.

Dr. DAY—I can reply to that. I would say that Mr. Nesbitt, who has conducted all these cases for the prosecution, is here ; and I would suggest that any undertaking given by Dr. Anderson should be subject to the approval of Mr. Nesbitt.

The PRESIDENT—If Dr. Anderson is prepared to make any proposal to the Council in writing, it had better be handed in.

Dr. HARRIS—Did I understand Mr. Mowat to say that Dr. Anderson said he thought he had not done anything wrong?

Mr. MOWAT—The doctor is quite prepared to admit he has.

Dr. HARRIS—I ask that because Dr. Anderson admitted to-day before this Council that he had done wrong, and apologized verbally for it.

Mr. MOWAT—The doctor is quite prepared to cry "*Peccavi.*"

The PRESIDENT—While Dr. Anderson's solicitor is preparing his submission, the Council may proceed with other matters.

Dr. Harris moved, seconded by Dr. Fulton, that By-law No. 56, to appoint a Committee on Discipline, be now read a second time, and referred to a Committee of the Whole. Carried.

Dr. Harris reads by-law.

Council in Committee of the Whole. Dr. Williams in the chair.

The by-law was read clause by clause, and on motion, adopted.

Dr. Campbell moved, seconded by Dr. Rogers, that the first blank in the by-law be filled with the name of Dr. Day, of Belleville. Carried.

Dr. Rogers moved, seconded by Dr. Campbell, that the second blank in the by-law be filled with the name of Dr. Bray, of Chatham. Carried.

Dr. Day moved, seconded by Dr. Rogers, that the third blank in the by-law be filled with the name of Dr. Logan, of Ottawa. Carried.

Dr. HARRIS—The clause will now read, "Dr. Day, of Belleville, Ontario; Dr. Bray, of Chatham, Ontario; and Dr. Logan of Ottawa, Ontario, are hereby appointed the committee for the purpose of said section for the ensuing year."

On motion this clause was adopted.

On motion the Committee rose. The President in the chair.

Dr. Harris moved, seconded by Dr. Williams, that the report of the Committee of the Whole on the by-law appointing the Discipline Committee, with the blanks in the by-law filled with the names mentioned, be adopted. Carried.

Dr. Harris moved, seconded by Dr. Rogers, that the by-law be read a third time, passed, numbered, and signed by the President, and sealed with the seal of the College of Physicians and Surgeons of Ontario, as follows. Carried.

(Copy of By-law.)

By-law 56, Council of the College of Physicians and Surgeons of Ontario.

APPOINTING A COMMITTEE ON DISCIPLINE.

Under and by virtue of the powers and directions given by subsection 5 of Chapter 121, 50th Victoria, entitled, "An Act to amend the Ontario Medical Act," and enacted as follows :

First,—The Committee for the purpose of said section shall consist of three members, three of whom shall form a quorum for the transaction of business.

Second,—The said committee shall hold office for one year, and until their successors are appointed, provided that any member of such committee, notwithstanding anything to the contrary herein, until all business brought before them during the year of office, has been reported upon to the Council.

Third,—The Committee under said section shall be known as the Committee on Discipline.

Fourth,—Dr. Day, of Belleville, Ontario; Dr. Bray, of Chatham, Ontario; Dr. Logan, of Ottawa, Ontario; are hereby appointed the Committee for the purposes of said section for the ensuing year.

J. A. WILLIAMS,
Chairman, Committee of the Whole.

[Seal]   R. A. PYNE,
Registrar, College of Physicians and Surgeons of Ontario.

June 16th, 1893.   Adopted in Council.

CL. T. CAMPBELL,
President, College of Physicians and Surgeons of Ontario.

Dr. FULTON—It was intended by the Chairman of the Finance Committee to recommend to the Council that the sum of $20, which has been paid to the examiners as a retainer fee, be discontinued, but through some oversight it did not appear in his report, and as he is absent at present, I will now take the liberty of making a motion to that effect.

Dr. Fulton moved, seconded by Dr. Williams, that the payment of $20 to the examiners as a retainer fee be discontinued, it being considered that their remuneration, independent of this amount, is quite sufficient.

Dr. ROGERS—The reason that was put there in the first place, I think, was on account of the homœopathic examiner, because if that was taken off, he really would not receive any pay at all.

Dr. HARRIS—So far as that is concerned, it could be provided for.

Dr. FOWLER—I think before it is voted upon it would be desirable some statement should be laid before us, showing what the remuneration likely would be without this $20.

Dr. GEIKIE—I know the examiners consider their duties very onerous. I have not looked into the thing, and I have not heard anybody speak about it, but I think the diminution of the amount would perhaps lead to some difficulty, and to the withdrawal of some examiners, who say the work is very great on account of the large number of candidates and the length of time the examinations take, and I may say, the great devotion of the examiners to their work.

Dr. FULTON—They are paid $10 a day with expenses, the same as the members of this Council are paid; and in consequence of their remuneration being the same as ours, the Committee considered this $20 superfluous.

Dr. WILLIAMS—On page 235, the provision for the appointment of examiners is, "Each examiner shall receive the sum of $20, and in addition thereto he shall receive thirty-five cents for each paper he may have to read over the number of fifty. He shall also receive $10 per day for each day's attendance at oral examinations and meetings of the Board of Examiners, with the same allowance, hotel and travelling expenses when absent from home, as is received by the members of the Council. The oral examinations shall continue for seven hours each day until they are completed." It would seem the examiners get the same pay as members of the Council, and in addition to that they get thirty-five cents a paper for each paper over fifty, and a retainer fee of $20. And the Finance Committee, in looking at this matter, thought they were paid better than members of the Council, at least to the extent of that $20 retainer fee; they thought the papers they read were generally taken home, and that the thirty-five cents apiece for these papers was reasonable pay, and that while they were in attendance at the examinations, if they got the same pay as members of the Council get, it should be satisfactory, and the Finance Committee thought there should be a saving of at least the $20 for each examiner, and at the same time the examiners would be reasonably well paid, at least as well paid as members of the Council.

Dr. ROGERS—Last year when this new arrangement was brought up, the $20 was placed there because it was for reading the first fifty papers. The first suggestion was we were to give them twenty-five cents a paper, or fifty cents a paper, but it was thought as the homœopathic examiner would have only four or five papers, he would hardly receive anything for the whole of his work, as the other examiners would get paid from the large number of papers they would have to read.

Dr. WILLIAMS—Would he not be getting the $10 a day and the $3.50 for expenses, the same as you would get, even if he had not a paper to read?

Dr. ROGERS—No. Supposing he had four or five or ten papers, he would read those papers for nothing.

Dr. WILLIAMS—Wouldn't there be $10 and $3.50 hotel expenses paid?

Dr. Rogers—When he was here. But they do the work at home. I am only pointing out the reason why, on the first fifty papers, he was to receive $20; it was as a certain amount of compensation for the first fifty papers, intead of thirty-five cents each. I consider it is a small amount of money for the large amount of work they do, if they take fifty papers and fairly, and honestly, and conscientiously read them, and read them properly. They get $20 for reading fifty papers, and after that, if it goes above fifty, they get at the rate of thirty-five cents, and if you cut that $20 off, then, for the first fifty papers, they do not get one cent. I think that was the way it came to be put there. I would be very sorry, for one, to see it taken off, unless you make a special fee for the homœopathic examiner, and I do not think even then it is fair to our examiners. They are good examiners, and I think they ought to be paid as well as you can pay them.

Dr. Johnson—I do not see why the fee that is received by the members of the Council should be set up as apparently the extreme standard of any fee that should be collected by any man for any work that he does for the Council. I think that the fee that is received by the members of the Council for their attendance might be called a very small fee for the work we have to do, and I think certainly for the work the examiners do, the fee they receive need not necessarily be compared in size with that received by the members of the Council. The whole matter was thoroughly threshed out last year— thoroughly gone into ; gone into very much more exhaustively than we can go into it now—and there were a great number of points brought up then on the consideration of this matter, and it was decided then the fee of $20 was not an unreasonable fee to give the examiners as a retainer. I think at that time that I, at least, upheld the idea of giving the examiners the same fee for the examination of the different papers that they receive at Toronto University, which is fifty cents a paper. It was afterwards decided that thirty-five cents would be sufficient, as they already received a $20 retainer. I think the matter was so thoroughly gone into last year that it is, perhaps, wasting time to touch it this year.

Dr. Rogers—I think so. It was settled thoroughly last session, and I object to it being taken up now.

The President put the motion, calling for the ayes and nays, and declared that the nays had it, and the motion was lost.

Dr. Logan called for a vote by division.

The President put the motion by Dr. Fulton, seconded by Dr. Williams, " That the payment of $20 to the examiners as a retainer fee be discontinued, it being considered that their remuneration independent of this amount is quite sufficient," and called for a show of hands, and after counting the vote declared the motion lost.

Dr. Moore, on behalf of ₍the Committee on Registration, reports that the Committee, having examined the certificates and diplomas presented by Peter R. McMonagle, find they do not entitle him to registration, and moved, seconded by Dr. Henry, that the report be adopted, as follows. Carried.

REPORT OF REGISTRATION COMMITTEE.

To the Medical Council of the College of Physicians and Surgeons of Ontario :

GENTLEMEN,—The Committee on Registration have examined the certificates and diplomas presented by Peter R. McMonagle, and find that they do not entitle him to registration.

All of which is respectively submitted.

J. W. ROSEBRUGH, *Chairman.*
Per V. H. MOORE.

Adopted in Council, June 16th, 1893.

CL. T. CAMPBELL, *Chairman.*

Dr. MOORE—I want to call the attention of this Council, with the permission of the chair, to the fact that Mr. J. Ross Robertson, of the *Telegram* newspaper, has invited this Council, if they can possibly, to visit the Hospital for Sick Children to-morrow; and he has also sent up to us a copy, for each member of this Council, of the annual report, which has been laid upon the desks of the members. Mr. J. Ross Robertson, I believe, has done a very great deal for the hospitals and for other charitable institutions in this city, and he was very anxious the Medical Council should go as a body and visit, not only the Lakeside Home, but also the Hospital for Sick Children on College Street, and has extended to us this invitation.

Dr. HARRIS—I had the privilege of being with Dr. Moore at the time of his interview with Mr. Robertson, and I can freely endorse what Dr. Moore has said as to the hearty invitation extended to us. I can also state that Mr. Robertson is very enthusiastic over the Hospital for Sick Children, and is doing a very good work there, and he is anxious that not only the members of the Medical Council, but members of the profession throughout Ontario should visit it.

The PRESIDENT—We will now take up the case of Dr. Anderson. I have received the following document :

"Dr. Anderson's case having been taken up, and the report of the Committee having been read, he admits that the report and findings of the said Committee are correct, and that his name is liable to be erased from the medical register; and he undertakes and agrees not further to offend in the premises, and asks the Council to suspend

9*

action on the report of the Committee so long as he, in good faith, complies with all the rules of the Medical Council, and hereby undertakes to so comply, and agrees that the Medical Council may, at any time, in their discretion, act in any manner they see fit on the said report of the Discipline Committee; one week's notice of intended action to be given by registered letter, addressed to said Anderson's last known post-office address.

" Dated at the Medical Council building, Toronto, the 16th day of June, 1893.

" (Signed) WILLIAM ANDERSON.
" (Signed) H. M. MOWAT."

Dr. DAY—I have just been thinking over that matter, and I wish to say that the " one week's notice " will have to be changed to three days, for the reason that the Council always get through their meeting by Saturday ; therefore, if we came here on Tuesday, and decided to take action, we could give him only three or four days' notice of that.

. Mr. MOWAT—As long as it is reasonable.

Dr. DAY—Make it three days, so it can be brought up and decided at the same meeting.

Dr. Harris moved, seconded by Dr. Rogers,

That whereas, Committee on Discipline reported to this Council in the case of Dr. William Anderson as appears by the printed report of the proceedings of the Discipline Committee, and as appears by the report in the case on file in possession of the Registrar ;

And whereas, the said William Anderson has been called upon to show cause why the Council should not act upon the report of the said Committee, as appears by the notice served upon him ;

And whereas, the said William Anderson has appeared upon the said notice in person and by counsel, Mr. H. M. Mowat, and the Council has been addressed by the counsel for William Anderson, showing cause to the said notice, and the said Anderson has signed a submission, which is attached to the said report of the Discipline Committee ;

And whereas, the offences charged and reported as proved by the said Committee, are not within the premises contained in sub-section 2 of section 34 of the Ontario Medical Act as amended ;

And whereas, as to the said facts stated in the report of the said Committee on Discipline, the Council now resolve to act, and hereby adopt the said facts, and report as to the finding of the facts in the case of the said William Anderson ; be it therefore

Resolved, That upon the application herein, and upon the enquiry herein before the said Discipline Committee, and upon the report of the said Committee, and upon the facts herein found and adopted by the Council, and upon reading the said submission,

That the name of William Anderson, now appearing in the register of the College of Physicians and Surgeons of Ontario, be retained upon the register, subject to the right of the Council to deal with the said report at any time as per said member. Carried.

Dr. Day moved, seconded by Dr. Harris, that Dr. Anderson be called into the room, and that the President inform him in the usual way of the decision of the Council.

The PRESIDENT—Dr. Anderson, the Council has given your case careful consideration during this session; you have had a fair trial before this Committee, and even though you were not present, due justice, I think, was done by the Committee, and your interests were guarded as carefully as they possibly could be. You have been present at the Council, and by your own voice and the voice of your solicitor you have stated your case, and the desire of the Council has been to deal as mercifully as possible with you. It is the desire of the Council always to deal mercifully in cases of this kind. You have, however, been found guilty of the offences charged; and while the Council wishes to be merciful it has been no easy matter for it to exercise its prerogative of mercy in this case, because the seriousness of your offence cannot be too strongly reprobated; the fact that you, as a member of an honourable profession, have, so far as the evidence goes, sold your rights and privileges as a member of that profession to the service of unqualified men, and have acted as a shield for unscrupulous men to defraud the public is a most serious matter. The Council, in its judgment and in its desire to be merciful, has taken the lenient view of the case that you have perhaps in this matter offended not realizing the heinousness of the offence; and in view of the submission you have made, and the promise you have submitted to the Council, they are prepared to believe that in the future you will abstain from further offending in a like manner. And they have decided that in the meantime further action on your case is deferred; and your name, therefore, remains on the register.

Dr. Bray moved that the Council do now adjourn for half an hour, in order to give the Education Committee time to complete their report.

FRIDAY, *June 16th*, 1893, 9.30 *p.m.*

Medical Council met in accordance with motion for adjournment. The President in the chair, called the meeting to order.

Dr. Harris presented Report No. 2 of the Education Committee.

Dr. Harris moved, seconded by Dr. Geikie, that the Education Report No. 2 be now received and considered and adopted by the Council.

Report read clause by clause, and, on motion, adopted as follows:

EDUCATION COMMITTEE REPORT NO. 2.

To the President and Members of the Ontario Medical Council :

GENTLEMEN,—Your Committee on Education beg leave to submit Report No. 2.

The Announcement for 1892-93 has been carefully looked over and a few slight changes are recommended.

The Registrar is authorized to make all necessary clinical changes in the Announcement for 1893-94.

It is recommended that section 5, clause 6, be changed so as to read : "The Examiners shall return the schedules to the Registrar with values inserted within seven days of notice sent by the Registrar. From these schedules a general schedule is to be prepared by the Registrar, and no change of value can be made after such schedules are returned by the Examiners to the Registrar."

The general schedule so prepared is to be examined as to its correctness by the President and the results announced by him.

Clause 10, section 5, to read thus : "That it be an instruction to the President that he shall in no case report a candidate as having passed an examination when on any subject he makes less than the minimum of marks set by the Council for a pass on that subject; but in any case where he thinks there are special reasons for granting a license to such candidate he shall report the same to the Council for its action."

On page 17, Therapeutics is erased from clause " C " of sub-section 5 of section 13, and is placed after Diseases of Women as a separate clause marked " L."

A few alterations are made in the text-books mentioned on page 15 of Announcement, which see.

For Board of Examiners for 1893-94, see page 7 of Announcement.

Appended with this report are the reports of the Board of Examiners and the correspondence referred to in said reports, and asked for by the Council.

W. T. HARRIS, *Chairman.*

Adopted in Council.

CL. T. CAMPBELL, *President.*

REPORT OF BOARD OF EXAMINERS.

October 20th, 1892.

To the President and Members of the Medical Council of the College of Physicians and Surgeons of Ontario :

GENTLEMEN,—I have the honour to submit for your consideration the report of the Board of Examiners of the College of Physicians and Surgeons of Ontario and the results of the professional examination held in Toronto, in September, 1892.

For the primary examination 35 candidates presented themselves, 15 of whom passed, 20 failing to satisfy the Examiners.

For the final examination 45 candidates presented themselves, 35 of whom passed, 10 failing to satisfy the Examiners.

The number of each candidate with the number of marks obtained upon each subject of the examination will be found recorded in the schedule by the Registrar.

The number of marks in each case were taken from the schedule of the Examiners, and finally were examined and certified as correct by the Chairman on behalf of the Board.

The examinations were as practical as possible.

I have also the honour to submit for your consideration a detailed statement of the deliberations of the Board as recorded by the Registrar, being a true copy of his minutes upon such general and special matters as engaged the attention of the Board, the desire of the Board being to secure for all an honest and fair examination.

In pursuance of the notice issued by the Registrar, the Board of Examiners met this day, the 20th of October, 1892, at the hour of 3 p.m. Present, Drs. Saunders, Peters, Acheson, MacDonald, O'Reilly, Burt, Hearn, Small, Waugh, Fraser, Grasett.

Dr. Fowler, the President, took the chair and called the Board to order, and read the instructions provided by the Council for the guidance of the Examiners, and then directed the Registrar to proceed at once with the marks made by the candidates.

The Registrar read aloud the marks made by the candidates in the primary examination, which were now considered.

The standing of the final candidates was next considered, and each candidate's standing read aloud, the result being announced by the Chairman in each case and recorded by the Registrar as the schedule will show.

Moved by Dr. Grasett, seconded by Dr. Waugh, that the schedule of the Registrar be referred to the Medical Council as the correct report of the Board of Examiners, and that the same be signed by the Chairman on behalf of the Board, for presentation to the Medical Council. Carried.

Dr. Fowler now presented and read a letter he had received from one J. A. Sangster, when it was moved by Dr. Peters, seconded by Dr. Waugh, that the communication of Mr. J. A. Sangster having been carefully considered by the Board of Examiners, it is decided that no action can be taken in the premises. Carried.

The Registrar then read a report regarding the personation of one candidate by another at the examinations, when it was moved by Dr. Burt, seconded by Dr. Grasett, that the communication from the

Registrar in *re* Messrs. Kraussman and Jones, relating to personation, the former by the latter, at the Fall Examinations in 1892, be referred to the Council for their action. Carried.

The communications from Mr. J. A. Sangster and the Registrar will be found appended hereto.

Drs. Peters and Saunders now addressed the Board *re* the separating of Therapeutics from Pathology, no action being taken, when, on motion, the Board adjourned.

All of which is respectfully submitted.

FIFE FOWLER,
Chairman, Board of Examiners.

TORONTO, *October 20th*, 1892.

To the Board of Examiners of the College of Physicians and Surgeons of Ontario :

MR. CHAIRMAN AND GENTLEMEN,—I beg leave to call your attention to the perpetration of a fraud during the examination upon Chemistry on the afternoon of Wednesday, September 14th.

When the candidates were handing in their papers, a candidate handed me a paper with the name George Kraussman written upon it. He then signed his name in the book as George Kraussman.

Being suspicious that something was wrong, I asked him if that was his name. He stated most emphatically that it was, and seemed inclined to be angry when I doubted his word. Another student, who was leaving the room at the same time, was asked what this candidate's name was, and he replied, " He told you his name, and I suppose he knows it." When I asked him if he would identify him as Kraussman, he said it was not his business identifying men for me.

I told the candidate who handed in the paper that I was certain he was not Kraussman, and that I would ascertain who he was. This ended the interview.

When I came down to the vault to put away the papers, I found George Kraussman waiting for me. He expressed sorrow for what had happened, and said he had got the candidate to write on the subject of Chemistry for him, and hoped there would be no more about it. I told him it was a very serious matter, and one that would require to be taken notice of, and that I had already reported the matter to the solicitor of the Council, and that I would be guided by his advice. As this is the first case of the kind where personation has been detected, and knowing the difficulty that exists in preventing personation, Mr. Osler thought the Council should deal severely with offenders of this kind.

He also said that the act of the man who undertook to write the paper and personate Kraussman, had forged Kraussman's name, and that the offence was therefore a very serious one under criminal law, but as the Council had such power in their hands to deal with offenders of this kind, he would not advise taking any proceeding against the candidate under the criminal law, but would recommend that the Council deal with the matter as they thought proper. The name of the candidate who personated Kraussman is A. J. Jones, from St. Catharines, Ontario. Both are equally guilty, and should be dealt with in the same way.

(Signed) R. A. PYNE, *Registrar.*

For Mr. J. A. Sangster's communication to Dr. Fowler, President, College of Physicians and Surgeons of Ontario, see proceedings of Council, 14th June, 1893.

———

11 Alpha Ave.,
TORONTO, *June 1st,* 1892.

J. A. Williams, Esq., M.D. :

DEAR SIR,—I beg leave to place in your hands my application to have my answers to the Primary Examination held by the College of Physicians and Surgeons of Ontario, reread, and especially my marks obtained at the oral examination reconsidered.

I would take oath that the following five statements respecting the oral examination are correct :

1. I correctly tested for and recognized both salts in Chemistry, for Dr. Acheson told me so, and that was all that was required of us on that subject.

2. I correctly answered all his questions in Toxicology, and he seemed very well pleased indeed, for he told me " That is all," long before the time was up.

3. I correctly answered every question in Materia Medica and Pharmacy.

4. I made but one mistake in Physiology, but Dr. Fraser, who also presided over the Histological Specimens, told me that I had recognized the specimen, remarking, " That's right."

5. I did fail to answer two or three, not more, questions in Anatomy, and yet I was asked some twelve or fifteen.

Thus, I am forced to believe, Sir, that even if I have obtained less than the required marks in one or two subjects on the written papers, yet I feel certain that I have more than made the required percentage in that subject or subjects when the marks of the oral and written are added together.

This is my second primary examination, and I would feel too keenly its loss through injustice or mistakes, for I am convinced that there has been either (1) gross injustice done me, either wilfully or unintentionally by the presiding examiners, or (2) some mistake in transferring the marks. In either case, Sir, I trust that the error will be erased, and that the injustice done me will be promptly rectified.

I am, Sir, your obedient servant,

J. A. SANGSTER.

TORONTO, *June 28th*, 1892.

J. A. Sangster, Esq., Toronto, Ont.:

DEAR SIR,—I beg leave to inform you that the Medical Council decided as follows: That they have very carefully looked into your appeal and cannot see any reason for changing the decision of the examiners. I also beg leave to inform you that there will be an examination held in Toronto, beginning on the second Tuesday in September next.

Yours faithfully,

R. A. PYNE, *Registrar.*

---

11 Alpha Ave.,

TORONTO, *June 30th*, 1892.

Dr. Pyne:

DEAR SIR,—I have only just received your communication in reply to my note of yesterday, asking for the result of my appeal to the Council.

Please communicate to me the names and addresses of the examiners of that Council, and that of any substitution that may have been made in it during the last sitting of that body. I also ask for permission in company with an uninterested party to look over my papers which you infer have been reread, and also to have access to the oral examination.

It may be only fair to state that should I fail to obtain the above information or to be satisfied with the way the examiners have treated me, I purpose to appeal to the Ontario Government, in fact, have already drafted an appeal to Sir Oliver Mowat's Government, with fifteen or twenty members of which I shall singly communicate, but I hold my action with the Ontario Government until I may hear from you, assuming that that will be in a few days—days and not *another four weeks.* I may also say that in the event of your refusing the above information, or should Sir Oliver Mowat fail to ferret out what I consider the injustice, I shall take still other means of discovering what appears to me to be the " Nigger in the fence," and not leave a stone unturned in my determination to unearth the matter.

Yours, etc.,

J. A. SANGSTER.

TORONTO, *July 2nd*, 1892.

J. A. Sangster, Esq., Toronto, Ont. :

DEAR SIR,—I am in receipt of your letter of the 30th June, and in reply I beg to say that if you will be good enough to name any day and time that you can call, I will be pleased to give you all and every information in my power as to your examination, and will gladly place your papers before you for identification, and trust I will be able to satisfy you that you have not suffered through any mistake of mine, or from any injustice at the hands of the Board of Examiners. Awaiting your reply, believe me,　　　　Yours faithfully,

R. A. PYNE,

Registrar.

---

11 Alpha Ave.,

TORONTO, *July 7th*, 1892.

Dr. Pyne :

DEAR SIR,—I am in receipt of yours of 2nd, and in reply would say that I shall be able to call at your office on Saturday afternoon at 2 o'clock promptly, if that will do you.　　　　Yours, etc.,

J. A. SANGSTER.

TORONTO, *July 9th*, 1892.

(*Saturday, 2.03 p.m.*)

Dr. J. Thorburn met this day in my office, as did also J. A. Sangster, who appealed from Examiner's decision.　His papers were shown him, and he identified them as his, also his marks, and he appeared satisfied that everything was correct.　Dr. Thorburn and myself asked him questions, and explained to J. A. Sangster any matters he desired to know in connection with the examinations, and he (J. A. Sangster) withdrew.

R. A. PYNE, *Registrar.*

JAMES THORBURN.

TORONTO, *May 30th*, 1893.

To the President and Members of the Medical Council of the College of Physicians and Surgeons of Ontario :

GENTLEMEN,—I have the honour to submit for your consideration the report of the Board of Examiners of the College of Physicians and Surgeons of Ontario, and the results of the Professional Examinations held in Toronto and Kingston, in April, 1893.

For the primary examination, 205 candidates presented themselves ; 7 of the candidates did not complete the examination, owing to illness or for other reasons. One hundred and ninety-eight candidates completed the examination, 112 of whom passed ; 86 failed to satisfy the examiners ; the percentage of the candidates passed being 52 per cent.

One hundred and twenty-eight candidates presented themselves for the final examination, one of whom was taken ill. One hundred and twenty-seven completed the examination, 85 of whom passed ; 42 failed to satisfy the examiners ; the percentage of successful candidates being 72 per cent.

The number of each candidate, with the number of marks obtained upon each subject of examination, will be found recorded in the schedule by the Registrar. •

The number of marks in each case were taken from the schedule of the examiners, and finally were examined and certified as correct by the Chairman on behalf of the Board.

The examinations were as practical as possible.

In Anatomy, wet and dry preparations were used, embracing dissections of the whole human body, together with the viscera, bones, models, etc.

In Materia Medica and Pharmacy, specimens were used.

In Physiology and Histology, microscopical specimens were used.

In Chemistry, practical work was required in the laboratory.

The examiners in Medicine, Surgery, operative and other than operative, gave clinical examinations in the General Hospitals, Toronto and Kingston.

The examiner on Pathology and Therapeutics used gross and microscopical specimens, etc.

The examiners on Midwifery and Medical and Surgical Anatomy used the subject and models, instruments, etc., and examined the candidates upon their various uses and application.

I have the honour also to submit for your consideration a detailed statement of the deliberations of the Board, being a true copy of the minutes of the Registrar upon such general and special matters as engaged the attention of the Board.

The final meeting of the Board was characterized with unanimity, the only desire being to secure for all a fair and honest examination.

In pursuance of the notices issued by the Registrar, the Board of Examiners met this day, the 30th ot May, 1893, at the hour of 2 p.m., in the College building. Present—Drs. Burt, Saunders, Grasett, Wáugh, Peters, Hearn, Fraser, McDonald, Small, Acheson.

Dr. Fowler, the President, took the chair, and called the Board to order, and read the instructions provided by the Council for the guidance of the examiners, and instructed the Registrar to at once proceed with the marks of the candidates.

The Registrar read aloud the marks made by the candidates upon each subject, and each candidate's standing being read aloud, the result being announced by the Chairman in each case and recorded by the Registrar, as the schedule will show.

Dr. Saunders presented and read a letter he had received from one P. B. Wood, upon which no action was taken. Letter will be found attached to the end of report.

The consideration of marks being now completed, the Board confirmed the Registrar's schedule, and ordered it to be signed by the Chairman on behalf of the Board as their work.

Moved by Dr. Grasett, seconded by Dr. Saunders, that the report of the Board of Examiners and schedule be now adopted and signed by the Chairman, and that the same be presented to the Medical Council of the College of Physicians and Surgeons of Ontario as the correct return of the Board of Examiners for the examinations held in April, 1893. Carried.

Moved by Dr. Peters, seconded by Dr. Saunders, that it is the opinion of the Board of Examiners that it is advisable that the subject of pathology and bacteriology and therapeutics be separated in the examinations, and that separate papers be set in each subject, with or without separate examiners in each subiect. Carried.

Moved by Dr. Grasett, seconded by Dr. MacDonald, and

Resolved—That six hours per day be the amount of time devoted by the examiners to the oral examinations. Carried.

On motion the Board adjourned.

All of which is respectfully submitted.

FIFE FOWLER,
Chairman, Board of Examiners.

———

H. J. Saunders :   NEW YORK, *May 3rd*, 1893.

DEAR DOCTOR,—In examining your papers of final work on medicine, you will come across a paper written by a student who misunderstood a word in one of your questions. I had been reading Cholera out of Osler's work on medicine just the night before the day of examination, and was telling my fellow-student that we would get a question on Cholera sure, as it would probably visit this country this coming summer, and it would be necessary for us to understand the nature of the disease ; and in my anxiety I overlooked the question, and thought it was Cholera instead of Chorea.

Now, Doctor, I know you will not feel like giving me anything for that question, but my dear sir, when you consider that I picked it out and wrote on this question as first one, and that I spent so much time on it, that I did not get time to write on the question on Hydatids, Cancer, etc., and that I had but a minute to write on Erythema, can you not, under these circumstances, give me something for that question ? I did well on the Oral, and if you will do this, and give the question a fair consideration, you will be doing me a just kindness, and I shall appreciate it very much. Otherwise, I am afraid my Written will pull me down, so that I must fail.

I am here taking a course at the Polyclinic College and Hospital, and am seeing a great deal of practical work. Sincerely hoping you will give my appeal a fair consideration, and do what you can for me,

I remain, very truly, yours,

PETER B. WOOD.

———

Dr. MILLER—Might I ask the Chairman of the Committee if he proposes that there should be a supplemental examination in the fall of 1893?

Dr. HARRIS—That matter was not taken up in committee. It was not referred to us at all ; and Dr. Geikie, I believe, has prepared a resolution which will perhaps cover the ground.

Dr. Geikie moved, seconded by Dr. Moore, that an examination will be held next September, beginning on the second Tuesday in September, in Toronto ; the fee of $20 to be charged to each candidate who has been unsuccessful at any previous examination, the usual fee to be charged in other cases.

Dr. GEIKIE—I move this resolution because it has been forgotten, and it appears to me that it would not do to let a whole year go without holding an examination.

Dr. BERGIN—I think we ought to ask the treasurer before we put this resolution, because I understand we cannot very well afford to hold that examination.

Dr. MILLER—Last year there was a surplus.

Dr. GEIKIE—Under the new arrangement a great deal of saving will be effected in the fall examination, and we cannot possibly go a whole year without doing injury.

Dr. MILLER—The treasurer's figures show that we received $1,450 for the professional examination in the fall of 1892, and that the expenses were $886, so that we had a surplus.

Dr. WILLIAMS—According to the report we have adopted, this announcement stands subject to clerical alterations made by the Registrar ; and on page 18, section 3, sub-section 12, the announcement provides for a fall examination.

Dr. MILLER—Only in that year.

Dr. WILLIAMS—This announcement holds good for this year except for the clerical corrections made by Dr. Pyne. If he struck out that fall examination, I would not call that a clerical alteration. That stands subject to clerical alterations by the Registrar.

Dr. BERGIN—Let the same time and same fee and same everything else be put in this by-law.

Dr. MILLER—Have you no right to make a clerical omission of that. It is a very serious matter either having, or not having, an examination.

Dr. WILLIAMS—I object to the resolution altogether. The announcement now fixes it subject to change of date, and the Registrar is authorized to make clerical changes ; and I hold the change of date is merely a clerical change required in the announcement.

Dr. MOORE—Quite right.

Dr. WILLIAMS—He has not a right to say there shall or shall not be an examination. The announcement fixes it.

Dr. GEIKIE—Withdraw the motion.

Dr. MILLER—I do not think the mover should be allowed to withdraw it. I think it requires a substantive motion. It was clearly understood last year that the resolution might be permitted to pass upon that occasion, but there were some members of this Council who thought it ought not to occur again.

Dr. ROGERS—If Dr. Miller will move that sub-section 12 of section 3 be excluded—

Dr. MILLER—No. I merely say the motion proposed by Dr. Geikie is a proper and correct motion, and a very necessary one if you propose holding a supplemental examination.

Dr. WILLIAMS—I object to a supplemental examination. We have established the examinations, and this resolution provides for it. All that is necessary is for the Registrar to change the necessary dates on which it is to be held.

Dr. DAY—The resolution was passed last year in this way : It was to be considered a supplemental examination for that year only, and that it was left open to have them, or not have them, in the years following. I remember that distinctly. Whatever your announcement may say, I do not know, but I know that was the understanding ing come to; and I opposed a fall examination, thinking it would be too expensive; and the construction put upon that part of it was an examination to be held for 1892, and that all future years would provide for themselves.

Dr. MILLER—That is clearly the understanding which I had of it.

Dr. GEIKIE—Let the resolution be put.

The PRESIDENT—There is no harm in putting the resolution.

Dr. ROGERS—I think there is harm.

Cries of "Question," "Question."

The PRESIDENT—It simply re-enacts that clause, but if you think that clause is still in force—

Cries of "Question."

On the motion being put the President declared it carried.

Dr. GEIKIE—It is understood that the dates and fees shall be the same as last year?

The PRESIDENT—Yes.

Dr. Harris moved, seconded by Dr. Moore, that Miss M. Wasson be paid the sum of $10 for her services to the various committees as stenographer and typist.

Dr. HARRIS—I would like this motion carried because I know this young lady has done a great deal of work. I know she has done it for my committee—the Education Committee—and for other committees, and her work has been well and carefully done. Carried.

At the request of Dr. Johnson, the President vacated the chair and it was taken by Dr. Bergin, M.P.

Dr. JOHNSON—I wish to propose a vote of thanks to the President for the able way in which he has managed the affairs of the Council during this session. It appears to me, and I have been here now some three or four sessions, that during this session we have got through more work in a limited time than we have ever done before; that the meeting of the Council has been most harmonious; and everything slipped along as easily as it possibly could. I attribute that in a great measure to the ability shown by our President in the way in which he has managed this meeting; and I have much pleasure now in proposing the vote of thanks to Dr. Campbell as President of the Council.

Dr. ORR—I have great pleasure in seconding that motion. I can thoroughly and heartily endorse every word that has been said by Dr. Johnson. I think the proceedings of the meeting have been carried on most amicably, and the business gotten through during this session of the Council, I think, is quite equal to the amount of work done, if not more than that which was done last year.

Dr. Harris—Mr. Chairman, I do not wish to prolong the debate, but I can rise with the greatest pleasure to endorse what has been said by the mover and seconder of this resolution, and I am sure that every member of this Council must fully and thoroughly appreciate the great ability that Dr. Campbell has shown while he has been in the chair.

Dr. Bergin—Mr. President, I have very great pleasure in presenting to you the thanks of this Council for your conduct in the chair, and I beg to add my own tribute to the great ability with which you have conducted the affairs of the Council, and I do not think any former president need take offence when I say that during the term I have been here—the many years I have been here—the affairs of this Council have never passed off so harmoniously, never has so much good temper been shown, and never has business been despatched as rapidly as during this meeting of the Council.

Dr. Campbell—I thank you, gentlemen, for the compliments you have paid me, and if I have filled the chair to your satisfaction, I am abundantly repaid for the trouble taken in connection therewith.

Dr. Williams moved that the President again take the chair.

Dr. Miller—The resolution which has been moved is certainly a very deserving one, but we have two other officers who are probably more hard worked than yourself. With all due deference to the ability with which you have discharged the duties encumbent upon you, the duties performed by our Registrar and Treasurer are certainly of the most onerous nature; the duties of the latter having become so through the operations and exertions of people who are desirous that the Medical Council should be conducted in the best possible manner, and with the very best possible results to the profession, and more particularly to them. I therefore beg leave to move that a very cordial vote of thanks be tendered to the Registrar and Treasurer for the ability with which they have discharged the duties of their offices, and the courtesy with which they have treated the members of this Council.

Dr. Moore—I have very great pleasure in seconding that resolution. It is not only known to members of the Council, but it is known to almost every medical man in the Province of Ontario, as well as to every medical student, the kindness and courtesy extended to them at all times and on all occasions by our esteemed Registrar. How we would succeed in filling his place were anything to happen to him, is almost a mystery to me. And in saying this much for the Registrar, I can say quite as much for our esteemed Treasurer ; he has not only filled this office for the last year, but for a great many years, and he not only has filled it with honour to himself and credit to the Council, but on many occasions when we were behind hand, when we did not have money enough to pay our bills, he put his hand in his own pocket and paid them for us. I have, therefore, very great pleasure in seconding that resolution. Carried.

Dr. BERGIN—I would like to pass a vote of censure on the gentleman who deprived me of the pleasure of naming Dr. Aikins.

The PRESIDENT—The Registrar and Treasurer have heard the vote of thanks ; and the motion is now formally presented, and the thanks of the Council tendered to them.

Dr. GEIKIE—There is one resolution that I think should be moved, and that is a special one to the Committee on Discipline.

Dr. DAY—Oh, stop.

Dr. GEIKIE—Making special mention of the Chairman, Chief Justice Day he should be called. I think his duties have been well discharged, and they are very difficult to discharge well. Let anyone of us be raised to the position, and we can realize it. I have great pleasure in moving that the thanks of this Council be given to the Committee, but very specially to the Chairman of the Committee, Dr. Day.

Dr. HARRIS—I have a very great deal of pleasure in seconding the motion tendering the thanks of this Council to Drs. Day, Bray and Logan, who have discharged the duties relegated to them very ably. Carried.

The President here tendered the thanks of the Council to the Discipline Committee.

Dr. DAY—On behalf of the Committee, I thank you for passing the resolution. I have no doubt you mean it. All I can say is we have striven to do our duty faithfully. I must say my colleagues are quite as much entitled to commendation as I am. And while it pleases you to pass the resolution you have, I am under the impression that our conduct in like measure has been displeasing to somebody else.

Dr. Johnson moved, seconded by Dr. Harris, and

Resolved—That in accordance with the by-laws, the Registrar do now read the minutes of this last meeting of the Council, which was accordingly done. The minutes were found correct, and on motion, confirmed, and the President directed to sign the same.

Dr. Johnson moved, seconded by Dr. Harris, that the Council now adjourn and stand adjourned. Carried.

CL. T. CAMPBELL,

President, College of Physicians and Surgeons of Ontario.

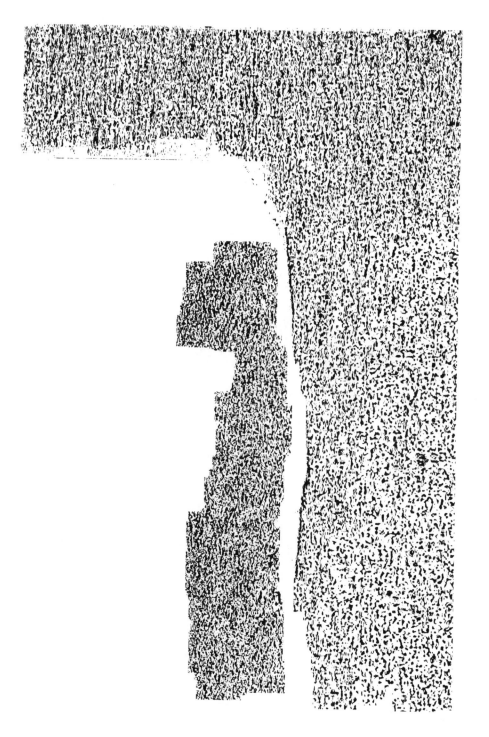

9 781397 327109